The Names of the Wyandot

Also by John Steckley from Rock's Mills Press

Gibbons: The Invisible Apes
Parrots: The Flock Among Us
The Memoirs of Alexander Brodie

The Names
of the
WYANDOT

John Steckley

Rock's Mills Press
Rock's Mills, Ontario • Oakville, Ontario
2023

Published by
Rock's Mills Press
www.rocksmillspress.com

Copyright © 2023 by John Steckley.
All rights reserved. No part of this publication may be reproduced, distributed, or transmitted in any form or by any means, including photocopying, recording, or other electronic or mechanical methods, without the prior written permission of the publisher, except in the case of brief quotations embodied in critical reviews and certain other noncommercial uses permitted by copyright law. For permission requests, contact the publisher at customer.service@rocksmillspress.com.

Contents

CHAPTER ONE
Introduction: A Lesson about Indigenous Names and Naming • 1

CHAPTER TWO
How Wyandot Names are Constructed • 13

CHAPTER THREE
Gender and Names • 29

CHAPTER FOUR
Clan Naming • 43

CHAPTER FIVE
Nicknames • 67

CHAPTER SIX
Names Shared with the Wendat and the Haudenosaunee • 75

CHAPTER SEVEN
Naming the Incomers • 93

CHAPTER EIGHT
Names in the Narratives • 109

CHAPTER NINE
Wyandot Names in the 19th Century • 119

CHAPTER TEN
Translations • 147

References • 285

CHAPTER ONE
Introduction: A Lesson about Indigenous Names and Naming

Almost 30 years ago, I first experienced the sacred nature of Indigenous naming. It took place in northern Ontario. The one doing the naming was an Anishinaabe elder, senior in the centuries-old Midewiwin or Mide spiritual society, as well as a university professor colleague of mine in what was then called "Native Studies" at Laurentian University. He had been given tobacco by his daughter as a sign of respect to come up with the name. The one being named was his newly-born granddaughter, so this was a very special and important naming for him.

There was a fairly large group in attendance in the Midewiwin lodge, the sacred fires burning with smoke rising high. The Midewiwin elder presented the name to us, which had come to him in a vision. He repeated it several times and had us say it too. He explained the nature and significance of the name, which was associated with the haunting call of the loon, a familiar sound in the north country. When the ceremony was over, I walked out of the Mide lodge with a much deeper respect and understanding of Indigenous names, naming, and name-givers.

Ignorance of Indigenous Names and Naming

Mainstream North American society has an ignorance of Indigenous culture and history that is becoming well-known, and increasingly commented on. What has not been an important part of that commentary is the extent of that ignorance concerning the meaning and nature of Indigenous names. I have never seen or even heard of a book dedicated to names in general or those that an individual Indigenous person has. I have looked but found nothing.

Yes, certain Indigenous names have a kind of narrow mainstream cultural visibility, but this visibility is one-dimensional, lacking the multi-dimensional vision needed to truly understand both the names and the nature of naming in Indigenous societies.

One good example of this is the famous Lakota warrior Crazy Horse or Thašunka Witko. His best-known name is generally said to have come from a vision he had of a warrior and his horse riding out of a lake, with the horse floating and dancing in an unusual manner to avoid being shot. But his father had the name before him, and before his father another man in the patrilineal line. It was a traditional name, not one unique to him. When Crazy Horse reached a certain level of maturity, his father gave up the name for another. That sounds like a clan name.

The Lakota man had other names as well. His birth name was Among the Trees, and the nickname his mother gave him was Curly, because his hair, like hers, was relatively light and curly. Light Hair was another such nickname. And, after a particular military victory, he was called Shirt Wearer, a name for a war leader. I cannot claim to be particularly knowledgeable about Crazy Horse and Lakota naming, but these customs sound familiar to me from what I know about Wyandot names and naming. There is more going on than what is generally known.

Who Are the Wyandot?

The Wyandot are Iroquoian in language and culture. They are closely related to the Wendat, more distantly to the Haudenosaunee peoples (Mohawk, Oneida, Onondaga, Cayuga, Seneca, and Tuscarora), and, more distantly still the Cherokee. Since first contact with European settlers in the early 17th century, they have been forced to move several times,[1] first from their homeland in what is now Ontario, then from temporary communities around the upper Great Lakes. In the early 18th century, they moved to the Detroit area, where the Anderdon band still lives. Later that century some moved to Ohio where in Upper Sandusky and elsewhere they established a new homeland, only to be driven out in 1843 by settler expansion. They went first to Kansas, where a community still exists, and then to Oklahoma, where their only federally recognized tribe lives today as the Wyandotte Nation of Oklahoma.

They have gone through a series of identifying tribal names. Wyandotte tribal historian Charles A. Buser, in a piece called "101 Names," half-jokingly, but also seriously, claims that there were at least 101 names given to the Wyandot.[2] In Charles Garrad's epic work *Petun to Wyandot: The Ontario Petun from the Sixteenth Century*, in Appendix E "Names for the Petun," he presents eight full pages of such names (Garrad 2014:555–63).

They were first called Petun, meaning 'tobacco', a French version of the Tupi-Guarani term for 'smoke', tobacco being first domesticated in South America. The people were called Petun because they were major tobacco traders, exchanging the tobacco that they received in trade themselves from the tribes further south that grew the crop.

The Wendat called them by a name that referred to the area in which the people lived at the time of contact, around Blue Mountain, part of the Niagara Escarpment. We don't know whether the people themselves used this name.[3]

Ekyǫnǫtaterunǫ	People of where there is a mountain.
eky-	cislocative – where
ǫ-	feminine-zoic singular patient – it
-nǫt-	noun root – mountain or hill
-a-	joiner vowel
-te-	verb root – exist + stative aspect
=runǫ	populative clitic – people of

There are a good number of shortened versions of this name, Tionontate and

---

1. For a clarifying mapping of the dispersal of the Wyandot from Ontario to Ohio see Wyandot Lloyd Divine's *On the Back of a Turtle*, "Map 2.1. The Huron-Wyandot Dispersal and Migrations," Divine 2019:59.

2. www.wyandotte-nation.org/culture/history/general-history/names-given.

3. Their fellow Northern Iroquoians, the Onondaga 'People of the Hills' and the Seneca 'Great Hill People' both have names incorporating the noun root for 'hill, mountain' The -ky- reflects usage in the Wyandot dialect as well as three dialects of Wendat. See the discussion of dialect later in this chapter.

Tionontati often being used, the initial Wendat form -ti- as opposed to -ky- reflecting a different dialect.

Interestingly, at least four Wyandot names involve the noun root -nǫt- 'mountain or hill':

Hǫnǫtara	He is on top of a hill or mountain.	male
Onǫkyentawi?	She is or has a sleeping hill or mountain.	female
Shǫnǫkyakǫ	He breaks a hill or mountain into many pieces.	male
Skonǫtarǫ	She is crossing a hill or mountain again.	female

The people were often called 'Huron' during the late 17th and the 18th century. The word 'Wyandot', based on a particular pronunciation of 'Wendat', emerged in the 18th century. There is no good translation of what it means. Recently, a tribal linguist of the Wyandotte Nation of Oklahoma introduced the word 'Wąndat', taken from three stories found in the narratives recorded by Barbeau in 1911–2 (Barbeau 1960:302–4, 306–7, and 311–2).

Sources of Wyandot Names

The Wyandot people and others interested in their names through the centuries are fortunate in that there are a variety of rich sources of material available, more than for many Indigenous peoples. But while this is true, there are two widespread problems with the sources: the often great variety of ways in which names are represented, and the lack of translations when names are presented. The latter can be illustrated with the example of the Wyandot name of Adam Brown, a much-respected leader in Wyandot history, and his wife and son.

Adam Brown and His Untranslated Name

Adam Brown was a settler boy between the ages of eight and twelve when he was captured in West Virginia in 1755–6. A short biography of this man was written by Charles A. Buser and published on the Wyandotte Nation of Oklahoma website (see references cited). He was taken to Detroit, adopted by the Wyandot, made a member of the Deer clan, and given a clan name. That name is presented in the literature in many different ways, but never translated. Neither were the names of his wife and son.[4]

As it was a clan name, others would have borne the name before him. The first person so recorded had the first name of Antoine: the godfather of a baptized child in 1759, Antoine's name written as 'taennenha8e'ti' (Toupin 1996:879). The same year, his name was recorded as 't'ahonnenha8iti', when giving a gift at a memorial ceremony (Toupin 1996:944). In 1765, his name was written as 'Taonnenha8iti', when such a ceremony honoured him (Toupin 1996:958).

We first see Adam Brown's name, written as 'ta8ennenha8iti', in 1776, with the baptism of his two-year-old daughter Agnes (Toupin 1996:901). Their daughter

---

4. Ekyǫnętat 'Where an evergreen stands, or evergreens stand.' and Hutaseti 'He is hiding himself.' See Translations.

Angelique was also baptized at two in August 1783 (Toupin 1996:933), Adam's name written as 'ta8enne 8eti'.

Later Adam Brown's Wyandot name was recorded in treaties. On Treaty #2 in 1790, it was written as 'Ta hou ne ha wie tie' (Lajeunesse 1960:173). In the Treaty of 1805, his name appears as 'Tahunehawettee'.[5] His grandson Peter Dooyentate Clarke had the name written as 'Ta-haw-na-haw-wie-te' (Clarke 1870:39). Mine appears to be the first attempt in the written record to actually translate his name. Here it is, possibly for the first time in writing:

Tehǫnęhawehtih	He does not have all of the corn.
te-	negative
-hǫ-	masculine singular patient – he
-nęh-	noun root – corn
-a-	joiner vowel
-we-	verb root – be together
-ht-	causative root suffix
-ih	stative aspect

The *Jesuit Relations*

The earliest written source of Wendat and Wyandot names is the *Jesuit Relations*, yearly reports of the Jesuit missions in New France, throughout most of the 17th century and part of the 18th. Almost all of the 238 Wendat/Wyandot names contained within these documents are Wendat, only a few Wyandot. However, we can learn from those Wendat names as well. A number of names mentioned there are shared by the two peoples. This is discussed in chapter six.

Father Pierre Potier

By far the most prolific source of Wyandot names is the work of Belgian Jesuit Father Pierre Potier (1708–81). He recorded Wyandot names in two nearly identical censuses of the Wyandot community in 1747, as well as the Wyandot names of the parents and godparents of 729 of the 1,581 baptisms that took place from 1729 to 1796, 39 marriages, and a good number of death announcements and mortuary ceremonies honouring the anniversaries of the deaths of many different people over the years. The latter included long lists of the names of those who gave gifts for that honouring.

Potier arrived in New France on October 1, 1743, and spent eight months in Wendake (Lorette) learning Wendat. In 1744 he went to live and work with the Wyandot, who then had a community in the Detroit area. As he learned their dialect, he would write down the differences between the Wyandot he was hearing and the Wendat that had been earlier recorded. He usually did this by writing superscript letters where the differences were in the grammar and dictionary he was copying out. Sometimes he did that with names as well. Here are several examples.

---

5. www.wyandotte-nation.org/culture/treaties/treaty-of-1805/.

Name	Wendat Feature	Wyandot Feature	Reference
r 8ïench on	no -r- after the -ch-	-r- after the -ch-	Toupin 1996:203
g Taronniahak	-ny- (as -ni-)	-ngy- (as -ngi-)	Toupin 1996:214
g Skandieretsi	-ndy- (as -ndi-)	-ngy- (as -ngi-)	Toupin 1996:241

Many of the names in Potier's writing have been made available to modern scholars and Wyandot through the dedicated scholarship of Jesuit Father Robert Toupin (1924–2000), who compiled a collection of Potier's writings in *Les Écrits de Pierre Potier* (1996). This monumental reference work was indispensable for my study of Wyandot names.

Even with Potier's knowledge and linguistic ability, the names recorded in his writing can vary somewhat, sometimes significantly different in their spelling. See the example of the name 'He has a river in his mouth'.

The 19th Century: Treaties, Landholder Maps, Allotments, Rolls and a Voters' List
For 19th-century Wyandot names, both in the language itself and translated into English, the primary source is the Wyandotte Nation of Oklahoma website: www.wyandotte-nation.org/. It is incredibly rich in files for Wyandot and others wanting to know more about the people and their history. There are 20 treaties from 1785 to 1867. They give you a good idea of who the chiefs and councillors were. These are all male. There are maps with landholder names in Ohio in 1836, and the allotments in Kansas (1855) and Oklahoma (1888). There are official rolls of the people, Ohio, Kansas, and Oklahoma, and a voters' list by clan of 1874. These present both males and females.

One drawback of this source is that the spelling of the names is often very bad as compared with the precise linguistic work of the Jesuits. To a greater degree, the same name can be written a number of different ways. A good illustration of this can be seen in the many ways in which 'Teyaṛǫtuyęh: Between-the-Logs' was recorded. Still the sheer volume of the material is helpful and made possible chapter nine.

James B. Finley
In 1840, the Rev. James B. Finley published *History of the Wyandott Mission, at Upper Sandusky, Ohio, Under the Direction of the Methodist Episcopal Church*. His work included 30 names, most of which I have yet to decipher. His writing of the language was highly idiosyncratic. His adopted Bear clan name, which he would have heard many times, was one of the best recorded ones at Re-waw-waw-ah (Finley 1840:38). It is a name of some significance and is more accurately written as 'Hariwawayi': 'He holds, grasps a matter' (see discussion in chapter seven).

John Wesley Powell
In 1881, John Wesley Powell (1834–1902), geologist, explorer, professor, and a

leading scientist of his time, published *Wyandot Government: A Short Study of Tribal Society*. His primary informants were Matthew Mudeater and Nicholas Cotter.

He presented a male and female name from each of the eight clans that he listed. Eleven of the names were easily transferred to literal translation, but five I have yet to figure out.

William Elsey Connelley

The next major source of Wyandot names is a prolific author who several times worked for the Wyandot, William Elsey Connelley (1855–1930). He recorded 73 names in *The Wyandots. Archeological Report of the Minister of Education Annual Reports 1899* (Connelley 1900:92–123), and nine names in *Wyandot Folklore* (Connelley 1899b). In the latter source, all of the names are immediately identifiable. In the former source there are 28 names that I can't translate. Even though in a few such cases he provided a translation, I cannot analyse them, and they may be more connotations of the name rather than literal meaning. There are five cases in which he says that the meaning of a name "is lost," when it can be interpreted and would have been known by people that he did not speak with. I have translated these names.

Marius Barbeau

The last source, Marius Barbeau (1883–1969) has played a very important role in the preservation of traditional Wyandot culture. He was a French-Canadian folklorist/anthropologist of note, a founding figure in both areas of study in Canada. After graduating in 1910 from Oxford University, he got a job in 1911 working for the National Museum of Canada. That was his home base for the study of French-Canadian folklore and the stories and culture of several Indigenous people.

His first fieldwork was in 1911–2, starting with the Wendat, then the Wyandot of Anderdon, Michigan, and finally and most extensively with the Wyandot living in Oklahoma. His unpublished 44 pages of 1911 fieldnotes, and his short but important discussions of names in his collection of Wyandot and Wendat stories in English, *Huron and Wyandot Mythology* (1915), provide important information concerning Wyandot names. In 1911–2 he collected 40 stories or narratives in the Wyandot language from some of the last speakers of the language at the time. This collection makes rescuing or re-awakening the language possible. Unfortunately, his attention was directed elsewhere after that time—primarily to French-Canadian folklore, and to important studies of the Haida and Tsimshian of British Columbia. Consequently his 1960 publication of the collection, *Huron-Wyandot Traditional Narratives in Translation and Native Texts*, needed more complete analysis, which I tried to achieve in *Forty Narratives in the Wyandot Language* (2020).

Chapter Summaries
CHAPTER TWO: HOW TO CONSTRUCT A WYANDOT NAME

Chapter two will probably be the most difficult chapter to read and comprehend for many people who are not linguists and have had little or no exposure to the Indigenous languages of North America. These languages are quite different from their European counterparts. Hopefully, terminology such as *modals, inclusive vs. exclusive first person*, and *aspects* do not deter the reader from continuing through the book. Keep in mind that almost every Wyandot name is a verb, that the structure of these verbs is very rule-governed, and that there is what I have called a "simplicity principle" in play in these names that keeps them from being too complicated for speakers or non-speakers.

CHAPTER THREE: GENDER AND NAMES

Gender is a factor in the discussion of the names of the Wyandot. First of all, in the Wyandot language, pronominal prefixes generally point to the gender of a name (although some are deceiving). Second, some noun and verb roots are gendered in the sense that they are used significantly more often for names of one gender than they are for the other. If the noun root for 'sand' appears, the bearer of the name is likely to be female. If the noun root for 'tree' appears, it is almost certain that the bearer will be male. Finally, and quite significantly, there is a gender bias in the recording of names, more in some sources than in others. Male names are recorded much more often than female names. Some sources are better or worse than others in this matter. These three topics will be discussed in chapter three.

CHAPTER FOUR: CLANS AND NAMES

Many Wyandot names belonged to specific clans. The leading men and women of the particular clan, no doubt with the assistance of members of the lineage most often associated with the name, would determine the successor of a clan name once the previous owner had died or had gone on to take a new name. The process common to Wyandot, Wendat and Haudenosaunee, was well described by Jesuit Father Jerome Lalemant in the *Jesuit Relation* of 1642. His nephew, Jesuit Father Gabriel Lalemant, would be given the important Deer clan name of Hatironta 'he attracts, draws' (a fact usually omitted in his biographies),

> [I]t is arranged that, if possible, no name is ever lost; on the contrary, when one of the Family [clan or lineage] dies all the relatives assemble, and consult together as to which among them shall bear the name of the deceased; giving his own to some other relative. He who takes a new name also assumes the duties connected with it, and thus he becomes a Captain [chief or other leader] if the deceased has been one. That done, they dry their tears and cease to weep for the deceased [a Wendat expression]. In this manner, they place him among the number of the living, saying that he is resuscitated, and has come to life in the person of him who has received his name. (JR23:165–7)

Of course, the same applied to the significant female names as well.

John Wesley Powell, in his important work, *Wyandot Government: A Short Study of Tribal Society* (Powell 1881), wrote about Wyandot names and naming in the following way, under the heading "Name Regulations." He obtained his information from interviewing Matthew Mudeater (1812–78) and Nicholas Cotter (1822–1887), both of whom had been Principal Chiefs during their lives. Notice that Powell mentions the council women:

> It has been previously explained that there is a body of names, the exclusive property of each gens [clan]. Once a year, at the green-corn festival, the council women of the gens select the names for the children born during the previous year, and the chief of the gens proclaims these names at the festival. No person may change his name, but every person, man or woman, by honorable or dishonorable conduct, or by remarkable circumstance, may win a second name commemorative of deed or circumstance, which is a kind of title. (Powell 1881:64)

CHAPTER FIVE: NICKNAMES

Another kind of name, which we will be calling 'nicknames' here, is included in the list of Wyandot names. They are independent of clan, and do not usually continue after the death of the individual so named (but see their use as surnames in chapter nine). This chapter includes the nicknames that they gave the Frenchmen they encountered in the Detroit area during the 18th century. These will be found in this chapter and in chapter seven.

These nicknames were common to North American Indigenous people. The famous name of Pocahontas (more accurately Pocachantesu), from the Powhatan confederacy of Eastern Algonquian[6]-speaking tribes, was a nickname usually translated as 'she is playful'. It was given to her in childhood for how she acted with other children, allegedly a kind of 'flirting' with the boys of white settlers when she danced outside the palisades. Her more traditional names were Matoaka or Matoax (Mansky 2017), which she received at birth, and a name given later of Amonute, sometimes translated as 'little bone woman'. Someone was likely to bear these names both before and after her, unlike the name Pocahontas.

CHAPTER SIX: NAMES SHARED WITH THE WENDAT AND THE HAUDENOSAUNEE

There are a great number and variety of Indigenous languages in North America. If we look solely in Canada, we can say that there are eleven different groups (a non-linguistic term) of such languages.[7] Eight of these groups are language families. These are groups of distinct languages that are related to each other. What is meant by that is that they have a significant number of cognates, words, and parts of words that have a common origin and a similar sound and at least a similar meaning. Numbers, for example, are easily determined to be cognate. Look at numbers in French and English. 'One' and 'un(e)', 'two' and 'deux', and 'three' and 'trois' are cognates. This does not include borrowings, like the Wendat and English shared word 'Ontario', meaning 'it is a large lake' in Wendat.

---

6. Algonquian (Algonkian) is the language family with the greatest number of member languages in North America.

7. For more complete information, see the discussion in Cummins and Steckley 2013:23–27.

The remaining three are called 'language isolates'—Haida, Kutenai and Tlingit—as they have no known related languages.

Wyandot is a dialect of a language that also includes the 17th-century Wendat dialects and the more uniform single dialect of Wendat that followed. In *Words of the Huron* (Steckley 2007:35–45), I discussed in terms of phonetic features the early contact dialects of Wendat, including reference to Wyandot evidence from the 18th century. Here in simplified form are five of the contrasts and similarities.

Dialect Features

Southern Bear	Northern Bear	Rock	Wyandot
-tr-	-kr-	-tr-	-tr-
-ky-	-ky-	-ty-	-ky-
-ngy-	-ngy-	-ndy-	-ngy
-ndr-	-ndr-	-nnr-	-ndr
-u-	-u-	-o-	-u-

You can see that for these five features, Northern Bear and Wyandot are consistently the same, and Southern Bear is different in only one feature. The Bear tribe of the Wendat was the one that lived closest to the Petun, the primary ancestors of the Wyandot. Rock is different in all the features. Eventually the forms I am calling Rock here became what was written in the Jesuit dictionaries

The language family to which Wyandot belongs is called Iroquoian, the branch Northern Iroquoian. The branch includes Wendat, the Haudenosaunee languages Mohawk, Oneida, Onondaga, Cayuga, Seneca, and Tuscarora. Cherokee is the sole member of the Southern Branch.

In chapter six, we will be looking at names that have cognates shared between Wyandot and Wendat, and, in a separate section, shared with the Haudenosaunee languages.

Chapter Seven: Naming the Incomers

What did the Wyandot do when it came to giving names to individuals of the settler society moving in? There were different strategies used for different groups. People of high authority received what can be called 'titles'. In the eighteenth century, Jesuit missionaries were typically adopted, and usually given names that belonged to their predecessors named by the Wendat. Tradesmen—blacksmiths, woodworkers, masons, and shoemakers—received names that said what it was that they did, using a verb root meaning 'to make'. A good number of the incomers received nicknames, often chosen with a sense of humour.

Chapter Eight: Names in the Narratives

The names discussed in this chapter are all ones that exist in the fiction of traditional stories. One name refers, however, both to a fictional rich and powerful man who gets tricked by a Wyandot, and, in fact, as a title for the British king. Three of the names come from the origin story, as the first woman on earth and her twin grandsons. The story, entitled "The Old Bear and the Nephew," contains the name of a spirit and of three uncles that help their nephew. In other narratives there are the names of four young men, and joking names shared between a bear and a rabbit. Then there is the person who has the name of a mythical spirit—'It is a white lake'.

Chapter Nine: Wyandot Names in the 19th Century

As settler society imposed itself more and more upon the Wyandot in the 19th century, naming changed. The development of surnames was one of the main such changes, most of them translations into English of male Wyandot names, others still written in some form of the original Wyandot. Some few traditional names still remained, but their number seriously dwindled.

Chapter Ten: The Translations

This is by far the longest chapter in the book. This does not include all the possible names. I have only presented names that I feel that I can translate with a significant degree of accuracy. Doing so, I have excluded a good number of names that I just could not figure out. A few of those are discussed in chapter nine.

The reader might notice in this chapter, or have detected earlier, that the way the words are represented will be different from that of any of the sources. There are four fundamental reasons for that. One is that there are several weaknesses in the writing of the Jesuits regarding nasal vowels, glottal stops, and pre-aspiration (see the following chart). And the names are often written in Wendat and not Wyandot. Second is that my writing of the names is intended to have them grammatically and morphologically complete. Names are often shortened in the sources, particularly at the beginning of the word. So I often have to add parts that are not in the original written sources. This means adding letters, sometimes confidently, other times making educated guesses.

Thirdly, in my opinion, Barbeau over-differentiates phonetically, including between recordings of the same name. My intentions are to simplify for the non-linguist reader and to be consistent.

Fourthly, my writing is intended to reflect language change that took place in the later years of the language. This includes having a -u- where earlier writers have an -o-, and an -m- to replace a -w- when it is followed or sometimes preceded by a nasal vowel.

System Used in This Book	Jesuit System
Nasal Vowels	
ą	an, 8oin
ę	en, 8oin
ǫ	on,
Glides	
y	, or j
w	8
Consonants	
h	ʻ (pre-aspiration before a consonant)
ʔ (glottal stop)	-k

CHAPTER TWO
How Wyandot Names are Constructed

The vast majority of Wyandot names are one word. That word is almost always a verb, like most words in the language. Only a few of the names are nouns by themselves. The composition of a name usually involves both a noun root and a verb root. The noun root precedes the verb root. Linguists say that the noun root is incorporated into the verb. A Wyandot verb has a minimum of three parts: a pronominal prefix, a verb root, and an aspect.

The Three Necessary Parts of a Wyandot Verb
PRONOMINAL PREFIXES IN WYANDOT NAMES

I will begin this part of the chapter with a warning. Entering into the world of the Wyandot language from an Indo-European language such as English, French, or Spanish, you would not suspect how complicated pronominal prefixes are in the language. For me it was the hardest part of learning the language. New considerations included conjugation, agent and patient, dual vs. plural, first person inclusive vs. exclusive and the indefinite third person.

There are five different conjugations, based on the first sounds of a noun or verb root. The most common one by far is the consonant conjugation. It usually, but not always, has the root following it begin with a consonant. The four other conjugations, in which the roots begin with vowels are a-, e-/ę, yę-/i- and u-/ǫ-. All five appear in Wyandot names.

There are two potential players in Wyandot pronominal prefixes: agent and patient. The agent is the most commonly found. It is always the subject. Sometimes it stands alone, and sometimes it is used with a patient. The patient is the object when both players are present. When it is on its own it is the subject. This often, but not always, happens with a verb that takes the stative aspect. It can appear with the other aspects as well. What an aspect is will be discussed shortly.

The first set of examples all take the consonant conjugation pronominal prefixes:

Ahanęhutaha	He planted, stood up the corn. (male)
-ha-	masculine singular agent – he
Tehǫmandušrakwa	They (f) often grab his robe. (male)
-hǫma-	feminine-zoic plural agent – masculine singular patient – they (f) – him
Ǫndaižu	It is a great arrow. (male Wolf)
-ǫ-	feminine-zoic singular patient – she/it (with stative aspect)

Ahurȩwa He floated. (male)
-hu- masculine singular patient – he
(with punctual aspect)

There is a distinction between dual and plural with agents, but not patients. Three Wyandot names on the list take the dual:

Dual Form		Plural Form	Conjugation
Ayitǫhǫh	We two (exclusive) used to say	Awatǫhǫh	a-
Ayižatǫ	We two (exclusive) are marking, writing.	Awažatǫ	consonant
Ndikaratase.	They two (feminine) have twisted loins.	Ȩdikaratase	yȩ-/i-

Wyandot exhibits clusivity, the distinction between the 'we' that includes the listener(s) (inclusive) and the 'we' that excludes the listener(s) (exclusive). The first two examples given above have exclusive forms. They are the only names in the collection that do. No Wyandot names have the inclusive.

The indefinite can mean 'they' (rather like the word 'people' in English sayings such as 'people say') or 'one'. There are 12 examples of this in the translated name list.

Sayurewatha	He often criticizes, opposes them.	consonant conjugation
sayu-	masculine singular agent + indefinite patient – he – them (ind)	
Taǫtrạndeyȩh	They (ind.) are joined. (male)	a- conjugation
-aǫ-	indefinite agent – they	

FIRST AND SECOND PERSON

1st person singular agent

| tuh yaraskwan | (from) there I have departed, left. (male) | a- conjugation |

1st person singular patient

| Tayehšatȩ | Carry me on your back! (male) | consonant conjugation |

feminine-zoic singular agent + 1st person plural patient

| Ǫmanduyarha | It often bears ill-will towards us. | consonant conjugation |

There are no Wyandot names that use the second person (you, your) in any way.

MASCULINE

Masculine pronominal prefixes usually involve an -h-. This -h- was not easily heard by French and English speakers so it was often not part of the recording of names, particularly after an -s-. When there is a patient, the singular masculine agent can be represented by an -s-.

Masculine Singular Agent (no patient)
Ahandatureha	He has found a village.	consonant conjugation

Masculine Singular Agent with First Person Plural
Sǫmandeyareskwa	He used to raise us up.	consonant conjugation

Masculine Singular Agent with Indefinite Patient
Sayuerakǫ	He has done many things for them.	consonant conjugation

Masculine Singular Patient (in some cases it refers to something happening to him)
Ahurewa	He floated.	consonant conjugation

Masculine Plural Agent[1]
Tehǫmayandra	They (m) look at him.	consonant conjugation

Masculine or Feminine-Zoic Plural Agent With Masculine Singular Patient
Hǫmamenǫkyǫ	They disobey or reject his word.	consonant conjugation

Feminine-Zoic

The term *zoic* here refers to the fact that such pronominal prefixes can refer not just to female humans, but to animals and things generally as well.

Feminine-Zoic Singular Agent
This is by far the most frequently occurring pronominal prefix with names, most with the consonant conjugation -ya- at or near the beginning of a name.

Yandarekwi	She is living, has lived there long.	consonant conjugation
Yariwase?	It is new news, a new matter, law.	consonant conjugation

Feminine-Zoic Singular Patient
This has the second-most common pronominal prefix with names, most represented by a simple -u-. This most often occurs with the stative aspect.

Utrǫnyǫwąh	Sky is coming out of the water.	a- conjugation
Uture	It is cold.	a- conjugation

Feminine-Zoic Dual Agent
Ndikaratase	They two (f) have twisted loins, flanks.	ye-/i- conjugation

Indefinite Agent (with no patient)
Taǫtrąndeyeh	They (indefinite) are joined.	a- conjugation

---

1. When a group of people are referred to, either all male, or male and female, then this pronominal prefix is used.

Indefinite Agent with Masculine Singular Patient
Tehumayęs   They (indefinite), people, one often cannot see him.   consonant conjugation

Indefinite Patient
Ekyayumęndata   It is at the end of one's or their word, voice.   consonant conjugation

VERB ROOTS

The two most common verb roots in Wyandot names relate to size. A verb root meaning 'be large, great' is found as -(y)uwanę- and -uwat-. I am not sure why one form is used in a particular case and not the other. The second most common is -e(t)s- 'be long, tall'. One peculiarity of this verb is that sometimes it takes what appears to be the habitual form -es-, but has a stative meaning of 'be in a state' rather than 'often, regularly'. I have no good explanation for this. In the labelling, I am calling it habitual.

Tsundak**wanę**h	It is a very large barrel, drum.	consonant conjugation
Yarǫntu**wanę**h	It is a big, large tree.	consonant conjugation
Shayę'**tsuwa**t	He has a very large forehead.	consonant conjugation
Skahšęndu**wat**	She has a very large, great name.	consonant conjugation
Skangy**wes**	It is very long moosehide.	consonant conjugation
Shand**etsi**	He has a very long arrow.	consonant conjugation

ASPECTS

Aspect was a new term to me when I first started studying Wyandot over 40 years ago. There are five aspects. Most names take the *stative* (in a state). The stative often does not add any sound to the end of the verb. The other aspects are the *habitual* (often, regularly), *punctual* (happening once), which in names requires one of two modals (factual, future), *purposive* ('going to' as intent or prediction), usually signified by an -e-, and *imperative* (command or request), which requires both a particular prefix and suffix. The following are examples:

Hangyayęhwi	He **is** clean**ing** off his fingers. (male)	stative
Ekyǫnętat	Where an evergreen stands, or evergreens stand. (female)	stative
Aǫnęta	She **often** falls. (female)	habitual
Ateyašǫtata'	Her heart **often** shakes (female)	habitual
Ayandatǫgyah	She **has made** (*factual*) a village (female).	punctual

Etsuskwa	She **will** (*future*) be able to smell again (female).	punctual
Haskutaše	He is going to have a skull of such a size. (male)	purposive
Tayeąndrak	Look at me! (male)	imperative[2]
Tayehšatę	Carry me on your back! (male)	imperative

Expanding the Basic Verb

More parts can be added to a verb. These include pre-pronominal prefixes, voice, root suffixes and aspect suffixes. The first group involves the imperative prefix (see the last two examples), modals (factual and future), and non-modals. The latter includes the coincident, partitive, repetitive, cislocative, the translocative, the dualic, and the negative.

Pre-pronominal Prefixes

Modals

There are two modals that appear in Wyandot names: the *factual* and the *future*. They generally take the punctual aspect.

Factual

The factual -a- is a modal that usually takes the punctual aspect, but sometimes takes the purposive aspect. Its usual 'tense' is the recent past.

Ahandaturęh*a*	He has (just) found a village.	(with the punctual)
Tahaky*e*	He is not going to abandon it.	(with the purposive)

Future

The future usually takes the punctual aspect, sometimes the purposive, but not with names.

Ehędihaǫ	They (m) will say, speak.	(with the punctual)
Etsuskwa	She will be able to smell again.	(with the punctual)

Non-Modals

Coincident

The coincident -ša- always comes first when it is in a verb. It means 'at the same time'. When a dualic -te- follows it, the translation is often 'in the middle'.

Šamętaha	At the same time it concluded, finished.

2. The imperative suffix takes the same form as the punctual.

Šatehaǫmętsati   He is in the middle of the land.

Partitive

The partitive -i- appears at the beginning of a verb and has the general meaning 'such'.

Iwanderes	My waist is long.
Iyatǫk	She often talks, says.

Repetitive

The repetitive appears in many Wyandot names, represented by -s- or -ts-. The former suggests that an almost silent -h- marking the masculine will follow. It gives meanings such as 'again' and 'very' (the latter typically with verbs that meant big or large).

Shandatsuwaht	He has a **very** large pot, kettle.
E**ts**uskwa	She will be able to smell **again**.
Skahwęndes	It is a **very** long island, or she has **very** long calves.[3]

Negative

The negative usually takes -te-, unless followed by the factual -a-.

Teyanǫęs	She does **not** often fall into deep water.
Tahakye	He is **not** going to abandon it.

Dualic

The dualic -t(e)- refers to a 'two-ness' in names. This can literally refer to 'two' but can extend that meaning into unexpected areas (i.e., actions with two legs or two eyes) When it appears with the translocative -a- the meaning is 'every.'

Tehandakwaye	He has **two** drums, barrels.
Tehat	He is standing (involves two legs).
Teharǫnyayandra'	He often looks at the sky.
A**tu**ehtes	**Every** one of his nails is long.

Translocative

The translocative is translated as 'away' or 'go'. It takes an -a-.

Šiy   **a**we   She or it goes far.

VOICE

There are two prefixes situated between the pronominal prefix and the root that indicate voice. Both give the pronominal prefix a- conjugation forms. The reflexive takes -atat-, the semi-reflexive -at-. There is only one example of the reflexive with names. The semi-reflexive tends to express a passive voice, but can represent a middle voice, with

---

3. The noun roots for 'island' and 'calf' are virtually the same.

the subject being both doer and the one done to.

Reflexive

Tehatatatǫh	He surrounds it (i.e., with arms wrapped around a tree) (male)

Semi-Reflexive – Passive

Ateyašǫtata'	Her heart often shakes (female)
Taǫtrąndeyęh	They (indefinite) are joined. (male)

Semi-reflexive – Middle voice

Hutaseti	He is hiding himself (male)
Utriwąndet	She holds an important matter, responsibility close to her. (female)

NOUN ROOTS

Most Wyandot names contain noun roots. They come before verb roots, usually separated by a joiner vowel -a-. The four most common noun roots in Wyandot names are -rǫny- 'sky', -(w)(m)ęnd- 'word, voice' -ri(h)(w)- 'matter, affair,' and -rǫt- 'tree, pole, or log'.

Urǫnyureta	She regularly examines the sky.
Skamęndat	She, it is one voice.
Harihužah	He stirs up matters (e.g., is quarrelsome).
Teyarǫtaye'	Two trees.

ROOT SUFFIXES

Root suffixes come after the verb root or another root suffix. There are 11 root suffixes in Wyandot: causative, causative-instrumental, dative, dislocative, distributive, frequentative, inchoative, instrumental, progressive, transitional and undoer.

Causative

The usual meaning of the causative root suffix -t- is 'to cause or make'.

Huhšruyuti	He is causing an axe to penetrate it. [verb root -uyu- 'penetrate']
Skweyatęsti	She again thickens the water, liquid. [verb root -tęs- 'be thick']

Causative-Instrumental

The causative-instrumental root suffix -st- shares functions with both the causative and the instrumental. It only appears twice in Wyandot names, both with the same verb root.

Thawęntaestih	He strikes it with a stick. [verb root -ae- 'strike']

Dative
The dative root adds the meaning of 'for the advantage or disadvantage of someone.'

Utesędi	She is grinding corn for her.
	[verb root -te- 'grind corn']

Dislocative
The dislocative means 'going to' both in the sense of being about to do something, and in travelling to do it. It is usually followed by the purposive aspect.

Haskutaše	He is going to have a skull of such a size.
	[verb root -a- 'be a size']
Taurhęšre?	Day is dawning, going to dawn.
	[verb root -rhę- 'dawn']

Distributive
The distributive root suffix means 'many times, many places' and ends with -ǫ-.

Araskwahǫ	She leaves many times.
	[verb root -araskwa- 'leave']
Tǫndešrisǫ?	Where she presses against the sand in many places.
	[verb root -is- 'press against']

Frequentative
The frequentative root suffix refers to something being done frequently (more so than with the habitual aspect). It only appears with the stative aspect and always has the patient as subject. It takes the form -skǫ-, and with names taking the repetitive prefix, adds 'very' to the word.

Shahęteskǫ	He very frequently leads.
Shutetsęnskǫh	He is very frequently a healer, curer.

Inchoative
The inchoative adds the meaning of 'coming into being' to a verb root. It takes the form -ha- when it combines with the punctual aspect.

Amęteha	She came to know.
	[verb root -ęte-]
Šamętaha	At the same time it concluded, finished.
	[verb root -ęta-]

Instrumental

The main function of the instrumental root suffix -kw- is to add a sense of 'at such a place.' Sometimes it is a nominalizer, changing a verb root into a noun stem (see third example).

Yandare**kw**i	She is living, has lived at such a place, there long.
Hǫndeskǫta**kw**i	He is turning to face the sand in such a place.
Skękyuh**kw**es	She has a very long family, lineage.

Progressive

The progressive -(h)aky- adds the meaning of 'go about, around, along', or 'continues, continuing' to the verb root. It follows the stative aspect and takes another aspect after it.

Taurhędi**haky**e	When, or where day(light) continues to come. [verb root -rhę- 'for light to come']
Awenyǫ**haky**eʔ	She is going to pass by many times. [verb root -e- 'go, come, walk']

Transitional

The meaning/function of the transitional -(h)w- or -m- is difficult to describe precisely. For at least some verbs it adds the notion of putting into a state.

Huyę**hw**i	He is cleaning it off. [verb root -yę- 'be clean']
Ayanyę**m**iha	She learned how to do it; she knows how. [verb root -nyę- 'have skill, ability']

Undoer

The undoer shifts the verb root's meaning to its opposite. It typically takes the form -wa-.

Huhšraę**wa**hs	He often loses his axe. [verb root -ę- 'have']
Ahurę**wa**	He floated. [verb root -rę- 'be stable']

ASPECT SUFFIXES

Aspect suffixes come immediately after aspects. They include the diminutive, plural, and past.

Diminutive

The diminutive either indicates small size or a relationship in which one is older or senior in some way to others, such as with one's children, siblings, nephews/nieces, grandchildren, and pets. It generally appears with the stative aspect.

Thatęri²**a**	He is (the younger one) left behind.
	[verb root -ęri- 'leave behind']
Tsundaskway**ah**	It is a very small domestic animal, pet.
	[verb root -a- 'be a size']

Plural

The plural aspect suffix -s- shows that there are a plurality of objects, including body parts.

Shastahǫretsi²**s**	He has very long bone marrows. (male)
	[verb root -ets- 'be long']
Tehažahšuwanę²**s**	He has two large arms. (male)
	[verb root -uwanę-]

Past

This indicates past tense and takes a different form with each aspect. The habitual aspect is used in all but one instance in this collection of names:

Amęses**kwa**	She used to value, cherish, esteem it. (female)
	[with the habitual aspect is -s-]
Watriwanǫ**nę**	It, she was taken care of in a matter in the past. (female)
	[the verb root plus stative aspect is -nǫ-]

CLITICS

Clitics are attached to a word but are not strictly part of it. They typically follow an already completed word (see Woodbury 2018:85). Two clitics are used with Wyandot names. The augmentative clitic -ywę- looks like it is cognate with the verb root -(y)uwanę- 'be large'. Its only use in Wyandot is in names. The other clitic used in names is the external locative clitic, usually written as -ye-.

Handarey**wę**	He lives large, puts a lot into life.
Ǫtarey**wę**	It is a very big lake.
Yawinǫ**ke**	At the (beautiful) young woman.

The Simplicity Principle

Despite all these structural possibilities, we can still say that Wyandot names are relatively simple, non-complex words. The general range is three to six morphemes (meaningful parts), five being the norm, with a few seven-part words and one eight-part word. Wyandot names appear to follow a simplicity principle. What this means in basic terms is that morphologically, structurally Wyandot names do not contain many morphemes, and generally are one word in length. Further, when there are two words involved in a name, at least one of those words is very simply constructed.

As almost every animal name in the Wyandot language is a verb, this means that Wyandot has no names like Sitting Bull, Crazy Horse, Running Bear or Little White Dove, the last two names purely fictional and highly stereotypical, taken from a popular song that came out in 1959. Neither would be constructed in Wyandot—too complex. Running Bear would be like this, with three words:

Tehuratata'	He often, frequently runs.
te-	dualic
-hu-	masculine singular patient - he
-ratat-	verb root – run
-a'	habitual aspect
de	who
hanyǫnyę	He is a bear.
ha-	masculine singular agent – he
-nyǫnyę	verb root – be a bear + stative aspect

He often runs, he who is a bear.

The name invented for a song, Little White Dove, would be even longer and more complex. This is the simplest way I can imagine. This might be seen by an old-time speaker as an artificial construction:

iyu'	She is a dove[4]
de	who
yaa'tayęratah	She has a little white body.
ya-	feminine-zoic singular agent - she
-a't-	noun root – body
-a-	joiner vowel
-yęrat-	verb root – be white + stative aspect
-ah	diminutive aspect suffix

She is a dove who has a little white body.

---

4. This is probably not a verb, but a name formed by onomatopoeia, imitating the sound of a dove.

SIMPLICITY IN NAMES WITH THE COLOUR WHITE

You can see the simplicity rule operating with the general absence of colour terms in Wyandot names, except for the colour white. Unlike the other colour terms, it has a verb root -yęrat- 'be white', which can be used with a noun root.

Otarayęrat	It is a white lake.
otar-	feminine-zoic singular agent - it + noun root - lake
-a-	joiner vowel
-yęrat	verb root – be white + stative aspect

It is interesting in this regard that there are Wyandot surnames of the 19th century that contain the word 'white': White, Whitejaw, and Whitewing. No other colour terms translated from Wyandot appear.[5]

Other colour terms in Wyandot are long words in themselves in which the noun root for a something that is a particular colour is mentioned. Take the word for the colour black:

yatsihęstatsih[6]	It is called charcoal.
ya-	feminine-zoic singular agent - it
-tsihęst-	noun root - charcoal
-a-	joiner vowel
-ʔats-	verb root - call, name
-ih	stative aspect

Names that are Nouns

At the simplest level, there are 12 Wyandot names that are just nouns, five of them having to do with trees, particularly 'poplar' -nduyar-.

Honduyarha	His poplar
Omanduyarha	Our poplar
Yanduyarha	poplar.

Names with Two Words

One way to understand the linguistic limits on the complexity of Wyandot names is to look at the names that involve two words. In none of these cases are there two complex verbs.

---

5. See the discussion of the names Greyeyes and Black Sheep in chapter nine.

6. The Wendat and Wyandot called the Jesuits 'hatitsihęstatish' 'they (m) are called charcoal' because of the black robes they wore. See discussion of Black Sheep as a surname in chapter nine.

WITH PARTICLES

haǫ - (comes) from

Aserá'ye haǫ	She comes from the south.
aser-	feminine-zoic singular agent + noun root – south, noon
-a'	noun suffix
=ye	external locative clitic

Undatižu haǫ	She is from a large village.
u-	feminine-zoic singular patient - she
-ndat-	noun root – village, community
-ižu	verb root – be large, great + stative aspect

Ǫnǫdu haǫ	It or she is from a cave.
ǫ-	feminine-zoic singular patient – she or it
-nǫd-	noun root – depth, cave
-u	verb root - be in water' + stative aspect

ši – far

Šiw	ahate	She exists far from the path.
	ah-	feminine-zoic singular agent + noun root – path
	-a-	joiner vowel
	-te	verb root – exist + stative aspect

Ši	huwatenhwa	He often carries, or is carried from afar
	huw-	masculine singular patient - he
	-at-	noun root – body
	-enhw-	verb root – carry
	-a	habitual aspect

tuh 'there' plus a verb

In Connelley's list of names published in 1900, he had the following entry, "Wolf Clan Tōōh'ä." He gave its meaning as 'There, i.e., at the Wolf's house or the Wolf's position in the tribal camp" (Connelley 1900:113). He appears to have left out the verb that was supposed to go with the particle 'tuh' meaning 'there'. It may have been one of the following three male names.

Tuh yandawias	There the river often breaks.
Yandawias	A river often breaks.
ya-	feminine-zoic singular agent – it
-ndaw-	noun root – river
-ia-	verb root – break
-s	habitual aspect

Tuh yaraskwan		(From) there I have departed, left.
Yaraskwan		I have departed, left.
	y-	1st person singular agent – I
	-araskwa-	verb root – depart, leave
	-n	stative aspect

Tuh yarihǫkye		There a matter, affair is going to continue.
Yarihǫkye		A matter is continuing
	ya-	feminine-zoic singular agent – it
	-rih-	noun root – matter, affair
	-ǫky-	verb root – continue
	-e	purposive aspect

Independent Noun plus Simple Verb

Amęnye tehat		He is standing in the water.
Amęnye		in the water
	am-	feminine-zoic singular patient – it
	-ę-	noun root – water
	=ye	external locative clitic
Tehat		He is standing.
	te-	dualic
	-ha-	masculine singular agent – he
	-t	verb root – stand + stative aspect

Amęnye ire		He is walking on water.
	amęn-	feminine-zoic singular patient – it + verb root - be water + stative aspect
	-ye	external locative clitic - on
Ire		He walks
	i-	partitive
	-r-	masculine singular agent – he
	-e	verb root – walk + stative aspect: he walks, is walking

Ǫndišraʔ ires		He often walks on ice. (male)
Ǫndišraʔ		ice
	ǫ-	feminine-zoic singular patient – it
	-ndišr-	noun root – ice
	-aʔ	noun suffix
ires		He (often) walks.
	-i-	partitive
	-r-	masculine singular agent – he
	-e-	verb root – go, come, walk
	-s	habitual aspect

Yariuta? tehat		A rock, he stands.
yariuta?		rock
	ya-	feminine-zoic singular agent – it
	-riut-	noun root – rock, stone
	-a?	noun suffix
Tehat		He stands
	te-	dualic
	-ha-	masculine singular agent – he
	-t-	verb root – stand + stative aspect

Two Simple Verbs

Tsawę ahęhaǫ		He said again.
Tsawę		It is said again.
	ts-	repetitive – again
	-aw-	feminine-zoic singular patient – she or it
	-ę	verb root – say + stative aspect
Ahęhaǫ		He said.
	-a-	factual
	-h-	masculine singular agent – he
	-ęhaǫ	verb root – say + punctual aspect

Tsawę Hinǫ		Thunder speaks again.
Tsawę		She or it speaks again.
	ts-	repetitive – again
	-aw-	feminine-zoic singular patient – she or it
	-ę	verb root – say, speak + stative aspect
Hinnon		thunderer

Hǫdikakǫ ižuh		It is like they (m) were seized by the cold.
hǫdikakǫ		They (m) were seized by the cold.
	hǫnd-	masculine plural patient – they (m)
	-ikakǫ	verb root – be seized by the cold + stative aspect
ižuh		It is like

The longest names have five meaningful parts, the norm for one-word names as well.

Chapter Three
Gender and Names

Detecting Gender in Name Morphology

With names in Indo-European languages—for example, the Romance languages such as Italian, Spanish, and French—first or Christian names are often marked for gender. In Italian, for example, male names often end with -o- with the female equivalent ending with an -a-: Mario/Maria, Gino/Gina, Alessandro/Alessandra and Ludovico/Ludovica, for example. In English they aren't as uniformly marked, but people usually know very well which gender a name belongs to. The jokes people (usually males) who were given gender-neutral names such as Leslie (people like my good friend Les) have to endure is a sign of that.

Iroquoian languages are one of the relatively few Indigenous language families in which gender is expressed pronominally: the masculine and feminine-zoic prefixes mentioned in the previous chapter. That distinction is a very active one in Wyandot. It should be pointed out that although the presence of masculine pronominal prefix such as -ha- or -hu- 'he' usually means that the name belongs to a male, there are a few examples when it does not. For example, the name I have presented as Tehurǫnyureta 'He often examines, considers the sky', is presented in Potier's baptismal records in 1741 as "agn[es]. Horonhioreta" (Toupin 1996:849) and without the first-name abbreviation in 1743 (Toupin 1996:851), both times as the mother of the baptized.

In most cases when you have a -ya- or -u- and other such feminine-zoic agents or patients alone in a name, that name is a female one. But that is not always the case. This happens much more often than when a masculine pronominal prefix goes with a female name.

A small number of names are held, identical or nearly identical except for distinguishing masculine and feminine pronominal prefixes (marked below by **bolding**), both by males and females. There are also two animal names, otter, and osprey, which are shared across gender, but, like many animal names, do not indicate for gender, and one animal name that takes the feminine-zoic singular agent, most likely with the meaning 'it'. There is no evidence that I can find that these matched names belonged to the same clan.

Names Shared By Both Genders

Name	Meaning	Gender	Clan
Harǫnyieht	He scrapes or scratches the sky.	male	---[1]
Ayarǫnyiet[2]	She or it scraped the sky.	female	Porcupine

---

1. The three dashes indicate that the clan is not known to me.

2. This is also different in taking the factual and the punctual aspect, while the male form takes the stative aspect.

Hatrewatih[3]	He is opposing, resisting, criticizing it.	male	Snake
Utrewatih[4]	She is opposing, resisting, criticizing it.	female	---
Hǫnǫste	He is stingy. (nickname)	male	---
Ǫnǫste	She is cheap, stingy. (nickname)	female	Striped Turtle
Harǫtwanęh	He is a large tree.	male	---
Yarǫtuwanęh	It is a big, large tree.	female	Bear
Skękyuhkwes	She has a very long family, lineage.	female	Bear
Shękyukwes	He has a very long lineage.	male	---
Yarǫtayęrat	She, it is a white tree, pole, log.	female	---
Sharǫtayęraht	He is a very white tree, pole, log.	male	---
Skandare	It exists again.	female	---
		male	---
Tawinde[5]	otter	female	---
		male	---
Tsamęhuhi?	osprey, eagle	female	Large Turtle
		male	possibly Porcupine

Gendered Recording Bias

Unfortunately, there is a distinct gendered recording bias in the history of writing Wyandot names. Almost all major sources have more male than female names. The number of female Wyandot names recorded here amount to roughly 60 percent of male names. Potier in his reporting of the two censuses of 1747 had roughly equal numbers, as he included baptisms and other religious ceremonies. This helped to balance the two numbers.

A major part of this imbalance comes from the recording of the names of chiefs and other male leaders in treaties and council meetings with the French, British and Americans. I have one example in which there are female leaders present, but their names are not recorded This comes from a report of a council meeting held regarding the death of Father Pierre Potier in 1781. At the end we get the following mention of the leading Wyandot who were there:

---

3. A French Jesuit priest by the name of Salleneuve shared this name (Toupin 1996:236).

4. There is also a difference in that the female name takes the patient form, while the male name takes the agent.

5. Animal names often do not have pronominal prefixes.

Names of the principal chiefs present
Tiockouanohon   Joriha
Toienthet   Isoncainen
Cimrathon   Tharatohat
Tihockeres
With the principal women of the Nation. (Lajeunesse 1960:126)

This meant that between the 1780s to the 1810s female names were distinctly underrepresented, as there were few other significant sources during that period.

Noun Roots and Gendering
THE SKY -rǫny-: THE MOST COMMON NOUN ROOT IN WYANDOT NAMES

The noun root that is involved more than any other in Wyandot names is -rǫny- the noun root for 'sky'.[6] It was used by every clan except for the Snake clan. There are 42 such names that I have been able to translate (there are more that I haven't been able to as yet), 26 of which are male, 16 female. As this mirrors the gender bias of the recording, we can say that ultimately there probably is a gender balance in names with this noun root.

VOICE, WORD, AUTHORITY -mę̨nd- / -wę̨nd-

There is more of a gender balance of names found with the noun root that has the second highest number of occurrences in recorded names -mę̨nd- / -wę̨nd- 'voice, word, authority'. It appears in 28 names, with 14 female and 14 male names. It appears in the Deer, Snake, Bear, Large Turtle, Striped Turtle, Porcupine and Wolf clans. The significance of this noun root in the Wyandot language, which traditionally was an oral not a written culture, can be seen in the fact that the word for God employs it. The noun root is bolded in the word.

hamę̨ndižu   He is great in voice, word, authority God.

One of the female names, Skamę̨ndižu 'She is a very great voice, is great in authority' involves the same verb root, so we know that any woman bearing this name would be a significant person.

Gendered Noun Roots in Names
MATTER

Perhaps the most frequently occurring noun root in the Wyandot language is -ri(h)(w)- 'matter, affair, news, law, word'. Accordingly, the noun root is the third most common one in Wyandot names. So far I have 21, 16 of which are male, only five female. So it can be said that use of this noun root is more a feature of a male than a female name.

---

6. See examples in the next chapter of names from the Large Turtle, Striped Turtle, Wolf and Snipe clans. It is a good source of metaphors in the language. In Barbeau 1960:81 word #35, a word that literally means 'they (m) are a large, great sky', is translated as "they are conversing." In Potier 1920:371 the noun root is used with the augmentative clitic to refer to being 'pleasant'. This is used in two Wyandot names.

Name	Translation	Clan
Male (16):		
Harihǫtawan	He is deposing her, it from a position.	---
Harihužah	He stirs up matters (e.g., is quarrelsome).	Striped Turtle
Hariwae	He hits, strikes a matter.	---
Hariwaerǫ	He tricks in a matter.	---
Hariwakyǫditi	He is saying or doing something surprising.	---
Hariwandinyǫtak	He used to suspend, hang matters.	Striped Turtle
Hariwandutǫ	He tells about a matter, affair.	---
Hariwawayi	He holds, grasps the matter.	Bear
Huriwaętǫk	He deals with many matters.	---
Huriwahętǫh	He is leading in a matter, affair.	---
Huriyehteʔ	He who bears a position of importance.	Striped Turtle
Shuriwaętǫʔ	He put, placed very many matters.	---
Šateyariwate	Two equal matters or statements.	---
Taharihǫkye	His affair, news is not going to continue.	---
Teyarihuyęh	A matter is divided, at a dividing point.	Striped Turtle
Tsuriwaht	He is one affair, matter.	---
Tuh yarihǫkye	There a matter, affair is continuing.	---
Female (5):		
Ši Yariwate	A matter exists far away.	---
Utriwąndet	She holds an important matter close to her.	Striped Turtle
Watriwanǫnę	She took care of, protected a matter in the past.	---
Yarihǫnętaʔ	She often drops matters, affairs.	Snake
Yariwaseʔ	It is new news, a new matter, law	Bear

Trees, Poles and Logs

The fourth most common noun root involved in Wyandot names recorded in this study is -rǫt- which means 'tree, pole, or log'. There are 16 such names, 13 of which are male names. This points to a kind of gendering operating here.

Name	Translation	Clan
Male (13):		
Ahatrǫtamęrat	He got over a log.	Wolf
Harǫtwanęh	He is a large tree.	---
Karǫtuʔ	Log lying in the water	Large Turtle
Sharǫtayęraht	He is a very white tree, pole, log.	---
Sharǫtǫkye	He again abandons a tree, log, pole.	Deer
Tehurǫtatiri	A tree is not supporting him.	---
Tehutrǫturęʔ	He splits a log in two.	---
Teyarǫtandeyęh	Two trees are joined, close together.	---
Teyarǫtayeʔ	Two trees	Bear
Teyarǫtuyęh	It is between two logs: Between the Logs.	Bear
Tsurǫtaętandih	A tree falls, is falling again.	---
Urǫtǫndih	A pole is made; Warpole.	Porcupine
Yarǫtęntawih	It is a tree sleeping.	---
Female (3):		
Yarǫtuwanęh	It is a big, large tree.	Bear
Sharǫtat	He is one tree, log, pole.	---
Yarǫkyakǫ	A tree is broken into many pieces.	---

Branches, Treetops

The same gender pattern seems true for the noun root -ręh 'branch, treetops', with six out of nine examples being male.

Name	Translation	Clan
Male (6):		
Haręhaęžat	He is at the top of the treetops.	---
Haręhatase?	He is going around a branch.	Large Turtle
Haręhutǫn	He is many standing treetops.	Large Turtle
Haręhužah	He moves, shakes the treetops.	Porcupine
Teharęhǫt	He is not putting the branch into the fire.	---
Sharęhes	He is very tall treetops, or long branch.	Snake or Deer
Female:		
Utręhętǫ?	A branch hangs down.	Striped Turtle
Yaręha?tsih	She is called treetops, branches.	---
Yaręnyakǫ	Branch(es), or treetops are broken in many pieces	---

EVERGREENS

Interestingly, the reverse is true for the eight names that have the noun root -nęt- 'evergreen' in them.

Name	Translation	Clan
Female (7):		
Ekyǫnętat	Where an evergreen stands, or evergreens stand.	---
Skanętarǫ?	Evergreens are again distant from each other.	---
Skanętatih	On the other side of the evergreen tree(s)	---
Skanętatǫ	It became evergreen again (perhaps a forest).	---
Unęta?	Evergreen	---
Yanętayi	She is eating an evergreen. (female).	---
Yanęti	It is an entire, intact evergreen (female).	---
Male (1):		
Hanękinyǫndih	He is an evergreen sticking out.	---

Names with Corn -nęh-

Corn, of course, has been very important to the Wyandot for hundreds of years. So it should not be surprising that the noun root for corn -nęh- appears in clan names. What surprises me is that of the 10 names I have discovered and translated, eight are for males, and only two for females.

Name	Translation	Clan
Male (8):		
Ahanęhutaha	He planted, stood up the corn.	---
Hanęhanyǫʔ	Corn often arrives for him.	---
Hanęhasa	He is small, little corn.	Prairie Turtle
Hunęharahwih	He is turning corn upwards.	---
Ǫnęharawi	Corn has been put up, set up.	---
Hanęhurak	He used to attach corn.	---
Tanęhušreh	Water is not going to flow in his corn.	Snake
Tehǫnęhawehtih	He does not have all the corn.	Deer
Female (2):		
Yanęduk	She is putting corn in water.	---
Yanęhǫtak	Corn used to be in the fire.	---

It should be pointed out that when it comes to pounding corn, a woman's task, both names found are for females.

Utesędi	She is grinding corn for her.	---
Yateta	She grinds corn with it (female).	---

Names with -ašr- Axe

There are nine names I have discovered that use the noun root -ašr- 'axe'. In all nine cases it is a man's name. I have added to this list the one name using 'axe blade'. There should be no surprise in this as axes were often used as metaphors for war. Potier makes reference to the following series of metaphors (Toupin 1996:284) under the heading "Terms et expressions des Sauvages", all connected with warfare. The translations from the original French are mine. Unfortunately, he did not write the words in Wyandot:

Literal Expression	Metaphorical Meaning
To tie up the axe	to suspend warfare
To sharpen the axe	to wish to commence war
To throw the axe into the depths of the earth	to no longer listen to talk of war
To fish the axe out of the river	to recommence war
To take away the axe	to cause a cessation in the hostilities
To throw the axe to the sky	to cause open warfare
To drop the axe	to cause a cessation of arms
To retake the axe	to recommence war
To attach the axe to the door	to issue a challenge

EXAMPLES OF NAMES (ADDING ONE WITH THE NOUN ROOT FOR AXE BLADE)

Name	Translation	Gender	Clan
Hašrayetak	He used to bear an axe on a strap.	male	---
Hašręhaǫ	He is carrying an axe.	male	Snake
Huhšruyuti	He is causing an axe to penetrate it.	male	Large Turtle
Huhšraęwahs	He often loses his axe.	male	Deer
Hašrǫnęta	He often drops an axe.	male	---
Huskwehšandet	He holds the axe blade close.	male	---
Hušrandetak	He used to hold an axe close.	male	---
Ǫmašrutǫywę	Our large number of great axes	male	---
Tewašraye	Two axes	male	Bear
Tawašruwanęh	Where there is a large axe.	male	(Frenchman)

NAMES OF SAND -NDEŠ-

I have found 11 Wyandot names for which I have a translation[7] that use the noun root for sand: -ndeš-. Nine of the 11 bearing the name are female. Five of the six names where clan can be determined are members of Turtle clans, four Large Turtle, one Prairie Turtle.

Of course, it is easy to see the association of turtles and sand as they are often seen in the sand. For me, the gender factor here possibly relates to the dramatic sight of a female turtle digging in the sand to create a hole to lay her eggs in. I witnessed this when I was eleven years old and can still readily bring the picture to mind.

---

7. Powell 1881:60 Man of Smooth Large Turtle…Hu[n]'-du-cu-tá) (Throwing Sand). While the noun root for sand is clearly there, I can find no verb root that gives the sense of 'throwing' to the word. The verb root -ut- 'stand' might be used here.

Name	Translation	Clan
Female:		
Ǫndešinyętǫk	She regularly follows the sand.	Deer
Ǫndešǫngyahak	She used to make sand.	Large or Striped Turtle
Ǫndehšuręs	She often finds sand.	Large Turtle
Ǫndehšurih	She is covered with sand.	Prairie Turtle
Skandešrisǫh	She is again up against a lot of sand.	---
Tǫndešrisǫʔ	Where she hits the sand many times or places.	---
Tsǫndehšratęh[8]	It is very dry sand.	Large Turtle
Yandeša	sand	---
Yandešarǫs	She often pierces sand.	---
Male:		
Hǫndešaręmąn	He is floating (in) sand.	Large Turtle
Hǫndeskǫtakwi	He is turning to face the sand in such a place.	---

Gender and Common Verb Roots in Wyandot Names
BE LONG, TALL -E(T)S-

There are 23 names with this verb root, with a relatively balanced gender ratio of 14 males to nine females. The examples with -es- are a bit confusing as they take the form of the habitual aspect, but have the meaning of the stative aspect, which outside of names occurs with the verb root as -etsi-. For consistency's sake, I will still label them as habitual.

Name	Translation	Clan
Male:		
Atuehtes	Every one of his nails is long.	Bear
Shandetes	He is a very tall pine.	---
Shandetsi	He has a very long arrow.	---
Sharęhes	He is very tall treetops, or long branch.	Striped and Prairie Turtle

8. I am not absolutely sure about the gender of this one, as it was not presented. The feminine-zoic singular patient pronominal prefix suggests that the individual bearing the name was a female.

Name	Translation	Clan
Shastahǫretsis	He has very long bone marrows.	Deer
Shastaretsi	He has very long antler spurs.	Deer
Shękyukwes	He has a very long lineage.	---
Skangyeretsih	It is a very long bird's tail, pipestone, canoe point.	---
Sǫmanduyareskwa	Our poplar(s) used to be very tall.	---
Sutraʔtes	His quills are often very long.	Porcupine
Šateyarǫnyes	It is often as tall, as the sky. Half the height of the sky.	Large Turtle
Tsukares	Very long wood chips.	---
Tsunǫšes	It is (often) a very long house.	---

Female:

Name	Translation	Clan
Iwanderes	My waist is long.	Bear
Skangywes	It is very long moosehide.	---
Skanǫdes	It is often a very long mark.	---
Skahwęndes	It is a very long island. [She has very long calves.]	Bear
Skękyuhkwes	She has a very long family, lineage.	Bear
Tanduyares	Where the poplars are tall	Prairie Turtle
Tsaǫndešres	Her country is very long.	---
Tsuteses	It is very long ribbon work, lacework.	---
Yaʔtetsis	Tall or long bodies	---

To Carry -ęHAǪ-

Of the 14 names that involve this generally prolific Wyandot verb, 10 are female.

Name	Translation	Clan

Female:

Name	Translation	Clan
Ayatsitsęmah	She brought, carried flowers.	Wolf
Ǫtaręmaǫh	She is carrying a lake.	Bear

Skanderęhaǫh	Her waist is carrying again.	---
Tewasęhaǫh	She is not carrying a spoon, dish, or bowl.	---
Tsundihšręhaǫh	She is carrying ice again.	---
Uyehtęhaǫh	Throughout the summer	---
Wehtęhaǫh	She is carrying a field.	---
Yayetęhaǫh	She carries nails, claws, talons.	---
Yęhaǫh	She carries it.	Bear
Yętsęhaǫh	She is carrying bait for fishing.	---

Male:

Handaʔaręnhaǫ	He is carrying antlers, horns.	---
Hašręhaǫ	He is carrying an axe.	Snake
Hǫnǫręhawit	He is going to carry his scalp.	---
Ši Huwaʔtęhwa	He often carries or is carried from afar.	Large Turtle

To Bear -yehte-

The verb root -yeht(e)- refers to bearing something on a strap around the neck or shoulder. Of the 12 examples found with names, 11 are male. One reason for this can be found in what Star Young told Barbeau about the carrying of meat from the hunt:

> Star Young stated that in the old time the hunters used to carry the meat wrapped up in the pelt and fastened on the lower part of their backs by means of a rope or strap that ran across their shoulders, in front (Barbeau 1915:124 fn #1)

Name	*Translation*	*Clan*
Male:		
Hašrayehtak	He used to bear an axe on a strap.	---
Hawęndayehte	He bears an island.	Large Turtle
Humęndayehte	He bears a word, a voice.	---
Huriyehte[9]	He who bears a matter, a position of importance.	---
Hurǫnyayehte	He bears the sky.	Wolf

9. Potier 1920:250 "porter les affaires, etre chargé de q. commission, etre lieutenant de q. pour avoir soin de ses affaires [to bear the affairs, to be charged with some commission, to be lieutenant for someone, having care of their affairs]."

Huhšęndayehte	He bears a name around his neck/shoulder.	Bear
Hustayehtak	He often bears bark.	Porcupine
Ǫmayehtak	It bears us on a strap around its shoulder or neck.	Deer
Tsuahayehte	One bears a sack again.	Bear
Tsunǫyašehte	It again bears a beak	---
Urayehte	It bears air, wind.	---

Female:

Yaaʔtayehtak	She used to bear a body.	---

To Stand -UT-

There are 12 recorded names that use this verb root. Only one is female. A similar gendering exists with the other verb meaning to stand -t-, a verb that does not incorporate noun roots, of which five out of six are male.

Name	*Translation*	*Clan*
Male:		
Ahanęhutaha	He planted, stood up the corn.	---
Haręhut	He is or has a standing treetop.	---
Handutǫ	He is putting up many arrows.	Porcupine
Hangyarutah	His tail repeatedly stands.	Deer
Haręhutǫn	He is many standing treetops, branches.	Large Turtle
Huręndut	He is a standing stone, rock.	---
Ǫndayarut	It is a standing horn, antler.	---
Taharǫnyutęh	He stuck out in the sky.	Deer
Tewętut	A stick is not stuck in the ground.	---
Utęrut	It is a standing palisade, a tower (nickname).	Frenchman
Yangwirut	Standing corn tassels	Prairie Turtle
Female:		
Teutrǫnyuta	She or it does not (regularly) stand up in the sky.	---

To Stand -T-

Five out of the six names using the alternative verb root for 'stand' (-t-) are male. The difference between this and the previous verb is that this verb does not incorporate noun roots (except for the noun root for 'body'). The one gender exception involves the noun root for 'evergreen', which we have seen always involves a female name.

Name	Translation	Clan
Male:		
Ameye tehat	He is standing in the water.	---
Ameye	in the water	
Tehat	He is standing	
Tehaa'tat	He, his body is standing.	Striped Turtle
Tehatas	He often stands up.	---
Teyatak	It used to stand.	Large Turtle
Yariuta' tehat	A rock, he stands.	---
Yariuta'	rock	
Tehat	he stands	
Female:		
Ekyonetat	Where an evergreen stands, or evergreens stand.	---

Wyandot Names with a Twist

The verb root -tase- means to turn or twist. These are six names that contain the verb, all but one from a Turtle clan. All are male.

Name	Translation	Clan
Harehatase'	He is going around a branch.	Large Turtle.
Ndikaratase	They two (f) have twisted loins, flanks.	Snake
Teharhatase'	He is twisting, going around the forest.	Large Turtle
Tehatotaratase'	He is twisting, going around the lake.	Striped Turtle[10]
Tehatronyatase'	His sky is twisted; he is twisting the sky.	Bear
Taotowetsatase'	Where one twisted, turned the land.	---

---

10. One thing that I find curious about this name (Powell 1881:60) is that associated with the Snake clan's story of origin are songs, including ones entitled "He twists himself in the lake" and "I go around the lake" (Barbeau 1915:91, fn2).

Summary

We have seen in this chapter how gender is marked morphologically with pronominal prefixes, and how certain nouns and verbs were used more with males or females or balanced out between the two. This latter point teaches us a bit about gender associations that we might not know about otherwise.

The important point has been made that there exists a gender bias with more male names being recorded than female ones. This has meant for me that more can be said about male than female names. This reflects the culture of those who wrote down the names, which was more patriarchal than that of the Wyandot, whose names were being recorded. The recordkeeping of Father Pierre Potier was an exception to this. He and his colleagues documented over 1,500 baptisms, as well as other ceremonial occasions, particularly those honouring the dead.

Chapter Four
Clan Naming

Introduction

In an article entitled "Iroquoian Clans and Phratries" published in the prestigious academic journal, *American Anthropologist*, Marius Barbeau wrote:

> Each clan owned exclusively a list of animal names, a varying proportion of which referred to the clan animal; such proportion being large among the Wyandot (Barbeau 1917:402).

It is often not easy to detect the clan animal reference in a Wyandot clan name. Such names are often quite subtle in their meaning, not making explicit or literal reference to the clan animal. Take, for example, the following explanation of the connotations of the Large Turtle name Teharhatase? 'He is twisting, going around the forest':

> Name Räh'-hahn-tah'-sěh. Means "Twisting the forest," i.e., as the wind moves, waves, and twists the willows along the banks of the stream in which the turtle lives. (Connelley 1900:111)

In this chapter I will present a number of such names. In addition, you will read about names that as clan names have been passed down over the centuries. Three of them— Shastaretsi of the Deer clan and Hustayehtak and Haskutaše of the Porcupine clan—have been tied to five identified so-named people from the 17th until well into the 19th century.

Deer Clan

There are 38 translated Deer clan names in this collection, 25 male and 13 female. Few of these names have an obvious connection to that clan, based purely on a literal translation. One takes the word for 'deer' and adds the diminutive aspect suffix:

Uskęnǫtǫha	Little Deer	(male Deer)

Then there are names that refer to parts of the body of a deer:

Shastaretsi	He has very long antler spurs.
Shastahǫretsi?s	He has very long bone marrows.

The name Hǫnǫrawęǫt 'He has a bump or bulge on his scalp' is less obvious. Finley (1840:31) states that 'Lump-on-the head' is a Deer clan name, "denoting a buck fawn," the reference being to the beginnings of antlers.

Deer Clan Names in Connelley

William E. Connelley was a white historian, teacher and writer who is a good source of implications of Wyandot names as opposed to strictly literal translations. There are two reasons for this. First, he was provided with the broader meaning by his informants, who were probably used to doing so with non-speakers of Wyandot. Second, he did not have the knowledge to do the literal translations himself. Unfortunately, too often we only have the broader connotations, in large part because the way in which he recorded the name makes it very difficult to arrive at a literal translation.

The Deer clan names recorded by Connelley are the most informative of his clan name descriptions. This was probably because he was adopted as a Wyandot of the Deer clan by Catherine Johnson (Garrad 2014:539), Marius Barbeau's primary informant for the Wyandot language stories of 1911–2 that made up his *Forty Narratives* (Steckley 2020:3-4).

Unfortunately, the name given to Connelley himself is difficult to translate. In the Wyandot origin story, the rainbow helps the deer go up into the sky (Barbeau 1915:44) It should be no surprise, then, that a word referring to the rainbow should be a Deer clan name.

> From this circumstance, the Deer is sometimes spoken of as Deh'-hehn-yihn'-teh[1], – 'The Rainbow', or, more properly, 'The path of many colors made for the Deer by the Rainbow'. This is one of the oldest names for men in the list of names belonging to the Deer Clan. It is one of the Wyandot names of the writer. (Connelley 1899a:124)

The word does *not* literally mean 'the path of many colors.' There is no word for 'color' in the Wyandot language. The reference to 'many' is unlikely as the verb does not have the distributive root suffix, which contains a nasal -o- (i.e., -ǫ-). The noun root for 'path' -ahah- is absent.

Connelley also wrote the name as 'Dēh-hĕhn-yahn-'he' (Connelley 1899b:9). With either spelling it is difficult to analyse. The initial -deh- could be the definite article 'the, who, that which'. The noun root might be -hny-, cognate with the Mohawk noun root "-ʔnhy- rainbow" (Michelson 1973:130), the Oneida verb root -ʔnhyal- (Michelson and Doxtator 2002:854), and the -ʔnhny- that appears to be a noun root in the Cayuga word for rainbow (Froman et al 2002:255).

My incomplete analysis is as follows. I used the second writing, as a verb root seems possible with it.

De Hehnyateh	It is a rainbow.	(male Deer)
de	the	
he-	?	
-nhy-	noun root – rainbow	
-a-	joiner vowel	
-te-	verb root – exist	
-h	stative aspect	

1. This appears to be different from the Wendat word for 'rainbow ti·ondienhakennion' (Steckley 2010:49), which I cannot translate completely either.

Catherine Johnson's name he recorded as 'Yah-rōhn'-yäh-ah-wih' 'The Deer goes in the sky and everywhere' (Connelley 1900:113). I have recorded and more literally translated it as Yarǫnyą'wi' 'She is canoeing or floating in the sky'.

Her son Allen, who helped Barbeau interpret his mother's stories recorded in Wyandot, had his name presented by Connelley as 'Shrih'-āh-wahs' 'Cannot find deer when he goes hunting' (Connelley 1900:113). Barbeau presents it as meaning, 'he cannot find axe or game' (Barbeau 1915:xi). My own literal translation for what I represent as 'Huhšraęwahs' is 'He often loses his axe'. In an earlier chapter we saw that the noun root -ašr- 'axe' has broad metaphorical potential.

Connelley presents a particularly informative link of name with animal with 'Hähr-zhäh-tooh-ngk' 'He marks, i.e., the big buck comes to the mark to meet all comers of his kind of whatever number or size'[2] (Connelley 1900:109). A literal translation is 'Hažatǫh' 'He marks, writes'.

The same is found with the male Deer clan name: "''Mah'-yĕh-tĕh'-hah't' 'Stand in the water'. Refers to the habit of the deer, which stands in summer to get rid of the annoyance of flies." (Connelley 1900:113). I have presented and analysed it as 'Amęye Tehat' 'In the water he is standing'.

In *Wyandot Folklore*, he recorded Mrs. Alfred Mudeater's name as 'Mehn'-dih-deh'-tih'. He interpreted it as meaning:

> ... the echo; the wonderful talker; what she says goes a long way and then comes back again. Refers to the deer's voice echoing in the night when calling his fellows (Connelley 1899b:35).

My own more complete and literal translation is 'Yamęndindetih' 'She causes her voice to come'. In the origin story, the deer was the first animal to take the rainbow road into the sky (Barbeau 1915:44). When it spoke to the other animals, its voice had to go a long way.

Hers is the only female Deer clan name for which we have a record of more than one holder. The other was Christine, who in 1755 co-sponsored a mortuary ceremony (Toupin 1996:926). In 1757 and 1760, she was recorded as the mother of a baptized child, her name written as '8oindinde'ti' and 'a8oindeti' respectively (Toupin 1996:875 and 881).

Some of his translations and connotations just do not seem to work. His recording of a male Deer clan name 'Shäh-rahn-tah' is loaded with difficulties that severely hinder translation. The meaning he gives is "The young buck drops its spots, i.e., the fawn changing color." (Connelley 1900:109). The noun root -yarę- for spots, and the verb root -ǫnet- 'drop' are not present. There is no Wyandot word for 'color', and the word for 'young male buck'—given earlier—is not involved.

He does not mention a gender for the next name, presented as 'Tŏŏh-mĕh's A pond: a deer lick'. (Connelley 1900:110). I have no translation for this. Neither the noun root for 'lake' -ǫtar- or the verb root 'lick' -yahnęs- appear to be in this word.

---

2. Perhaps, then, the female Deer clan name I have recorded as 'Yanǫduwanęh She has, or it is a large mark, line, or sign' relates to a similar kind of mark made by a female deer.

Likewise with no gender specified is the Deer clan name 'Nēhn'-gah-nyohs': "It describes the act of a deer throwing up its hair when angry." (Connelley 1900:110). It does not relate to any word for hair or fur that I have found.

Next, with the gender not specified, is 'Nahn-dōōh'-zhoh. An old deer' (Connelley 1900:113). It does not have the verb root -'tǫ- 'be old' . I do not yet have a literal translation.

Gender again not specified, we have Connelley's 'Tĕh'-skŏŏk-hĕh-ng' 'At (or in) the deer lick' (Connelley 1900:113). It does not link to any literal translation I can make.

Shastaretsi

One of the most revered of Wyandot names is Shastaretsi, the name most often associated with being the principal or grand chief of the people. He was also chief of the Deer clan and the Deer phratry during the 18th century and presumably before that as well. It is a name for which we have references to five people:

Shastaretsi	He has very long antler spurs
s-	repetitive - very
-ha-	masculine singular agent – he
-star-	noun root – antler spurs
-ets-	verb root – be long or tall
-i	stative aspect

As with other Wyandot names there are many variations of the spelling of the name. In Charles Garrad's master work *Petun to Wyandot: The Ontario Petun from the Sixteenth Century* (2014), he told of having recorded "more than 60 variations of this name." (Garrad 2014:538). I have added a new variation myself with the addition of the barely pronounced but grammatically necessary -h- after the initial -s-.

Shastaretsi #1: 17th-Century Chief

The recorded history of the name begins a little more than a decade after the first dispersal of the Wyandot ancestors in the mid-17th century. On June 2, 1661, Jesuit Father René Ménard wrote that three Frenchmen were travelling to where the ancestors were living at the time, Black River, Wisconsin, their second diasporic home. Father Ménard wrote that "They have a present to be given to Sasteretsi on my behalf…" (JR46:143).

In 1682, when the Wyandot were at Michilimackinac, where Lake Huron and Lake Michigan meet, there was recorded the oratory of Kandiaronk or Rat speaking on behalf of the Wyandot in the name of the chief of the people, Shastaretsi:

> Some Hurons, or Tionnontatez, comprised under the name of their chief Sataretsi (spelling varies), arrived at Montreal … communicated their first word[3]… through

---

3. By this is meant the first aspect of a speech represented metaphorically by a single word.

their Orator, Soüoïas,[4] in French the Rat.... Speaking in the singular number under the name Sateretsi—they had come down at the request of Onontio their father ... to learn his will.... The same Soüoïas, after a pause, said; Onontio, thy son Sataretsi hath just stated that he made an alliance with Ouiatanon[5]... He intreats Onontio to receive and to protect them as he does Sataretsi....Onontio, thy son Saretsi styled himself formerly thy brother; but he has ceased to be such, for he is now they son.... Onontio, thy son Sataretsi hath an upright mind. Sataretsi stand before the eyes of Onontio, his father. (NYCD 1855: 178–179)

This passage has led an unfortunately large number of scholars over the years to conflate Kandiaronk and Shastaretsi.[6] They were two different people. Kandiaronk did not belong to the Deer clan, and unfortunately for prospects for learning more about the name, this great orator and politically savvy Wyandot was the only one recorded as bearing this name.

In a work first published in 1703 in French and English, *New Voyages to North America, Giving a Full Account of the Customs, Commerce, Religion and Strange Opinions of the Savages of that Country*, based on his travels in New France from 1683 to 1692, French traveller and occasionally imaginative recorder of places and people, Louis Armand, Baron de Lahontan, added considerably to the recorded story of Shastaretsi. In his discussion of the matrilineal descent of the Wyandot, he posed the question:

Now it may be ask'd how the name of *Sastaretsi*, has been kept up for the space of Seven or Eight Hundred Years among that People [the Wyandot], and is likely to continue to future Ages? (Lahontan 1970, volume 2: 461)

Horatio Hale in 1883 reported a similar story telling of the longstanding authority of the name/title Shastaretsi, when he articulated the belief of his informant Anderdon Chief Joseph White, bearing the Wolf clan name Ǫmandurǫ? (written as Mondoron) 'it is difficult for us', that a Shastaretsi had led his people from the St. Lawrence to their home by Lake Huron, where they were first encountered by Europeans. Then, just before he died, this Shastaretsi wrote on a birch-bark scroll directions to where they could live in the Detroit area (Hale 1883:480). In the story he told, they followed Shastaretsi's directions to get there.

Shastaretsi #2: Matthias the King
Writing in 1744, early French historian Jesuit Father Pierre François Xavier Charlevoix spoke about the position being like that of a king. Later on, the term 'half-king' would be used:

---

4. It could be that this is a mangled spelling of the Wendat word for muskrat, Tsisk8aia.

5. This refers to the Algonquian-speaking Miami.

6. See the list of 10 presented in Garrad 2014:539.

> ... Sasteratsi, whom our French call the King of the Hurons, is in fact the hereditary Chief of the Tionnontatez, who are the true Hurons. (Charlevoix 1923, vol. 1:286)

According to the 1747 census, Matthias Sastaretsi was living in a Deer clan longhouse in which there lived 39 people (Steckley 2014:224 and Toupin 1996:211–2, and 245–7). He was the chief of the Deer clan, phratry and the grand chief of the Wyandot (Toupin 1996:226–7 and 259–60) at that time. His death in October of that year during a trip to Quebec to visit the French governor Onnontio (Toupin 1996:922) was a severe blow to Wyandot leadership at the time.[7]

Shastaretsi #3: A Generous Chief
We first read about this next Shastaretsi in 1758, when he opposed a French proposal to ally against the Haudenosaunee (Johnson 1922:795). In 1759 and 1760 he was recorded as giving mortuary gifts at five different ceremonies, showing the generosity of a chief (Toupin 1996:943–5, 947, 953, and 955). This Shastaretsi died in 1765; we know this as there was an annual mortuary ceremony for him in 1766 (Toupin 1996:959).

Shastaretsi #4: The First to Sign
The last treaty upon which there is a Shastaretsi signature is Treaty #2, which resulted in a large piece of land in southwestern Ontario being signed away in 1790. 'Sastaritse' was the first of 13 Wyandot signatures (Lajeunesse 1960:173).

Shastaretsi #5: The Last of a Long Line
William E. Connelley (1855–1930) was the fifth and last Shastaretsi. In his words, he was "an adopted Wyandot of the Deer Clan, raised up to fill the position of Sahr'-stahr-rah-tseh, the famous chief of the Wyandots known to history as the Half-King" (Connelley 1899b:9).

THE RAT: NOT ANOTHER NAME FOR SHASTARETSI

A New York Colonia Document published in 1855 records the 1682 words of Kandiaronk or Rat speaking on behalf of the Wyandot in the name of Shastaretsi, the chief of the people:

> Some Hurons, or Tionnontatez, comprised under the name of their chief Sataretsi (spelling varies), arrived at Montreal ... communicated their first word[8] ... through their Orator, Soüoïas[9], in French the Rat. ... Speaking in the singular number under the name Sateretsi—they had come down at the request of Onontio their father ... to learn his will. ... The same Soüoïas, after a pause, said; Onontio, thy son Sataretsi hath

---

7. This was compounded by the death around the same time of Tayešatę 'Ride me', the Wolf clan and phratry chief.

8. By this is meant the first aspect of a speech represented metaphorically by a single word.

9. It could be that this is a mangled spelling of the Wendat word for muskrat, Tsisk8aia.

just stated that he made an alliance with Ouiatanon....[10] He intreats Onontio to receive and to protect them as he does Sataretsi.... Onontio, thy son Saretsi styled himself formerly thy brother; but he has ceased to be such, for he is now they son.... Onontio, thy son Sataretsi hath an upright mind. Sataretsi stand before the eyes of Onontio, his father. (NYCD 1855: 178–179)

This passage has led an unfortunately large number of scholars over the years to conflate Kandiaronk and Shastaretsi.[11] They were two different people.

A leading figure and orator or speaker for the Wyandot from the 1680s to the Great Peace of Montreal in 1701, in which he played a major role, Rat was known by several names: Kandiaronk or Kondiaronk, 'Soüoïas or The Rat' (NYCD9 1855:178 and JR64:257 and 281), and also as Adario (as Baron Lahontan called him). None of these names appear to have been passed down to others.

The name 'Rat' is linked with the Wyandot words Soüoïas, Soiaga or Soüaïti, which might be a Wyandot cognate with the Wendat 'tsisk8aia' meaning 'muskrat' (Steckley 2010:41), the same name written badly in three different ways. His mark or signature on the document of the Great Peace of Montreal has an image that looks to me like a muskrat seen from above. Beside it were written the words "marque du rat chef des hurons."

Of the two names Kandiaronk and Kondiaronk, the former is the most likely, with a cislocative or dualic -t- combining with a -ya- of the feminine-zoic singular agent. A -k- before an -o- is much less likely. It is written with the Wendat feature -ndy- where Wyandot would have -ngy-. A potential translation might be the following, with a possible reference to the slight webbing of the digits on the back paws of a muskrat.

Kangyaro̧k	Its fingers often, regularly cross.
k-	dualic
-a-	feminine-zoic singular agent – it
-ngy-	noun root – finger
-a-	joiner vowel
-ro̧-	verb root – cross
-k	habitual aspect

The name Adario is a little confusing as you do not find an -a- followed by a -d- in Wyandot or Wendat. There should be an -n- in-between. There is a noun root -ndar- 'cheek', and -io- is most likely the verb root 'be great', for a combination meaning 'large cheek', which might apply to the muskrat.

So what we may have here are three nicknames referring to the muskrat. However, I cannot be sure. I may well be taking this too far.

As to the clan of this man, I wrote in 2014 that he may have been of the Wolf clan (Steckley 2014:214). But further research has left me uncertain.

---

10. This refers to the Algonquian-speaking Miami.

11. See the list of 10 presented in Garrad 2014:539.

Snake Clan
THREE NAMES FROM THE CLAN ORIGIN STORY

This collection has 21 Snake clan names, 11 female and 10 male. At one point, two of those names were held by the same woman, Sarah Dagnett, both of which relate to the Snake clan's story of its origin ("The Snake Clan," Barbeau 1915:90–1, and 1960:12, 101–4). In that story a young woman falls in love with a handsome and charming male snake, who becomes her husband. In the course of the story her legs join together; she is halfway to becoming a snake.

The first name of the woman has is presented by Connelley as follows: "Yah’-äh-täh-sĕh. Means, 'A new body'. Said of the snake when she slips off her old skin, as snakes do once a year." (Connelley 1900:111). I believe it also refers to the changing of the woman's body in the story. My presentation of the name is Yaaʔtaseh 'Her body is new'. Its significance can be seen in part as it is the only Snake clan name that is recorded more than once. The earlier recorded holder of the name was a godmother at a baptism in 1772, the name written as ,aatase (Toupin 1996:895).

Sarah's second name relates to a later part of the story. When the woman realizes that her husband is in fact a big snake, she flees. In Connelley's words:

> The act of the woman in leaving her husband's lodge is called Ooh-dah-tohn-teh. It is perhaps the first name for wom[e]n in the list belonging to the Snake clan. It means, 'She has left her village' (Connelley 1900:117–8, as quoted in Barbeau 1915:341)

I have written the name as Aǫndatǫti 'She abandoned, left her village, community'.

She fled to the seacoast and met a man with a canoe who offered to help her escape her husband. When the man and the Young Woman in the canoe had gone some distance they heard the Snake-Man coming in pursuit, calling to his wife and entreating her to return. He came to the water, and waded in a way in his effort to follow her, always crying out to her to return. This act of the Snake is called Kāh-yōōh-mĕhn-dä'tah by the Wyandots, and signifies entreating without avail, or crying to one your voice does not reach, or does not affect. This word is one of the oldest names for men in the list belonging to the Snake Clan. James Splitlog of the Wyandot Reserve is so named. He is one of the very few left of the Snake Clan. (Barbeau 1915:341)

Barbeau presents James Splitlog's name as kuyumɛndĕta and käyuméndèta (Barbeau 1911:14 and 35 respectively).

For me, a more accurate representation of the name is: Kayumǫndata. There is no way in the context of this word that the -eta- can be applied to any verb in Wyandot. The word as I have presented it can be translated and analysed as follows:

Kayumǫndata[12]	When one's voice, word ends. (male Snake)
k-	cislocative – when
-ayu-	indefinite patient – one
-mǫnd-	noun root – voice, word

---

12. Barbeau 1911:14 and 35, and Connelley 1899b:87–8 and 1900:117–8 (see Barbeau 1915: 341–2).

-a-		joiner vowel
-ta-		verb root – end + stative aspect

Potier wrote of a man who lived during the 1730s to early 1750s who had a name that seems identical or close to it. He appears to be Porcupine clan. His nickname of 'le manchot' ('the one armed') represented him as one of the leaders of that clan (Toupin 1996:226). The name appears as follows:

Name	Reference
tio8endata	Toupin 1996:204
tion8oindata	Toupin 1996:241
tiaon8endata	Toupin 1996:827
etiao8endata	Toupin 1996:833
tia8endata	Toupin 1996:837–8, 840, 846, 852, 855 and 863

I put them in two separate entries in the translations, the latter as Ekyayumęndata, which is a name shared with the Wendat. I believe this to be different but am not yet sure how.

Burning Tongue: Clan Chief

The first Snake clan name that is recorded is that of Hundahšateyę' 'His tongue is burning'. He was recorded in 1682 as 'Ondahiaste chen', one of three leaders representing the Wyandot in a meeting in Montreal on August 15 (NYCD9:181).

The next person with the name recorded appears prominently in the baptismal record from 1731 to 1744 as a godfather of 12 people, four of them adults (Toupin 1996:829–30, 832, 835, 840, 842–3 and 853). That is the highest number of any Wyandot. He had adopted a boy, whose father was unknown to Potier, who was adopted at 10 and was 13 years old in 1747 (Toupin 1996:206 and 242). In that year Burning Tongue was the clan chief (Toupin 1996:226, his name written only as Mathias), but not an elder (Toupin 1996:228). He was clearly appreciated by Potier, as on his death notice in 1747 were written the words "bon chretien et tres fidel[e] françois" ["good Christian and very faithful to the French"] (Toupin 1996:922). Strangely, considering the prominent status of the two name-holders just described, the name does not appear again in the written record.

The Invisible Snake

Charles Lofland's Snake clan name was presented as: "'Teh'-hooh-mah'-yehs" meaning 'You cannot see him,' or 'He is invisible'" (Connelley 1899b:36). I have analysed this as:

Tehumayęs		They (indefinite), people, one often cannot see him. (male Snake)
	te-	negative
	-huma-	indefinite agent + masculine singular patient – they or one – him
	-yę-	verb root – see
	-s	habitual aspect

I believe this describes well how difficult it is sometimes to see snakes nearby.

THE TWISTED LOINS

Ndikaratase	They two (f) have twisted loins, flanks. (male Snake)
nd-	feminine-zoic dual agent – they two (f)
-ikar-	noun root – flank, loins
-a-	joiner vowel
-tase	verb root – twist, turn + stative aspect

This may be related to the part of the Snake clan origin story when the young woman and the male snake are both snakes.

Bear Clan
BEAR CHARACTERISTICS

The Bear clan has the second highest number of names in this collection, at 45. James B. Finley stated that "Between-the-logs, Three-logs [actually Two Logs], &c., refers to the Bear tribe [i.e., clan], denoting the manner in which the bear crouches, or sleeps" (Finley 1840;31).

Teyarǫtuyęh	It is between the logs, trees, poles.
Teyarǫtaye'	Two logs, trees, poles.

I imagine that included in the "&c" might be the Splitlog name:

Tehutrǫturę'	He splits a log, tree, pole in two.

Barbeau reported a similar subtle tree reference for a male Bear clan name with Robert Dawson's name that he presented as "'Tā'tatäñą' 'wrap around a tree." (Barbeau 1911:16). My version of the name has it as: 'Tehatatatǫh He surrounds it' (i.e., with arms wrapped around a tree). This fits with the tree connection with males discussed in the previous chapter.

The female Bear clan name that I presented as Tsamęndakaę 'She speaks very slowly' was given by John Wesley Powell as "Tsá-ma-da-ka-é (*Grunting for her Young*)." (Powell 1881:60)

Two female Bear names relate to caves:

Ǫnǫdu	It is a cave, or she has a cave.
Ǫnǫdu-haǫ	It or she is from a cave.

A male Bear name refers to claws: Atuehtes[13] 'Every one of his nails is long'.

---

13. Powell 1881:60: A-tu-e-těs *(Long Claws)*.

Another name describes how you see and hear what a bear does before you actually see the bear:

Uskwirǫta'ta   It (often) shakes bushes, undergrowth. (male Bear)

Several Bear clan names appear in the written record in a number of incarnations. The male Bear name that has the most, Hariwawayi 'He holds, grasps the matter, will be discussed in chapter seven.

SHE IS CARRYING A LAKE

One of the female Bear names with more than one recorded holder over the years is that of Mary McKee, who provided stories in Wyandot and English for Marius Barbeau. I have presented the name as Ǫtarǫmaǫh 'She is carrying a lake'. Barbeau wrote the name without the initial ǫ- and presented two alternative translations. The one that matches the one presented here is "carrying a pond." The alternative was "holding mud" (Barbeau 1915:xi). I suspect that Barbeau might have been hypothesizing that the noun root -tar- 'clay, mud' was in her name. In 1734, the record of a baptism has the mother's name presented as "Ontaren8a" (Toupin 1996:835; see Steckley 2011:203), the nasal vowel plus -w- later to become an -m-.

SHE OFTEN TIES KNOTS

Another female Bear name that has several reported holders is Kwęndinde?s 'She often ties knots'. In 1729 we find Anastasia as a godmother at the baptism of a girl receiving the same Christian name (Toupin 1996:826). In 1743, there is Maria, the mother of a newly baptized child, whose Wyandot name was written 'ok8endindes' (Toupin 1996:852). In 1747 we have someone, probably Maria, who has a new Wyandot clan name, with her old name, 'ka8indes', in brackets following (Toupin 1996:214). In 1755, there is a mortuary anniversary of someone called 'k8indindes', most likely Maria (Toupin 1996:926).

Her probable successor is the mother of a son baptized in 1774 (Toupin 1996:898). In 1790, Father François-Xavier Dufaux, who knew little of the language, wrote that 'guannedides' was the mother of a newly-baptized son (Toupin 1996:978). So, from 1729 until 1790, we have what could be four different women who bore this important clan name. Over a century later, Mary Splitlog had the name (Barbeau 1911:14 and 35). The unresolved question is how a name referring to knots would belong to the Bear clan. There probably was a story, later forgotten, that explained it.

Large Turtle Clan
NAMES AND THE ORIGIN STORY

The Large Turtle clan has the highest number of names in this collection with 47. There is a link, of course, between the Large Turtle clan and the large turtle that became Turtle Island. That is recognized in at least three names. In a female name we have: Ayanyęmiha 'She learned how to do it; she knows how'. Connelley wrote the following about the name "Nyĕh'-mĕh-ah. Means 'Accomplisher.' Refers to the work of the Big Turtle in the creation." (Connelley 1900:112).

The earliest written reference to this name is in Potier's census of 1747, with the name written as "anienh8iha" (Toupin 1996:211). Both Connelley, as we have seen, and Barbeau, recorded the name. Barbeau talks about the name being held by a Mary Williams Walker who was 83 years old in 1912 and worked as an informant regarding the stories (Barbeau 1915:xi).

Another apparent reference to the Turtle Island turtle in a Large Turtle name belongs to a male I have presented as Hawęndayehte' 'He bears an island'. The first apparent reference is a little confusing, as the name is in the < > brackets used by Toupin to add a name as part of the baptismal record in 1734 of a 12-year-old Fox boy (one of several Fox baptized that year) (Toupin 1996:835). More secure are the references in Barbeau with a "Thomas Walker Węndăyĕtĕ' carrying an island on his back" (Barbeau 1911:3, also see 10 and 49; and 1915:xii).

With one of the Large Turtle male names, Connelley writes "Têh'-häh-rōhn'-yooh-rĕh. Means 'Splitting the sky,' i.e., the Big Turtle is rushing across the sky, dividing it with his course" (Connelley 1900:111). Again this appears to be a reference to the origin myth. I have presented the name as: Teharǫnyuręs 'He often splits the sky in two'.

I should point out here that the Large Turtle clan has, with six, the largest number of recorded sky names of any clan. Mind you, it also has the greatest number of recorded clan names. These six also include:

Harǫnya'es	He often strikes the sky. (male)
Šateyarǫnyes	It is often as tall as the sky. Half the height of the sky. (male)
Teharonyateka'	His sky is not burning. (male)
Utrǫnyayęk	She is regularly seen in the sky. (female)
Yarǫnyawayih	She holds, grasps the sky. (female)

These too may be related to the origin myth.

CHARACTERISTICS OF THE LARGE TURTLE

There are also names that relate to physical characteristics and behaviours of a turtle.

Connelley gives the name of John Poynter, a Black slave whom Adam Brown bought and then adopted. He wrote the following:

> Named Sooh'-quĕhn – tah'–rah–nēh. Means the act of the Big Turtle in sticking out his head when it is drawn into its shell. A good translation would be "He sticks out his head." (Connelley 1900:110)

I have interpreted it as: Tsukętaranǫ 'It stretches itself out very many times'. Then there is the male Large Turtle name Huhšaę' 'He is a slow walker, is slow moving' (Barbeau 1911:2).

Striped Turtle Clan
NAMES OF THE ORIGIN STORY

There are 35 Striped Turtle clan names in my collection, two seeming to be shared with another clan. A very meaningful female Striped Turtle name was recorded by Connelley, as Wah-trohn-'yoh-noht-nĕh "She takes care of the sky," or "Keeper of the heavens." (1900:112). My interpretation of the word is Watrǫnyanǫnę 'She took care of the sky (in the past)'. This relates to the role that the Striped Turtle (sometimes called the Little or Small Turtle) played in the Wyandot origin myth, where it collected lightning to create the sun and the moon. Barbeau collected this story in English for his *Huron and Wyandot Mythology* (Barbeau 1915:37–47).

The storyteller was B. N. O. Walker, whose father was Striped Turtle and mother was Large Turtle. Although he was first given a Large Turtle name, which he writes as Cęnda''crę''te' (Barbeau 1915:x, see šendahšrehte' in Translations), in Barbeau's words, "he has since assumed the name of Hę''tǫ' or Hętǫ'' (*he leads, or is a leader*) of the Small or Striped Turtle clan, which was formerly borne by John Greyeyes, one of his relatives." (Barbeau 1915:x). In one of his writings, Walker wrote his name as HEN-TON (*Chronicles of Oklahoma* 6(1), March 1928, republished in www.wyandotte-nation.org/culture/history/biographies/bno-walker/). I present it more completely as Hahętǫ' 'He is leading, he leads'. The leading involved probably relates to the origin story.

STRIPED TURTLE CHARACTERISTICS

A good name description of a turtle is the female Striped Turtle name Tsušaę' 'She goes very slowly', a near equivalent of the male Large Turtle name mentioned before.

Connelley presents one female Striped Turtle clan name as "Trĕh-hĕhn-toh. Means, 'Tree shaking,' i.e., by the current, or flow of water against it." (Connelley 1900:112). This word does not contain the verb roots for 'shake' or 'move'. My interpretation of the word is Utręhętǫ' 'A branch hangs down'. It could be implied that the branch hangs into the water and is shaken by the motion of the river.

A term certainly descriptive of a turtle is the male name Handušrara[14] 'He has a shell on top'. Barbeau records this name for a Bill Bearskin (Barbeau 1911:4 and 30).

Porcupine Clan

There are 28 Porcupine clan names in this collection.

HE OFTEN CARRIES BARK

The Porcupine clan name with the longest written history is 'He often or repeatedly carries bark. He is a bark carrier'. Individuals bearing this name are recorded from the 1650s until the death of probably the last Bark-Carrier about 1860. This involves five individuals.

An analysis of the name runs as follows:

---

14. Barbeau 1911:4 and 30.

Hustayehtak	He often or frequently carries bark.
hu-	masculine singular patient - he
-st-	noun root – bark
-a-	joiner vowel
-yeht-	verb root – bear (often on a strap around the shoulder or neck)
-ak	habitual aspect – often

In 1900, Connelley added a behavioural context for the name in the following way: "As the porcupine carries it in his pocket-like jaws from the top of the hemlock, where it has been feeding" (Connelley 1900:110).

#1: A 17th Century Petun Chief

This name first appears in the written record in the *Jesuit Relation* written in 1654, in the account of Jesuit Father Simon Le Moine when he was travelling to the country of the Onondaga in July to September 1653. He was writing about the refugees from Wendat and Petun country:

> I have the consolation of confessing there at my leisure our former host of the tobacco [Petun] Nation, *Hostagehtak*. His feelings and his devotion bring tears to my eyes. He is a fruit of the labors of Father Charles Garnier. ... (JR41:97)

Father Charles Garnier spent his last years in the Petun village of Etharita, which was the principal village of the Wolf grouping (possibly a tribe) of the Petun. The fact that this first-recorded Bark Carrier had hosted the Jesuits when they were living in the country of the Wyandot ancestors tells us that he was a man of some significance among his people at that time. I have found no written record of reference to when and where he died.

#2: A Mislabeled Godparent

On June 11, 1730, a two-year-old girl was baptized. The one godparent listed was[15] *osta,eta* (Toupin 1996:827). Jesuit Father Robert Toupin believed that it was the name of the godmother, perhaps as this was the only godparent mentioned. However, a close examination of the baptism records demonstrates that when there was one godparent, it would not necessarily be of the same sex as the child.

#3: A Boy Named Franciscus-Xavier

On October 3, 1734, a 12-year-old boy, Franciscus Xavier *Hosta,etat* was baptized. No names of parents of godparents were mentioned (Toupin 1996:837). There is no later reference to him.

#4: Roundhead

The best-known individual to bear this name played a significant role in the War of

---

15. Use of what appears to be a female form is probably misleading, with the initial -h- not being heard or written, which often happened.

1812 as Tecumseh's second-in-command. The Shawnee leader's appreciation for this Wyandot man can be seen in what happened after General Isaac Brock publicly gave Tecumseh his red sash after their decisive victory over American Brigadier General William Hull in the Siege of Detroit in August 1812. The next day, the Shawnee man was seen not wearing the honouring sash:

> General Brock, fearing something had displeased the Indian, sent his interpreter for an explanation. The latter soon returned with an account that Tecumseh, not wishing to wear such a mark of distinction, when an older, and, as he said, abler, warrior than himself was present, had transferred the sash to the Wyandot chief Round-head (Drake 1845:127 as published in Divine 2019:171).

They both died in the Battle of the Thames in southwestern Ontario in 1813. His name is usually written as Roundhead (c.1760–1813), his nickname. A township and an unincorporated community in Ohio bear this name. This is the main name by which he is known to historians and others interested in Wyandot history. It will be discussed further in the chapter on nicknames.

On the Greenville Treaty of 1795, his name was written as Stayetayh, one of a good number of partial recordings of this name, a list which includes Stayeghtha, Stiahta, Tey-yagh-taw, and Ustaiechta (Horsman 2003). In the *Dictionary of Canadian Biography* his name was presented as STAYEGHTHA (Horsman 2003).

#5: Captain Bullhead (1785–c. 1860)

The next and probably the last person to bear this name was referred to in writing as Captain Bullhead. Like his predecessor, he fought on the British/Canadian side of the War of 1812. Connelley referred to this Bark-Carrier as "the last pagan Wyandot" (1900:8), living in the part of the Wyandot community separate from the "the more progressive portion of the tribe" (Connelley 1900:58). He respected him as a knowledgeable source concerning traditional songs, stories and practices: "He was a man of great intelligence and well informed in the history and traditions of his people (Connelley footnote in Walker n.d.:302; https://www.wyandotte-nation.org/culture/history/published/provisional-government/journal2/).

In another Porcupine name that relates to the animal's eating, Alfred Mudeater's name is presented by Connelley as Reh-hooh'-zhah, given as meaning "the act of the porcupine in pulling down the branches and nipping off the buds and bark" (Connelley 1899b:35). The literal meaning and more complete writing of the name adds the masculine singular agent pronominal prefix and is Haręhužah 'He moves, shakes the treetops'.

Quills are an obvious source of Porcupine clan names, as is their cognitive connection with arrows. There is Shutraʔtes 'His quills are often very long' (male Porcupine). Several names appear to include the noun root -n(d) 'arrow'. The most obvious one is Huʔndažuh 'His arrow or quill has killed, is killing'.

Then there is a male name presented by Connelley as "Ohn-dŏŏh'-tŏŏh. The meaning is lost" (Connelley 1900:110). I believe this word to be: *Handutǫ*[16] 'He puts

---

16. Powell 1881:60 "Ha-dú-tu *(The one who puts up Quills)"*

up many arrows'. There is another name that I believe might include the noun root -n(d)- . Connelley presents it as "Dah'-rah-hŏŏh-ngk. He throws up his quills for battle when angry." (Connelley 1900:109). The verb used is unclear.

During the 18th century, a very important Porcupine clan woman named Marguerite had the Wyandot name of Atsirǫnde 'She goes about on all fours' (as do porcupines). Although only 36 at the time of the census of 1747, hers was the first name mentioned for one of the longhouses, pointing to her being the matron of that house (Toupin 1996:202 and 240). Hers was also the first name mentioned in the list of female elders for the clan (Toupin 1996:229).[17] Unfortunately, I can find no record of anyone reviving the name after her death in 1785 (Toupin 1996:932).

Haskutaše: Five Generations

It is difficult to precisely translate the name 'Skutache'. I am suggesting that the complete word could have been the following. It is not unusual for non-speakers of the language to drop the initial sounds before an -s- when writing words in both Wendat and Wyandot:

Haskutaše	He is going to have a skull of such a size.
ha-	masculine singular agent – he
-skut-	noun root – skull
-a-	verb root – be a size
-š-	dislocative root suffix
-e	purposive aspect[18]

#1: A Man of Complicated Politics

The first Haskutaše in the written record appeared late in the 17th century. From what was written we can say that the individual bearing the name was someone the French authorities thought of as a troublemaker. I prefer to think of him as a person pursuing possible options that might aid the survival of his people. He was referred to as Scoutache and the misprinted Scoubache in the references that follow. In a summary of Governor Denonville's letters in 1685 to M. de Seignelay, we read:

> A man named Scoutache, who is among the Outawas, has told them that he, Denonville, was preparing to attack them, which has alarmed them. (NYCD9:274)

In a letter of the next year, June 12, 1686, Denonville wrote the following:

> I have had again the honor of advising you this fall that a man named Scoubache, a native Huron [Wyandot], has been to the Iroquois to induce them to make war upon us. It has since been discovered that his principal design was to betray all the Hurons

---

17. For a more complete understanding of the importance of this woman, see Steckley 2014:77–8, 94, 99–101, 115, 118, 122, 130, 158, 164, 175, 177, 180–1, 183–7, 195–6, 209–10, 213, 219, and 285.

18. The combination of the dislocative and the purposive gives the meaning 'going to'.

[Wyandot] at Michilimakinac, and that Traitor did in fact, conjointly with others like himself, deliver up to the Iroquois seventy Huron who were dispersed a-hunting between Lake Erie and Lake Huron, in the country called Saquinaw. (NYCD9:293)

According to Denonville then, Haskutaše was attempting to get the Haudenosaunee on his side by offering up 70 Wyandot prisoners to them. It seems unlikely to me that Haskutaše would betray his people. I feel that he was in some way trying to lessen the pressure of the Iroquois on his people through some independent strategy that was unknown to the French, but not necessarily anti-French, and certainly not anti-Wyandot. He might even have been attempting to trap the Iroquois through promising them non-existent prisoners. Lacking Haskutaše's written voice in the matter, it is hard to know what his intent was. Sacrificing his people to obtain a stronger personal relationship with the Iroquois does not seem a likely goal.

It is perhaps from his controversial reputation earned at this time that the story developed that he was the one who brought smallpox to his people. This was written by Peter D. Clarke:

> This malady was introduced among the Wyandotts by a member of the band, named Scoo-tush to gratify his curiosity he obtained a vial from some white physician containing vaccine matter, and who, on perceiving himself infected with the smallpox, and whilst in a high fever, waded out into Lake Erie, imitating the screams of a loon. He lived but a short time after coming out of the water. (This was on the Canada side of Lake Erie.). (Clarke 1870:55)

#2: An Ambassador of Peace
We do not know when this man revived the name. We do know he had the first name Louis. He first appears in the baptismal record in 1729, with the baptism of a 10-year-old daughter, Angelica, of whom Large Turtle clan member Ndechonngiaha was the mother (Toupin 1996:824). In a baptism held on July 23, 1733, he was the godfather of a 15-year-old boy called Louis (written in the Latin form Ludovicus) (Toupin 1996:833).

In 1735 he and what appears to be his new wife, Striped Turtle clan member Marie Tsondehe, had newborn twins, Catharina and Francisca baptized (Toupin 1996:939). I mention this as in 1739, he is referred to as the father of a son with Catherine tek8ennon,oti, who was Striped Turtle (Toupin 1996:845). They would have three more children baptized, in 1742, 1744 and 1747 (Toupin 1996:850, 852, and 857).

In 1747, Potier recorded that the Wyandot man was 56 years old, mentioned first in the listing of names in his house, a large one, in which the Porcupine clan and the Striped Turtle clan shared influence. His daughter Françoise was married to Tio8endata, who was a man of significance in the Porcupine clan, as was Nicholas Orontondi, who also lived in that house.

While he was not then an elder of the Porcupine clan, this Haskutaše's influence at that time can be seen in the fact that he was involved in a Wyandot peace initiative after Nicholas Orontondi's abortive attack on Detroit in 1747. The Chevalier de Bertel or Berthet, French commandant among the Algonquian-speaking Illinois people at that time wrote a letter that contained the following information concerning his peacemaking activities, partnered with Quarante Sols of the Bear clan:

> At the end of January, 14 Hurons of Sandosket, with Scotache and Quarante Sols at their head, come to Detroit to ask for the release of the three prisoners confined in irons, the remainder of the five who had been taken at Bois blanc Island, where they had been attacked by the French when Nicolas sued for peace. The deputation made such fair promises that Chevalier de Longueuil, though feeling great repugnance to the release of these three prisoners [consented to their discharge, on] the advice of the principal Frenchmen and Indians in the fort. (NYCD10:156–7)

He seems, then, to be continuing the independent style of political policy of his predecessor, speaking on behalf of his clan brother, Orontondi.

Louis must have died before 1763, as a testament and anniversary was held to honour his death that year (Toupin 1996:957).

#3: Tribal Orator

The name was resuscitated by 1780, as by that time he (with his name badly written as Sachetotache) was one of six chiefs who ceded on behalf of the tribe land to Father Pierre Potier (Buser 1989). He seems to have been a relatively young at the time, as on August 14, 1791, two girls were baptized each one being a "fille de sCoutaChe,"[19] (Toupin 1996:939). In 1782 he led a war-party in which two of his younger brothers died (Divine 2019:144).

Like his predecessors, he played an important role for this people. Garrad writes: "In 1786 the Tribal Orator was *Scotosh*, thought to be a half-brother to Sastaretsi … and additionally a nephew of and adopted as a son by *Tarhé*." (Garrad 2014:541)

In 1816, 'Scotash' took a trip to Washington to make a deal for his people (Buser 1989). In 1818, he signed two treaties, one with his name written as 'Scoutous', another as 'Scoutash'.

#4: A Clan Shift to Large Turtle?

The fourth Haskutaše was Allen Johnson Sr. (1848–1906), the husband of Catherine Johnson and the father of Allen Johnson Jr. (His wife was the teller of the tale of the bringing of smallpox, his son the interpreter.) The one who brought the deadly disease to the Wyandot was not named in this version, just called 'erǫme'', translated as "he person is (a man)" in the translation of the tale in the 1960 version (Barbeau 1960:96 #11), "an Indian" in the 1915 version (Barbeau 1915:81).

His name was written as Skuʔtac (Barbeau 1915:ix). Strangely, he appears to have

---

19. The capitals are as in the original, which, it should be noted, was not written by someone with the Wendat and Wyandot language experience of Potier. Father François-Xavier Dufaux went to work among the Wyandot in 1787–1796. His writing of the language as seen by the names he tried to record in baptisms was uniformly bad.

been Large Turtle clan, not Porcupine like the others. There is no readily apparent reason for that. Perhaps it was part of the falling apart of the Wyandot clan system, which took place during the 19th century.

#5: The Last One

The fifth and last recorded Haskutaše was presented in 1911 by Barbeau as skú$^{\text{?}}$utäc (1911:44), the name being held by a William Driver Jr. He appears to have been Large Turtle clan too.

Prairie Turtle Clan

The Prairie Turtle clan has a low number of recorded names in this collection, only 10. Unsurprisingly, one of the female Prairie Turtle names makes reference to sand: Ǫndehšuri 'She is covered with sand'. It is the only Prairie Turtle name for which I have found more than one recorded holder. There was an Anna in 1740 (Toupin 1996:847), a Louise who had the name in 1742 and was 40 years old in 1747 (Toupin 1996:210, 220, 254 and 850), and Barbeau writes of a woman with the name early in the 20th century (Barbeau 1911:48). No doubt there were women who bore the name in the intervening period, but did not have their names recorded in anything that I have seen.

There is a male Prairie Turtle name that I suspect comes from a story, perhaps an unrecorded story, concerning the origin of the clan: Tayeąndrak[20] 'Look at me'. In the census of 1747, he was listed as one of the males of the Prairie Turtle in the elders council (Toupin 1996:229).

Wolf Clan

There are 25 recorded Wolf clan names in this collection. There is on the record a name that mirrors that of the clan Hannâriskwa[21] 'He is a wolf (he used to chew bones)' (Toupin 1996:881). As it only appears once, and it is unusual that a clan's name is also a personal name, this might just have been an identification of the man's clan.

The Wolf clan name Hurǫnyayehte 'He bears the sky' was given to three different Jesuits (see chapter seven), two by the Wendat, and to Potier by the Wyandot.

RUNNING WOLVES

One Wolf clan name clearly linking it with the clan animal is Huskwindehti 'He is running with a group (e.g., a pack)'. The history of the name, including it becoming a surname will be discussed in chapter nine.

In the 1740s, and possibly in 1781, there is another Wolf clan reference to a wolf running in the male name Tehuratati 'He is running'.

The negative effect of running in the snow when it's very cold is found in the

---

20. Toupin 1996:186, 187, 208, 210, 238 and 245. This is one of two names in the collection in which an imperative is used.

21. Toupin 1996:881. As this name appears only once, and it is unusual that a clan's name is built into a personal name, this might just be an identification of the man's clan. Potier was adopted by the Wolf clan.

female name Teǫnęditakon 'Cold is seizing the front of her legs'. This could be part of a Wolf story that did not get recorded.

He is Sky in the Water

There seem to have been three men recorded as bearing this name from the 18th to the early 20th century. The earliest one was recorded in 1731 as being the father of an eight-year-old Snake clan boy (Toupin 1996:829).

The next recorded man who bore this name was a prominent figure in the council meetings and treaties of the late 18th and early 19th century. He had been captured as a child in a fight with the Cherokee, so had the nickname of Cherokee Boy. He was adopted and took his adoptive mother's clan. His son would have the surname of Cherokee.

His significance as a Wyandot leader is seen in the fact that he signed six treaties, one in 1795, 1805, 1815, 1817 and two in 1818 (Curnoe 1996:37), with five different spellings of his name.

John Wesley Powell wrote about him in 1881, in his *Wyandot Government: A Short Study of Tribal Society*. In presenting the connotations of the name, he drew a rather scary picture of a wolf at night: "Ha-ró-u-yû (One who goes about in the Dark; a Prowler)" (Powell 1881:60).

Connelley wrote about him in 1900, referring to his being "A famous Wyandot Chief", because of the treaties he signed, and gave the name as "Hăh-ròhn'-yooh" but he referred to the meaning as being lost, something he did for other names whose meaning was known, but not to him (Connelley 1990:113)

The third and last person with this name in the written record was Hiram Star Young, an important story provider both in Wyandot and in English[22] for Marius Barbeau (1915 and 1960). Barbeau believed him to be over 65 in 1911–2 (Barbeau 1915:x). The two stories that he told to Barbeau in Wyandot were a Wolf clan story entitled "The Wolf and the Young Hunter" (Barbeau 1915:103–5 and 1960:14–5 and 112–6), in which a wolf leader gives a young man a hunting charm, and "The Seven Stars" (Barbeau 1915:58–9 and 1960:74–77). Barbeau wrote the name as "hărŏñu'u" and gave the translation of "the sky on top (of the water)" (Barbeau 1911:31).

It is Often Difficult for Us

This name is another Wolf clan male name of importance in Wyandot history. It first appears in the written record as being the father or fathers[23] of children being baptized from 1735 to 1765 (Toupin 1996:837, 854, 865 and 887).

The significance of the bearer of the name becomes apparent in 1781, when a Mon-do-ro is reported as being one of the Wyandot chiefs attending a council meeting at Detroit, on April 26, 1781 (Curnoe 1996:72). The -onyw- sequence before the -a-

---

22. Stories in English include "The Bear and the Hunter's Step-Son" (Barbeau 1915:116–125), "The Sorcerer Roasting a Human Heart" (Barbeau 1915:164–5), "The Coming of the White Man Foretold" (Barbeau 1915:267–80), and "Wyandot War Adventure" (Barbeau 1915:275–80).

23. Four different mothers are referenced.

had become -m-. In 1789 he was one of the Wyandot leaders who, as Maudoronk, signed the Treaty of Fort Harmar. In 1790 he was one of the chiefs signing Treaty # 2, which led to the loss of land south of the Thames River from Port Bruce to Windsor (Curnoe 1996:72–3). He signed with a picture of a wolf (see Curnoe 1996:73).

A later bearer of the name would become Grand Chief of the Wyandot of Anderdon, from 1838 until his death in 1885. He was the last of the Wyandot chiefs in Canada, and, to my knowledge, the last person to bear his Wolf clan name.

Horatio Hale, in his "Wyandot Folk-Lore," relied significantly on information the chief provided for that work. He referred to him as "Mandarong," which he had translated as "Unwilling," which would seem to relate to the nameholder being difficult, a possible reference to how wolves relate to humans.

Hawk Clan

There are only two names that I can identify with the Hawk clan. One is Ǫndesǫk 'It is a hawk' (Toupin 1996:822). The name for the clan itself is hatindesǫk 'They (m[24]) are hawks' (Toupin 1996:260). The other is the name of the leader of the clan as recorded in the 1747 census, Ahandaturęha[25] 'He has found a village' (Toupin 1996:260). There is some question as to whether he belonged to that clan, or to the Wolf clan, a sister clan in the Wolf phratry, in which he was listed as an elder (Toupin 1996:229). This lack of names is not an indicator of the lack of significance of this clan, but more likely has to do with my lack of means of identifying people in the 18th century as being Hawk clan. The clan is referred to in a story in which clans were established (Barbeau 1915:82–9, 1960:11–2 and 98:101). In another story, this clan, along with the Prairie Turtle, spiritually defeated a lion by fasting, leading to the development of the "Lion Fraternity" (Barbeau 1915:95–7 and 1960:12–3 and 104–6).

Beaver Clan

There is no reference to a Beaver clan in Potier's writings of the 18th century. I have heard people say, and have read the claim, that Kandiaronk was Beaver clan (Garrad 2014:540). This could be a combination of the Wendat having such a clan ((Steckley 2007b:49 and 52), and because the image of his mark on the Great Peace of Montreal can be interpreted as being a beaver, although to me the tail does not look wide enough, but more like that of a muskrat.

But there seems to have been such a clan in the 19th century. Barbeau mentions a name as being Beaver clan. In discussing the source of the story of "The Two Giant Cousins and the Old Witch," told to him by Catherine Johnson, Barbeau explains that she said that she learned the story from her stepfather, who in turn learned it from his adopted father who was Beaver clan (Barbeau 1915:65 fn 4). This man had the name that I am presenting as Hungwąnduhrǫ? 'He has difficult rapids'. Barbeau inaccurately claimed that it meant 'He makes a dam'(Barbeau 1915:65 fn 4). The Wyandot noun

---

24. This is an instance in which the masculine plural form is used to refer to a collectivity of both males and females.

25. Toupin 1996: 176, 874, 194, 210, 220, 227, 229, 254, 260, 824, 828, 832, 837, 841, 847, 850, 861 and 874. See Steckley 2014:113, 117, 149, 156–8, 168, 200, 207–8, 212, 223, 230 and 283.

root for 'beaver dam or lodge' is -a'šr-. Maybe a dam was built because of the difficult rapids, and Barbeau was not given the connection between literal translation and connotations. As well, there was a man named John Beaver as a landholder in the Kansas Allotments in 1855 (Divine 2019:265).

Snipe Clan

According to Barbeau, the Snipe clan was "recently introduced" to the Wyandot (Barbeau 1917:296). I suspect that might relate to their living in Oklahoma next to the Seneca and Cayuga, both of which had Snipe clans. He also noted that the clan was "nearly extinct" (Barbeau 1915:xi).

In his collection of names of 1911, Barbeau mentions a particular Snipe clan name twice, belonging to a man called Jerry Charles: "tehătrŏnŭyu'ta?a through the sky" (Barbeau 1911:18 and 35). I have translated it as Tehatrǫnyuyu'ta? 'He penetrates the sky', a good name for a clan animal that is a bird.

There is also a controversial call on Barbeau's part. He has the name Hažatǫh 'He marks, writes' belonging to the Snipe clan (Barbeau 1915:xi). Following Connelley, I have assigned it to the Deer clan. There is evidence that the name existed in the 18th century, before there was a Snipe clan. There is one reference to hahiatonk h8nda 'She is the spouse of He Marks' (Toupin 1996:963) in a mortuary ceremony. I cannot say for sure whether this was the Frenchman Robert Navarre, who bore the name as well (Toupin 1996:235). Further evidence is that there is a cognate name in Wendat, 'hajaton' (Vincent 1984:335).

One other explanation is remotely possible. Barbeau wrote about the Large Turtle name Hawęndayehte? 'He bears an island' being loaned to or borrowed by Isaac White-Jaw of the Porcupine clan, later returned to Thomas Walker of the Large Turtle clan (Barbeau 1911:3 and 10). Maybe the Snipe clan borrowed the name for a short time.

Sturgeon Clan

The Sturgeon clan has a unique feature. With both the Wyandot and the Wendat, it has two names, one of which is sturgeon. For the Wyandot, Potier wrote the first part of the name as "Hotiraon (les eturgeons)" (Toupin 1996:227). For late 19th century Wyandot I would write it as hutiraǫ and translate it as 'they (m) are sturgeon'. The second part, which differs from the Wendat 'h8enh8en' referring to a loon (Steckley 2007:53), is the name 'tï,ataentsik', which is the name of the first woman on earth (to be discussed in a later chapter). The one name that is associated with the clan as its leading figure is presented with three names: his current clan name, a former clan name, and a French nickname: "s8ndak8a v. Agnioton…(Le brutal)" (Toupin 1996:224). I can come up with no translation for the second name, and the French name is very similar to that in English. His then current Wyandot clan name can be expressed as Sundakwa? 'eagle'. The initial -s- does not mean 'very' or 'again'; it is an initial letter that appears at the beginning of many animal names. It may be what linguists call a prosthetic, a sound that is added for other reasons than to cause the word's meaning to change.

Summary

We have seen in this chapter how names can have subtle connections with the clan animals they belong to, connections that are not obvious through just knowing literal translations. Further, some names have as many as five recorded people who carried the name through the centuries from the 17th to the early 20th. Names notable in the written record for being passed on through several generations are the following:

Name	Translation	Clan
Shastaretsi	He has long antler spurs	Deer
Yamęndindetih	She causes her voice to come	Deer
Yaaʔtaseh	Her body is new	Snake
Hariwawayi	He holds, grasps the matter	Bear
Kwęndindeʔs	She often ties knots	Bear
Ayanyęmiha	She learned how to do it; she knows how	Large Turtle
Shumęduwat[26]	He is very large in word, voice, authority	Striped Turtle
Hustayehtak:	He Often Carries Bark	Porcupine
Haskutaše	He is going to have a skull of such a size.	Porcupine
Ǫndehšuri	She is covered with sand	Prairie Turtle
Huskwindehti	He is running with a group (e.g., a pack)	Wolf

---

26. See discussion of this name in chapter nine.

CHAPTER FIVE
Nicknames

Introduction

In Marius Barbeau's *Huron and Wyandot Mythology*, in which stories were recorded in English and French, there was a Wendat story in which seven brothers turn into oxen. Near the end of the story, presented by Wendat priest Abbe Prosper Vincent, an early influence on Barbeau, the brothers had their names changed. In the English translation, probably done by Barbeau, we read

> Significant names, referring to their qualities and gifts, had first been given them when they were young children, upon the earliest signs of their inclinations. Now their new names were different. (Barbeau 1915:135)

Barbeau pointed out in a footnote that:

> This seems to have been in conformity with a Huron custom; that is, a child was first given a nickname, framed to describe one of the child's marked characteristics; and when he had become a young man,[1] he was given a traditional [clan-based] name, referring to mythological adventures or deeds of the past. (Barbeau 1915:135 fn1)

Nicknames played a significant role in traditional Wendat and Wyandot culture.

Leatherlips

In 2018, I published the politically titled "Rescuing Colonized Names of the Wyandot" in *Onomastica Canadiana*, the academic journal for the Canadian Society for the Study of Names. That year I had discovered that two Wyandot men who were significant both in the Porcupine clan and for the Wyandot in general were known primarily in history books and at historic sites by what I then called the "colonized" names of Roundhead and Leatherlips.[2] Roundhead was something of a hero of mine as he died in 1813 in the Battle of the Thames in southwestern Ontario defending my country, Canada, in the War of 1812. I wanted him to be known by his "real name" of He Carries Bark or Bark Carrier.

In a historic site near Columbus, Ohio there is a 12-foot-high limestone slab sphinx-like statue of the head and trailing hair of Leatherlips, created in 1990, interestingly including his forehead, eyes, nose, and chin but not his lips. If you search online, as I did, you will find an often-quoted explanation of his nickname: "The white settlers called him Leatherlips because of his admirable trait of never breaking a promise" (roadsideamerica/com/story/9791). No source for this quotation is given in anything I encountered online. I was bothered by the thought that settlers had imposed the name

---

1. This was of course true of females too.

2. The other names in the article I 'rescued' by giving more accurate representations and more precise translations to. None of them were nicknames.

Leatherlips, rather than respecting his—again—"real name" of Šateyarǫnyah' 'It is as big as the sky, half the sky'.

The mistake in my thinking back in 2018 was that I failed to adequately take into consideration Wyandot agency in this. Usually I spot that kind of weakness in other researchers and writers. This time I failed to see it in my own analysis. Wyandot agency involved giving and accepting names from other Wyandot at different stages of their lives and using them as primary identifiers if they so chose. There could possibly be an element of "keeping secret from outsiders" their more sacred and special clan names. Perhaps Leatherlips' Porcupine clan name of Šateyarǫnyah was treated like that, with his nickname of Leatherlips being his self-chosen public name.

What language did the name Leatherlips come from? For this to have come from the Wyandot language, two noun roots: -ʔndih- 'leather' and -nstr- 'lips' would seem to be necessary. At least one of these noun roots and possibly both of them would have to be incorporated into verbs. This would make the name more complicated than what the simplicity principle mentioned in an earlier chapter would require. Nicknames should certainly not be complicated.

It would seem that the name Leatherlips came from English. But that does not necessarily mean that it came from settlers and not his own people, some of whom by this time could speak English fluently. And even if it did initially come from the settlers, I would argue now that he would have chosen to accept the name, and use it freely, as his people had a tradition of doing so with nicknames. It was not purely an act of colonial oppression. It involved some measure of Wyandot agency or choice, not complete imposition.

Wyandot historian Charles Aubrey Buser informs us in a short biographical article that Leatherlips had several names in Wyandot:

> Leatherlips had three Wyandot names. The one most often used was **SHATEYAHRONYA** but he was sometimes referred to as **THATEYYANAYOH**. In later years he was called **SOUCHAETESS**, which means "Long Gray Hair".
> (Buser https://www.wyandotte-nation.org/culture/history/biographies/leatherlips/).

It is noteworthy that he did not include the name Leatherlips as a Wyandot name. None of the three names means Leatherlips. The first name he mentions is of course the one I referred to as his "real name." The second name I have been unable to translate. The third name has the verb root -es- 'be long' and the initial -s- repetitive that combine for 'very long', but it does not have any noun root related to 'hair', or the verb root -ndraʻtę- 'have gray or white hair.' Perhaps the Wyandot name and the proposed translation were separate, the latter being a English-based nickname that Leatherlips received when he was older.

French-Based Nicknames and Descriptors

One reason why I thought that the French and later the English/Americans might have initiated and imposed nicknames on the Wyandot came from reading Potier's census of 1747. Sometimes following a Wyandot's name was a descriptor that could be used by the French as a nickname, sometimes more likely a negative comment (e.g., "libertin," Toupin 1996:219 and "bon ivrogne" 'good drunk' Toupin 1996:239). They certainly were not translations of the Wyandot names. Here are representative examples:

Wyandot Name	French Nickname	English Translation	Reference
8ennenhario	le grand-male	The great/large male	Toupin 1996:203
Tio8endata	le Manchot	one-armed man	Toupin 1996:204
A8innon-i8oin	(f) la gross gorge	the big throat	Toupin 1996:205
Te horonhiotexa	piponette[3]	pipette, small pipe	Toupin 1996:206
Hannenratendi	L'etourneau	starling	Toupin 1996:207
Sandats8a't	le bijou	jewel	Toupin 1996:207
Nendeniont (f)	la mistasse violette	purple leggings	Toupin 1996:212
Harih8andiniontak	le glorieux	the glorious one	Toupin 1996:214
Sa8india (f)	la la douceur	the sweet one	Toupin 1996:217
Sa8oindgiandii (f)	la babillarde	the talkative one, chatterbox	Toupin 1996:218
Ochienda,ete	bas-jaune[s]	yellow stockings	Toupin 1996:221
Niendaharonk (f)	La puce	the flea	Toupin 1996:222
Te8askarandet	surdus	deaf	Toupin 1996:224
S8ndak8a	le Brutal	the brutal one	Toupin 1996:224

One negative descriptor which might have been a nickname was in Wyandot.

Clan Name	Nickname	English Translation	Reference
te8arachiande	L'onnonste	She is stingy.	Toupin 1996:213 and 247

The French would know this term as it was often enough used with respect to them. The Wyandot nickname for a man named Deruisseau who lived in Detroit in 1752 was 'honnonste', meaning 'he is stingy'[4] (Toupin 1996:262).

QUARANTE SOLS

The man often known by this name (1659–1707) was the chief of the Wyandot of St. Joseph River in Michigan, a talented and often recorded orator (see Steckley 2014:68–72 and Havard 2001:104, 145 and 152). He was a major player in the complex and sometimes dangerous politics of his people's survival early in the years immediately preceding and following the turn of the 18th century. He led his band to Detroit in 1703, before Sastaretsi and the main group of Wyandot made that move. Yet he is known in writing not by his Wyandot name(s), but by French and Anishinaabe nicknames.

3. His mother was called "la vielle [the old] piponnette" (Toupin 1996:250).

4. The mission's financial record for the time period 1746 to 1751 shows the Ruisseau family, husband and wife owing the mission for two supplies of boards (Potier 1920:697 and 698, as well as payment owed for masses given (Potier 1920:708 and 711). Still it is not clear who gave him that nickname, the French or the Wyandot.

Quarante Sols was what the French called him. We do not know the origin of the name, which can be translated as 'Forty Pennies', but historian Andrew Sturtevant suggests that that it was "probably a reference to what the French perceived as the man's avarice" (Sturtevant 2011:41 fn21). The French were suspicious of his motives.

The Anishinaabe name he bore was Michipichi. This seems to be a reference to Mishibizhiw, the dangerous 'great lynx' or 'underwater panther'. Was this a way of saying that he was an influential member of the 'lion fraternity' of traditional Wyandot stories (Barbeau 1915:95–7, 1960:12–3, and 104–6), connected with the mythic Qtarayǫrat 'It is a white lake' discussed in chapter eight? It is possible. Or it could be a way of saying that he should not be completely trusted.

In 1747, we find the name appears again with a brother and a sister Sohondinnonn "…andré (40 sols, le borgne [the one-eyed]…" (Toupin 1996:222) and "ts8ndeen anastasie la vielle [the old one] 40 sols" (Toupin 1996:221), both Bear clan members of the elders council (Toupin 1996:228). Her name is translated as 'She, it is joined again' (see Translations).

This may mean (if the second letter is really an -a-) 'He again wished for, had a vision of something' (see Translations). Written after his name on the elders council list are the words: "Saohetsaron atrio,e." They can be translated as:

Sayohetsaron		He encourages, exhorts them.
	sayo-	masculine singular agent + indefinite patient – he – them
	-hetsaron	verb root – encourage + stative aspect

Atrioye		It is in fighting.
	at-	feminine-zoic singular agent – it + semi-reflexive voice
	-rio-	verb root – fight + stative aspect
	=ye	external locative clitic

As the name before this has the word "general" after it and a sentence after that meaning "He is authority over those who are warriors," we can say that he was not a war chief, but was second to one (see chapter seven).

So we can assume that they are related to the first Quarante Sols. But as the name is a French nickname, we probably should not consider it passed down through the clan, but through patrilineage, their possibly being his son and daughter. Still, there was no Bear clan leader mentioned for that time, so there is still the possibility of the first Quarante Sols being Bear clan.

The Anishinaabe name was not passed down.

Tarhe: A Man with Two Nicknames

The Porcupine clan man named Tarhe (1740–1816) was a chief among the Wyandot in the late 18th and early 19th century. He signed treaties in 1789, 1795, 1805, 1814, and 1815.

In his informative biography about Tarhe on the Wyandotte Nation of Oklahoma website, Charles Aubrey Buser gave the nickname that he was known by:

Tarhe's ... name is intriguing. The English meaning is unknown. The name is not believed to be a clan property name and it apparently died with the man. It may have been given to him because of some particular deed or attribute of the man or boy. Old-time Wyandots said the name meant "at him" or "at the tree," or was perhaps the personification of "the tree". Tarhe's great height lends credence to the latter theory. He was six feet four inches tall in an era when few men reached six feet. (https://www.wyandotte-nation.org/culture/history/biographies/tarhe-grand-sachem/)

The name was not included in any of Potier's material of the 18th century. And, as Buser said, it disappeared after his death. That points to it being a nickname. The interpretations of the "Old-time Wyandots" can be explained. First of all, the -rh- can be seen as the masculine singular agent pronominal prefix. The -t- can be seen as the cislocative 'here or where'. And it could be that the interpretation 'at' comes from the external locative clitic, although that is not necessary given the presence of the cislocative. This interpretation may come from his name being one of the following two words:

Ethre		He comes from here.
	et-	cislocative – here
	-hr-	masculine singular agent – he
	-e	verb root – come or go + purposive aspect

Ǫtare		He came here.
	ǫ-	factual
	-t-	cislocative – here
	-a-	factual
	-r-	masculine singular agent – he
	-e	verb root – come or go + purposive aspect

Concerning the interpretation of 'at the tree', this could relate to the following word:

yarihiʔt		It is an apple tree, a tree.
	ya-	feminine-zoic singular agent – it
	-rihiʔt	verb root – be an apple tree, a tree + stative aspect

To change this to 'where there is an apple tree, a tree', using the cislocative, the initial -y- would change into a -k-.

Evidence for this being the meaning for his name comes from a much earlier (1632) reference. Recollect Brother Gabriel Sagard's description of the naming practices of the Wendat in *Le Grand Voyage du Pays des Hurons*:

> Pour l'imposition des noms, ils les donnent par tradition, c'est-à-dire qu'ils ont des noms en grand quantité, lesquels ils choisissent et imposent à leur enfants:

certains noms sons sans signification et les autres avec signification, comme *Yocoisse*, le vent, *Ongyata*, signifie la gorge, *Tochingo,* grue, *Sondaqua*, aigle, *Scouta*, la tête. *Tonra*, le ventre, *Taïhy*, un arbre, etc.

For the imposition of names, they give them by tradition, that is to say that they have names in great quantity, from which they choose and impose on their children: certain are without meaning, and the others are with meaning, as with Yocoisse, the wind, Ongyata, signifying the throat, Tochingo, crane, Sondaqua, eagle, Scouta, the head, Tonra, the stomach and Taïhy, a tree, etc. (Sagard 1990:206)

The -r- that is missing in the word for 'tree' here is found in his *Histoire du Canada,* first published in 1636, when the name is represented as Tarhy (Sagard 1866:307). The interpretation of the meaning is verified in the use of tarhi in words representing trees in Sagard's dictionary (Steckley 2010:371, entry 116.21).

I have uncovered no written evidence of the name existing between Sagard's time and Tarhe's, suggesting that it might have been a nickname. That appears to be true of most of the other names cited in this passage: Yocoisse, Ongyat, Scouta, Tonra.

In sum, I am suggesting that this is a nickname and not a clan name.

Tarhe also had the nickname 'Crane'. The French referred to him as Le Grue [crane], Le Chef Grue, and Monsieur Grue. In the treaties he signed in 1795, 1805, 1814 and 1815, his name has 'or (the) Crane' following Tarhe. The term for the bird in Wyandot is uhšinguʔt 'It is a crane.' I have not found this word used in association with him. This nickname might have come from French and English, but who initiated it is not known. It was likely given him as an adult because of his being tall, and perhaps a little thin. As you can see from the quotation immediately above, the name was recorded for the Wendat in 1632, in what I suspect is a nickname.

Wyandot Nicknames at the Turn of the 20th Century
Barbeau

In his fieldnotes of 1911, Marius Barbeau recorded a good number of what appear to be nicknames. Most are difficult to analyse. Marius Barbeau specifically mentioned six different people as having nicknames, five of them women. With most of these nicknames, I cannot readily connect the English meaning with the Wyandot word.

The easiest are of two of his story sources. Hiram Star Young, in addition to his Wolf clan name, had the nickname of Tihšǫ—Morning Star—as he was born early in the morning (Barbeau 1911:7 and 47). He was not the first Wyandot to bear this name, as a woman did in the 1740s (Toupin 1996:203, written as 'tichion'). Perhaps it was her nickname as well.

Mary McKee had the nickname of Turtle: ngyaʔwic (Barbeau 1911:17).

Mary Peacock had the nickname of Mush. She is probably the "Mary Mush" referred to as a landholder in the Oklahoma Allotments of 1888 (Divine 2019:293). The Wyandot word Barbeau gives is cáʔanęʔs (Barbeau 1911:16 and 22). I have not been able to analyse it.

Rena Scrimpshire had the nickname of Little Bundle: dŭcraʔa (Barbeau 1911:17 and 24). This could have the noun root -hušr- 'little bag', preceded by the definite article d', the -a?a- possibly being the noun suffix plus the diminutive. But there needs to be a pronominal prefix, which could be another -u-, which is conflated with the -u- in the noun root.

The adopted white wife of William Walker had the nickname nŭdú?a, which Barbeau identifies as referring to Red Bird. (Barbeau 1911:36). So far I have been unable to analyse the Wyandot word or link it with any bird name that I have seen recorded. It does not seem to match any of the terms for 'cardinal' in related languages.

Finally there is TùndƐndé' for Hilda Hicks (Barbeau 1911:46). So far I have been unable to analyse or translate this word.

There are also potential nicknames that Barbeau did not identify as such. I will mention one that I can translate. The entry for a daughter of an R. Dawson has "skänŏ'täwa" translated as "short legs" (Barbeau 1911:44). I would present it as Skanǫhtawak 'She has very short legs'. It could be nickname, or it could be a reference to a clan animal not specified.

Connelley and Nicknames

In 1900, William Connelley identifies three nicknames. Regarding Rev. James B. Finley (adopted Bear clan), he wrote: "He had a nickname: Hah-gyĕhh'-rĕh-wah'-nĕh. Means, 'Big Neck,' because the Wyandots say, he had the neck of a bull" (Connelley 1900:44). My version of it is:

Hangyaruwanęh	He has a large neck.
ha-	masculine singular agent – he
-ngyar-	noun root – neck
-uwanę-	verb root – be large
-h	stative aspect

Robert Robitaille, a settler adopted into the Bear clan had the Wyandot nickname 'Teh-hooh'-kah-quah'-shrooh', interpreted as meaning: "'Bear with four eyes,' so named because he wore spectacles when he was adopted" (Connelley 1900:36 and 110). My version is:

Tehukakašra	He has double eyes.
te-	dualic
hu-	masculine singular patient - he
-k-	semi-reflexive voice
-(y)ak-	noun root – white of the eye, eye
-ašra	verb root – be double + stative aspect

Connelley's detailed origin tale of Governor William Walker's brother's nickname is:

Name, Wah'-wahs. It means Lost Place. The name was given from the following circumstance. His mother was a woman of great influence with all the tribes of the north-western confederacy; she spoke the languages of most of them. It was often necessary for her to attend their councils. She was sent for to attend one of these on one dark night. Her period of maternity was fulfilled. She was expecting confinement, and objected, but the business of state could not wait on business of nature, and she was put into a wagon, and the journey for the council commenced. In the intense darkness the team left the path and soon was lost in the woods. The result was as she feared. She was seized with travail, and soon a son was born to her. To commemorate the circumstances under which he was born he was given the name of Wah'-wahs— Lost Place. (Connelley 1900:113)

While the story of the origin of the story appears to be true, I believe that the translation is different. The verb root for 'be lost' is -atǫ-, which is not in this word. To me, a more likely translation would refer to the shortened time of his mother's pregnancy:

Auwas		It was short for her.
	-a-	factual
	-u-	feminine-zoic singular patient – her
	-wa-	verb root – be short
	-s	dative root suffix + punctual aspect

In 1899, Connelley presented two names for William Walker. One was a Large Turtle name also recorded from 1747 to 1789 (Toupin 1996:203, 858, 879, 907, 909 and 938) that I write as Yatsistarǫ? 'It is a fire at diverse distances' (Connelley 1899b:36; see Translations).

Connelley did not identify a clan for the second name. Further, it does not seem to be anyone's name before or after William Walker. This points to its being a nickname. It is 'Hah-shah'-rehs', said by him to mean "overfull," and referring "to a stream overflowing its banks at flood" (Connelley 1899b:36). My analysis is the following:

Hašras		He often spills, overflows.
	ha-	masculine singular agent – he
	-šra-	verb root – pour, leak, spill, overflow
	-s	habitual aspect

Summary

We have seen in this chapter that nicknames were both common and important in Wyandot naming. The discussion of nicknames does not end here, but is continued in later chapters, especially in the ninth chapter, which deals with the surnames that came into play during the 19th century. These surnames, including such names as Big Foot, Blacksheep, Canada, Curleyhead, Greyeyes, Little Chief, Mudeater, Pipe (from a Delaware chief's nickname) and White Crow, involved nicknames that took on a new life in a different aspect of naming (see the discussion in chapter nine).

CHAPTER SIX
Names Shared with the Wendat and the Haudenosaunee

Introduction

Wyandot speakers who created and passed on names in their language shared much of their vocabulary (in terms of cognates or related words), grammatical structure, and naming practices with their close Northern Iroquoian relatives, the Wendat and the Haudenosaunee (Mohawk, Oneida, Onondaga, Cayuga, Seneca, and Tuscarora). It should not be too surprising, then, that there are a number of names that they shared with those peoples. The chapter that follows discusses some of those shared names.

Names Shared With the Wendat

As the Wyandot and Wendat share a language (but with two distinct dialects) and much of a cultural history, they also have a good number of traditional names in common. My research reveals that there are at least 64 such shared names. Access to more resources would doubtless reveal more.

Father Robert Toupin noted the sharing of names in his recording of Potier's work:

Les noms de certains Hurons (enons, taretande, atironta, sarenhès, taondechoren, souondakoua, otiokouendoron) se retrouvent dans la tradition des Attignaouantans d'avant la dispersion de 1649 [the names of certain Hurons [i.e., Wyandot] ... are found in the tradition of the Bear nation before the dispersal of 1649 (Toupin 1996:182).

He neglected to mention Aseraye haǫ 'She comes from the south', who was both Wendat Bear nation and Wyandot Bear clan.

SOURCES OF WENDAT NAMES

There are three main sources upon which I have drawn for Wendat names. My earliest source for the Wendat names is the collection of documents known as the *Jesuit Relations* (JR) of the 17th and early 18th centuries, which supplies an abundance of names particularly before the common dispersal of the mid-century. There are 273 such names. Unfortunately, there is a gender imbalance. Only 39 of those names are female, or roughly 18 percent.

A little caution has to be used concerning whether a name mentioned in this source is Wendat or Wyandot. In the *Jesuit Relations*, both Wendat and Wyandot were called "Huron," a practice carried on well into the 18th century.

For Wendat names of the 18th, 19th and 20th centuries, there is the excellent collection of names and their interpretation put together by Wendat Marguerite Vincent, who bears the name 'Tehariolina' (Vincent 1984), itself a shared name (see below). Unfortunately, as the primary focus is on the names of chiefs (reflecting the limitations of the sources she had to draw upon), there are almost no female names in the book.

Thirdly, there are 74 Wendat names recorded for participants in baptisms, marriages, and funerals at Lorette (Wendake) from 1762 to 1791 (Steckley 1998). Fifteen of them are female.

There are two possible interpretations of this sharing. One is that a Wendat bearing the name, or a part of a clan bearing the name, joined up with the people the French called the Petun (as they were serious tobacco traders), and thus became Wyandot. If a Wendat name appears after the dispersal, then this interpretation is unlikely. Another interpretation is that it reflects the two groups' common traditional heritage. I believe this to be true in the majority of cases.

In addition, Potier's census of the Wyandot in 1747 can include some Wendat in the community. I almost included a reference to 'a8oindité' in that census, declaring that the name, found among the Wendat (JR52:229 as 'Ouendité', and 53:105 and Steckley 1998:5 as 'A8endite'), was Wyandot too. However, when I looked more carefully at the reference, I found the following concerning her and her husband:

> Sohendinnon V. ok8endissena v. hannionenhak hatatiaθak [He speaks French]...le lorretain [the person from Lorette (Wendake) ... jongleur [shaman]
> A8oindité ... agnes... separés (Toupin 1996:226).

She was probably from Wendake too.

LIST OF SHARED NAMES: WYANDOT AND WENDAT

Here are 64 names that I have found to be shared by both peoples. There, of course, would be a higher number in a more complete sample of Wendat names. The clan referenced is Wyandot.

Wyandot Name	Meaning	Gender	Clan	Wendat Sources
Aęnǫs	not sure[1]	male	Bear	JR[2]
Ahanęhutaha	He planted, stood up the corn.	male	---	JR[3]
Ahatsistari	He moved the fire around, put coals on top.	male	---	Steckley,[4] JR,[5] Vincent[6]
Ahǫndešǫtih	He abandoned a country.	male	Deer	Vincent 1984:320

1. I suspect that it might involve the verb root -e- 'come, go, walk'.

2. "JR" indicates *Jesuit Relations*. JR9:251, 10:81, 235, 305, 11:135, 12:199, 13:61, 147, 171, 215, 233 and 235, 15:57 and 38:181.

3. JR33:129, 36:181, 37:109, Anotaha (42:253 and 43:43) and Anahotaha (JR45:245 and 255), from 1649 to 1660. For a telling of the story of the Wendat so-named see "Estienne Annaotaha: The Unwanted Hero" in Steckley 1992:27–39.

4. Steckley 1998:13 as Otsistari. For a telling of the story of the Wendat by this name, see "Eustache Ahatsistari: The Bravest of the Braves," in Steckley 1992:19–25.

5. JR21:287, 23:25 and 241, 26:183 and 273, JR31:21 and 39:179 and 181.

6. Vincent 1984:324, with the connotations of "celui qui n'a pas peur [one who does not have fear]," 325 and 329.

Aseraye Haon	From the south	female	Bear		JR,[7] Steckley 1998:3
Ehaneno	She is going, has gone away.	female	---		JR,[8] Steckley[9]
Ekyayumendata	It is at the end of their, one's word.	male	Porcupine		Steckley[10]
Hamendandinyot	His word, voice is suspended.	male	Wolf		Vincent[11]
Hanehasa	He is, has little corn.	male	Prairie Turtle		JR[12]
Hanehurak	He used to attach corn.	male	---		Steckley[13]
Hanekinyondih	An evergreen is sticking out.	male	---		JR[14]
Hahšendaseh	He has a new name	male	---		JR[15]
Hatirota	He draws, attracts.	male	Deer		JR[16]
Handutok	He often tells stories.	male	Porcupine		JR[17]
Hažatoh	He marks, writes.	male	Deer		Vincent[18]
Homaskatha	They desire him.	male	---		Steckley, Vincent[19]
Hondawatot	He has a river in his mouth.	male	Deer		Steckley, Vincent[20]

7. JR52:165, 58:137, and JR60:297-9.

8. JR37:93 as Ehawennon.

9. Steckley 1998:7: there is one female and one male example.

10. Steckley 1998:7 as Etia,o8endata.

11. Vincent 1984:461. "a8a8endadiont Sa voix est suspendue aux lèvres [His voice is suspended on the lips]."

12. JR34: 219–1649 as 'hanneusa'. This may not be a cognate.

13. Steckley 1998:9.

14. JR10:231 and 289 as Anenkhiondic. JR10:231 "when one speaks of Anenkhiondic in the Councils of Foreigners, the Nation of the Bear is meant." JR10:289 "chief Captain of the whole Country."

15. JR15:137. The name was written as 'ahiendase'.

16. The name was given in the *Jesuit Relations* as belonging to three different people in succession, including two brothers and Father Gabriel Lalemant, who arrived in Huronia in 1648 and was killed in 1649 (JR20:35, 23:151 and 167; 27:91, 103, 113; 27:289; 28:147, 151, 155, 159, 167 and 171; 33:121 and 133;34:157 and 57:37).

17. JR36:143 (1651).

18. Vincent 1984:335 as hajaton.

19. The Wendat name is represented in two dialects, one that reflects the same form as the Wyandot. Steckley 1998:10 as Honaskatha, Honaskanha, and Onaskannha, and Vincent 1984:142 as Homoaskatha (with a -t- before the final -ha).

20. Steckley 199811; Vincent 1984:123, 141, 165, 181, 303, 315, and 461.

Huskwehšandet	He holds the axe blade close.	male	---	Steckley[21]
Hukyukwanduro̜	He is of a valuable lineage, group.	male	Striped Turtle	JR,[22] Steckley[23]
Ihandehwatiri	He is supported by pelts.	male	Deer	JR,[24] Steckley[25]
Iža'ris	She cooks.	female	Large Turtle or Bear	JR[26]
O̜ndeso̜k	uncertain	male	Hawk	JR[27]
O̜hwarak	uncertain	male	Bear	JR[28]
O̜no̜rutęh	It is a scalp of such a nature.	male	Bear	JR[29]
Sayuhša'ih	He is finishing, killing them.	male	---	Steckley[30]
Shandatsuwaht	He has a very large pot, kettle.	male	---	Vincent[31]
Sharęhes	He is very tall treetops.	male	Striped Prairie Turtle	JR,[32] Steckley,[33] Vincent[34]
Ši Huwa'tenhwa	He often comes carrying, or carried from afar.	male	Large Turtle	JR[35]
Sho̜no̜nkyako̜	He breaks a hill into many pieces.	male	Bear	JR[36]

21. Steckley 1998:10 as "hoskwechiandet".

22. JR 22:135 and 139 Okhukwandoron, 26:37 as Atiokwendoron, 26:295 and 299 as Aotiokwandoron.

23. Steckley 1998:3 as Hok8adoron, Ok8andoron and Ok8adoron.

24. This name is recorded in the *Jesuit Relation* of 1669 as "Andehouakiri" (JR52:231), a child of five, for a Wyandot of the 18th century as "ihandeh8atiri". The -ki- or -ky- is a dialect form shared by Wyandot and the Northern and Southern Bear nation Wendat dialects (Steckley 2007:390).

25. Steckley 1998:8 as ,Ande8atiri, ,Andeh8ateri, Andech8atiri and Andeh8atiri.

26. JR36:122 as Aia´ris.

27. JR55:44-5 as Ondessonka.

28. JR36:123 and 133 (1651). I am not completely sure concerning this pairing.

29. JR20:23 "one of the best connected in all the village" and JR20:25 – 1640 – Rock nation.

30. Steckley 1998:13 as Sa,ochiai.

31. Vincent 1984:461 "tsadatso8an une large bouilloire [a large kettle]".

32. JR8:151 Saranhes and JR13:23 as Soranhes.

33. Steckley 1998:14 Sareness and Sarenes.

34. Vincent 1984:141 as Sharenhesé and 480 as Sharenies.

35. JR15:77, 17:33, 47, 81 19:151, 21:147, 157, 161 as Chihwatenhwa, 17:41, 191 as Chiwatenhwa, 17:95 as Chehwatenhwa, 19:151 as Chihouatenhoua. 23:59, 61 as Chihoâtenhoua, and 195 as Chihoatenhoua. For a telling of the story of this Wendat man, see "Joseph Chihoatenhwa: The Forgotten Martyr," in Steckley 1992:5–17.

36. JR13:217-9, 223 as Sononkhiacon

Shumęduwat	He is very large in word, voice.	male	Striped Turtle	JR[37]
Shutrižuskǫ	He very frequently fights, kills.	male	---	JR[38]
Skwatęre	She is missing it, is missed again.	female	Deer	JR[39]
Taurhęšre?	Day is dawning.	male	Striped Turtle	JR,[40] Vincent[41]
Teharęhǫt	He is not putting the branch into a fire.	male	---	JR[42]
Teharašahkwa[43]	He will grab, take.	male	---	JR[44]
Tehahšęndayeh	He has two names.	male	---	Vincent[45]
Tehatrǫnyatase'	His sky is twisted; he is twisting the sky.	male	Bear	Steckley[46]
Tehuratati	He is running.	male	Wolf	JR[47]
Tehurǫnyateka	His sky does not often burn.	male	Large Turtle	Steckley[48]
Tewašęnyę	uncertain[49]	female	---	JR,[50] Toupin[51]
Teyanǫęs	She does not often fall into deep water.	female	---	Steckley[52]

37. JR37:109 as Sowendwanne.

38. JR26:33 as Sotrioskon.

39. JR41:105 as Skouatenhré.

40. JR17:145.

41. Vincent 1984:72, 83, 87, 179, 324, 433 and 461.

42. JR38:171 as tearenhont.

43. Wyandot Toupin 1996:860 as tarachiak8a.

44. JR36:133 (1651)—captured by Iroquois.

45. Vincent 1984:147 and 161 Theachiendale and 324 as Teachiendali.

46. Steckley 1998:11 as Hotchonhiatase. When a Wendat word does not have a dualic with verb roots that take the dualic in Wyandot, it could either be a dialect difference or a case of bad copying.

47. JR36:137, 139, 37:93 and 111 as Torata´ti and 38:49 as Toratati.

48. Steckley 1998:10, without the initial te- of the dualic.

49. This name is a real challenge. The -tew- is either a negative or a dualic prefix. I strongly suspect that the noun root -aš- 'axe' is in the word. However, no verb really seems to fit.

50. JR58:139 as Téouachégnien and 60:45 as Teouachennien.

51. Toupin 1996:863 as te 8achinniont, 869, 875, 877–8, 881, 886, 893, 909, 942, and 973 as te 8achinien, 882 as te-8achinien.

52. Steckley 1998:14.

Thaǫndešrurę?	He splits the country in two.	male	Large Turtle	JR[53]
Teyarǫtuyęh	Between the logs	male	Bear	Vincent[54]
Tharatuwaht	He has two large heels.	male	---	JR[55]
Tihšǫywę	Large star	female	Striped Turtle	JR[56]
Tsǫndakwa	Eagle	male	Sturgeon	JR[57]
Tsamęhohi	Osprey	male	Large Turtle	JR,[58] Steckley,[59] Vincent[60]
Tshundeǫskǫ	He holds very many sweat lodges.	male	Striped Turtle	Jesuit Relations[61]
Tsundakwanęh[62]	It is a very large barrel, drum.	female/male	---	JR[63]
Undaętǫ	She puts, places many arrows.	female	Deer	Steckley[64]
Uskęnǫtǫha	Little Deer	male	Deer	JR[65]
Węhwęh	Loon	male	Large Turtle	Steckley,[66] Vincent[67]
Yandarekwih	She is living, has lived there long.	female	Snake	JR[68]

53. JR21:149 as Teondechorren, 23:75 and 87 as Tondechoren, 26:183, 197 and 23, 30:47, 37:105 and 169, 50:211, 55:267, 277 and 299, 57:75 as Taondechoren, 58:135, 149 and 197 as Thaondéchoren, 60:79 as Taondechorend, and 307 as Tandechorend.

54. Vincent 1984:461 "Tehotharon8alin Un arbre fourchu" [a forked tree].

55. JR9:271, JR12:97, 99, 101, 105, and 207 as Taratouan and JR17:3 as Tarat8ane. The final -t- is a Wyandot feature.

56. JR35:58–59 as Tichion8amie and Tichionwamie .

57. JR23:241 as tsondakwa and 26:205 as Sondakwa.

58. JR36:141 as Tsa8enhohi, 53:97 as Saouhenhohi, 66:165, 167, and 169 Latinized versions of the name.

59. Steckley 1998:16 as Tsa8enhoh8i.

60. Vincent 1984:123, 159, 315, 327, 329, 365 as Tsa8enhohi, 141 as Tsawanhonhi, 364 as Tsa8ehohi, and 461 as Tsa8enhoni. .

61. JR37:95 and 46:109.

62. Toupin 1996:848 as sondak8ennen, 851 as tsondak8annen and 964 as ts8ndak8annen.

63. It is female for the Wyandot and male for the Wendat. JR13:227-9 as Sondacouane, 13:231 263, 14:13, and 47, as Tsondacouane, 13:259 as Tsendacouane, and 14:51 as Sacondouane.

64. Steckley 1998:11 as Ondaenton.

65. JR37:109. The words "or Otindewan" were written after the name, possibly referring to a name the person had earlier. Unfortunately, the name does not appear elsewhere.

66. Steckley 1998:11.

67. Vincent 1984:87, 142 and 324.

68. This name appears once in the *Jesuit Relations*, as "Egandarekoui," a woman of 23, in 1674 (JR58:139).

Name	Translation	Sex	Clan	Source
Yanęduk	She is putting corn in water.	female	---	JR[69]
Yanęhǫtak	Corn used to be in the fire.	female	---	Vincent[70]
Yanęti	It is an intact evergreen.	female	---	Steckley[71]
Yanǫduwanęh	It is a large mark.	female	Deer	Steckley[72]
Yanyęutǫ[73]	uncertain[74]	male	---	JR,[75] Steckley,[76] Vincent[77]
Yaręhaʔtsih	She is called treetops, branches.	female	---	JR,[78] Steckley[79]
Yarhonnens	She often makes the forest fall.	female	Large Turtle	Steckley[80]
Yarihǫnętaʔ	She often drops matters, affairs.	female	Snake	JR[81]
Yanyewinde	It drags, or leads the snow.[82]	male	Deer, Snake[83]	JR[84]
Yawinǫke	At the (beautiful) young woman.	female	Bear	Vincent[85]
Yawinǫywę	She is a very beautiful young woman.	female	Snake	Steckley[86]

69. The name appears as Annendok (JR37:101, 1652 and 60:297, 1677).

70. Vincent 1984:461 as annennontak.

71. Steckley 1998:4 as Annente.

72. Steckley 1998:4 as Annd8annen.

73. Toupin 1996:865 as angnieoton and 971 as anienoton.

74. In Vincent 1984:167 she translates the name as meaning "plusieurs piquets de guerriers" [many poles of warriors]. While I recognize the verb root as -ut- 'to stand' and the distributive root suffix -ǫ- 'many' following it, I cannot find the noun root that she uses.

75. JR55:289, 291 and 311 as Annieouton.

76. Steckley 1998:4 as Annienhoton and Anniehaton.

77. Vincent 1984:141 as ayenoton and 167 as anienlonton.

78. JR36:205 – 1651 and JR45:53 – 1659.

79. Steckley 1998:5 as Arenatsi.

80. Steckley 1998:2 as Arhonens.

81. With the Wendat name we have one entry in 1674, where it tells us that she was the daughter of "Egandarekoui," suggesting that the latter would have been Snake clan with the Wendat as well as the Wyandot (JR58:139).

82. This is a very tentative translation.

83. See the discussion of this word in the list of names.

84. In the *Jesuit Relation* of 1652 the name "Annie8indet" appears in reference to a man killed in battle (JR37:111).

85. Vincent 1984:165 as "La8inonke", the -l- signifying a -y- sound (as in French), meaning "la belle fille Huronne" ("the beautiful Huron girl").

86. Steckley 1998:3 as ,8innon,8ann. This is not an exact parallel, but it is close enough to be considered cognate.

Patterns

Here are the patterns found in gender and Wyandot clan. The former probably reflects for the most part the gender bias of recording.

Gender Division
Male: 44   Female: 16

Clan Assessment

Wyandot Clan	Names Shared	Total Wyandot Names	Percentage
Deer	9	38	24.4%
Snake	5	21	28.5%
Bear	10	41	24.4%
Large Turtle	3	46	4.3%
Striped Turtle	9	34	26.5%
Porcupine	2	28	7.0%
Prairie Turtle	3	9	33.0%
Wolf	2	25	8.0%
Hawk	1	2	50.0%
Sturgeon	1	1	100.0%

The figures for the Hawk and Sturgeon clans should be ignored, as the numbers are too small to deal meaningfully with percentages. It looks like the Large Turtle and the Porcupine clans are distinctly underrepresented. However, two Large Turtle clan members were politically significant brothers in the *Jesuit Relations*: Ši Huwaʔtenhwa 'He often carries or is carrying from afar' and Thaǫndešrurę' 'He splits the country in two'. The Deer, Bear, Striped Turtle and perhaps Prairie Turtle and Snake clans are highly represented. I cannot say why. There are probably significant historical causes that created these name-sharing differences between clans.

Complicated Stories
Teyarihuyeh: Is This Name Shared with the Wendat?

The Wyandot name Striped Turtle Teyarihuyeh 'a matter is divided, at a dividing point', is an important name in this chapter, as will be discussed in connection with names shared with the Haudenosaunee. The question addressed here is whether or not it was shared with the Wendat as well. We have just seen that a good number of Striped Turtle names are so shared.

The Wendat name was written by Vincent as Tehariolin (the -l- having a -y- sound), which differs in the gender marked. It uses the -ha- of the masculine singular agent, while Wyandot and Mohawk use the feminine-zoic singular agent. Then there is the matter of the interpretation involved. Vincent translated the Wendat name as "non divisé" [not divided]. One difficulty here is trying to determine whether the te- prefix marks the dualic, negative, or cislocative. It is easy in the case of the Wyandot, as the verb root is recorded by Potier as always taking the dualic (Potier 1920:405 "ti-o,en"). That should stand for the Wendat as well, as this feature does not seem to be added by Potier in his dictionary. The word "non"—meaning he had not heard it among the Wyandot—could be mistaken.

Is the gender marker wrong too, the product of there being no fluent speakers for too long a time? Or is this a different name altogether, although similar? This being said, my interpretation is that they both are cognate terms, but that interpretation and pronunciation have been muddled due to the forces diminishing the fluency status of Wendat.

Tsamęhohi – Osprey

It took me a long time to settle on a specific interpretation of the name Tsamęhohi, both the bird referred to and what the name literally means. I published an article, entitled "Tsa8enhohi: The Vulture Seen through Huron Eyes," but I misidentified the bird (Steckley 1994). The -8- represents a -w- which reflects the Wendat dialect. In making this mistake, I was following the Jesuit missionary linguists in so doing. From at least the time of the oldest surviving Jesuit French-Wendat dictionary, we find the word interpreted as referring to the 'Vautour' ['vulture'] (Steckley 2010:45). Later Jesuit dictionaries followed suit (FHO, FH67:17 FH1697:232). But, as I made clear in "Tsa8enhohi: It's a Bird, It's a Vulture, It's ... an Eagle" in *Words of the Huron* (Steckley 2007:122–125), published 13 years later, my opinion changed.

In her presentation of the name, Vincent fell into the same trap. She often identified the bird involved as "Le Vautour" [The Vulture] (Vincent 1984:159, 315, 329 and 461).

The problem centres around the fact that European vultures are related to eagles, while the North American bird that bears that name is not so related, but is related to cranes. It is an example of convergent evolution,[87] in which species that are not closely related develop similar traits, in this case the food that the birds eat. The Jesuits took their 'vultures look like eagles' experience and wrongly applied it to what they saw in North America.

Vultures did not exist where the Wendat lived until the mid-17th century dispersal. They first appeared in Ontario in the late 19th century (see Steckley 2007:124).

The Wyandot used the term to refer to eagles generally. This can be seen in a story entitled "The Eagle and the Hunter" (Barbeau 1960:107-12), and in other stories as well (Barbeau 1960:155, 181, 194, 200 and 202).

Vincent also tried to break down or analyse the word. She analysed it as involving the noun root -węnh 'bud', and the verb root -o- 'be in water' to give the translation "un bourgeon qui immerge dans l'eau [a bud that emerges in the water]". Although osprey do dive into water to catch fish, making the verb plausible, the noun root does not have the same strength of possibility. The noun root for 'eagle' in the related language of Cayuga is -(a)węhe- (Froman, Keye, Keye and Dyck 2002:99).

It is important that this name in particular is understood by the Wendat, as it was the name of the grand chief, from 1685 to 1844, with a brief hiatus in the mid-18th century (Vincent 1984:81–2).

---

87. A better known example involves the flying squirrels of North America and the sugar gliders of Australia and nearby Pacific islands, which are marsupials and a kind of possum.

He Has a River in his Mouth
WYANDOT STORY

Hǫndawatǫt[88]	He has/puts a river in his mouth. (male Deer)
[hon-dah-wah-tont]	
hǫ-	masculine singular patient – he
-ndaw-	noun root – river
-a-	joiner vowel
-tǫt-	verb root – put in mouth + stative aspect

Hǫndawatǫt is spelled in a great number of ways in the literature. For that reason it is often difficult to identify. The name is significant both to the Wyandot and the Wendat. Vincent Tehariolina reported that it has metaphorical interpretations:

"Il a la rivière dans la bouche", expression symbolique pour dire "le bon nageur" ou "mieux "le bon harangueur" [He has a river in his mouth, a symbolic expression for saying 'the good swimmer' or, better, the good talker.] (Vincent 1984:165).

One interpretation of the Wyandot name I believe reflects Wyandot humour. Larry Hancks, in his list of Wyandot names, reports the following bad representation and incorrect translation: Daw-wah-towht; Cotton in the Throat, i.e., a big Adam's apple. The noun root for 'cotton, down, soft material', is homophonous with that for 'river', and 'lungs/liver'. In *The Deer and the Owl* (Barbeau 1960:29–32, 182–94), the two main characters have the same name 'He who is soft', and are competing for the same women, with some humorous results (see chapter eight Names in the Narratives). In *The Dogs and the Wild Cotton* (1960:48 and 273–4), a dog that understands Wyandot mistakenly believes that a bag of cotton contains liver.

The written record of this name as Wyandot begins with François-Régis, who in 1747 was shown to be an important person, being referred to as one of the "considerés" (Toupin 1996:260), one considered for chief status, or a significant person in his own right. His wife was Christine A8innonke (Toupin 1996:219 and 253), a Bear clan elder (Toupin 1996:228).

He was baptized in 1738 (Toupin 1996:844, and was a godfather for three boys named Regis in the early 1740s (Toupin 1996:848, 849 and 850). He died in 1747 (Toupin 1996:922).

An Alexius who was a godfather at a baptism in 1746 bore the name (856).

The apparent next person given the name was a Matthias who was a very active Christian. In 1759 he had a newborn child baptized (Toupin 1996:880), and gave the prized gift of an eagle feather at a mortuary ceremony (945). In 1761 he named a Matthias in a baptism (882), and in 1765 got married through the church (Toupin 1996:909). This was the same year that he and his wife had another newborn child baptized (886). There was another child in 1767 and yet another in 1769 (889 and 892). He gave three gifts in mortuary services in 1768 (961, 966 and 967). In 1771,

---

88. Toupin 1996:219, 234, 253, 260, 848-50, 880, 882, 884, 886, 889-90, 892, 906, 909, 922, 945, 961, 966-7, 969, and 972.

someone, probably Matthias, bearing the name gave white beads as a mortuary gift (972).

Matthias was possibly the same person that Buser (1989) identifies as probably being the "Sastaretsi", that is hereditary chief, with the name of Da-wa-tong, in 1778, and as Dawaton in 1780, when he signed the agreement ceding land to Father Pierre Potier. In 1782, for a similar agreement ceding land to Potier's replacement Father Hubert, he again refers to "Dawatong (the Sastaretsi)", but then conflates that name with a similar name of someone else who had influence at that time (see Ndoentet).

The last Wyandot to bear the name seems to have been John Hicks. In his entry in "Our Great Chiefs" for 1812, Buser wrote:

> John is often called the last of the hereditary chiefs.... Before moving to Kansas he lived in Ohio and served on Tarhe's tribal council.... John was also known as Donwattout. His father was a captive of German descent who had once lived in Maryland. John's mother was Wyandot, and it's said she could trace her lineage back to the Tionnonati (1989, https://www.wyandotte-nation.org/culture/history/general-history/our-great-chiefs/).

John Hicks signed a treaty of 1817 as Wottondt, and the September 17, 1818 treaty as Dauatont. After his death in 1853, I have seen no record of any Wyandot going by this name. His son Francis became principal chief, but did not, of course, inherit his name.

Wendat Story

In the Wendat dialect there is an -n- where Wyandot has the second last -t-. We can see from the literature that there were people bearing this name in Wendake at the same time as the name was still alive with the Wyandot. In Steckley 1998, we see a Louis Onda8anhont who was baptized in 1766 and buried in 1782 (Steckley 1998:110).

In Vincent's collection of names we find that the name belonged to Paul Picard (1788-1871), a community innovator who helped develop a much admired 'brand' of crafts that would become quite successful bringing money into the community of Wendake (Sioui 2007). When he died, his grandson J. O. Sullivan received the name (1875, Vincent 1984:324). Again, the spelling has great variation.

Date	Spelling	Individual	Reference
---	Ha8adonnonti	Paul Picard	Vincent 1984:123
1813	Hondaanont	Paul Picard	Vincent 1984:181
Early 1820s	Hodonanhont	Paul Picard	Vincent 1984:141
1838	Ohada8anonk	Paul Picard	Vincent 1984:315
1850	Honda8onhont	Paul Picard	Vincent 1984:165
	Ondawanhon		
1875	Ondas[89]oanhont	J. O. Sullivan	Vincent 1984:324
---	Anda8anhont	---	Vincent 1984:461
	Ho8adonnonti	--	Vincent 1984:461

89. I believe that the -s- here is a bad copy of an -8-.

There are nine recordings here, and nine different spellings. If the language had been given some kind of governmental support such as official status, then the spelling would have been standardized, and this would not be such a problem.

Sharing Names with the Haudenosaunee

This section will not nearly be as comprehensive as the previous one, as my sources aren't as extensive. What I want to demonstrate is that the Wyandot share names with the Haudenosaunee, and significant ones too. This includes some of the names of the 50 sachems (representatives in the general council) of the Haudenosaunee, and a few other leaders. I have not gone much further than that. These are the names of the chiefs who were established as male tribal representatives through the Great Law of Peace that unified the then five tribes of the Haudenosaunee into a political united confederacy known as the Iroquois. Wyandot shares eight of those names, something that I did not expect to find.

THE MOHAWK (KANIEN'KEHÁ:KA 'PEOPLE AT THE FLINT')[90]

Four of the eight sachem names that the Wyandot share with the Haudenosaunee are with the Mohawk. I do not know why. One of these names is Teyarihuyęh, which was discussed earlier concerning names shared with the Wendat. In Mohawk it can be written as Tehkarihoken[91], belongs to the Turtle clan and is the primary name of the nine Mohawk sachems. The plural tehadirihoken[92] refers to all their sachems.

In *The Iroquois Book of Rites,* Horatio Hale recorded the following possible translations:

> Opinions differ much among the Indians as to the meaning of this name. Cusick, the Tuscarora, defines it 'a speech divided,' and apparently refers to the division of the Iroquois language into dialects. Chief George Johnson,[93] the interpreter, rendered it 'two statements together,' or 'two pieces of news together.' Another native informant thought it meant 'one word in two divisions,' while a third defined it as meaning 'between two words.'…It may possibly mean 'holding two offices,' and would thus be specifically applicable to the great Canienga noble, who, unlike most of his order, was both a civil ruler and a war chief' (Hale 1883:77–8).

The individual that Hale was talking about was the best known historically of those Mohawk who bore this name (c. 1750–1830). He has an entry in the *Dictionary of Canadian Biography* ("Tekarihogen", volume 6 (1821–1835, www.biographi.ca/en/bio/tekarihogen_1830_6E.html).

90. At the Flint was a historically significant Mohawk village.

91. In the Jesuit Relations of the mid-17th century it was recorded in JR38:194–5 and 198–9 (as Teharihogen), 43:47 (as Tearihogen), 44:122–3 and 128–9 (as Te Garihogen), 204–5 (as Teharihoguen), 45:79 (as Teharihogen, 86–7 and 90–1 (as Tegarihogen), and 94–5 (as Tigarihogen).

92. The -hadi- is the Mohawk counterpart to Wyandot -hati- 'they (masculine or mixed)'.

93. George Martin Johnson (1816-1884) was a Mohawk of the Wolf clan.

A second shared sachem name is Šateyarihwate in Wyandot, which I have translated as 'Two equal matters or statements". Hale presents it as: "*Shatekariwate*, 'two equal statements,' or 'two things equal.'" (Hale 1883:154)

A third shared sachem name is Kwiyǫteh in Wyandot, which I have translated as 'it lives two ways'. Connelley was told that the name could be translated as: " Quin'-dĕh "Two lives," or "he lives in the water and in the air," or "in living he goes up and down." (Connelley 1900:113). Hale writes that the Mohawk version means:

> "double life," from *onnhe,* life. My friend, Chief George Johnson, who bears this titular appellation, tells me that it is properly the name of a certain shrub, which has a great tenacity of life. (Hale 1883:155)

A fourth shared sachem name is Ustamęšrǫt in Wyandot (a term for rattlesnake), which I have translated as 'it has a turtle shell rattle attached, rattlesnake'. Hale writes:

> "he puts on the rattles." Mr. Bearfoot writes, '*Oghstawensera* seems to have been a general name for anything denuded of flesh, but is now confined to the rattles of the rattlesnake.' (Hale 1883:155)

In the next chapter we see that a French Commandant of Fort Pontchartrain also was given this name by the Wyandot.

Again, one of my sources is the *Jesuit Relations*. There is one Mohawk name found there that is not one of the sachems: Assendassé[94] (Asendasé). It is shared with the Wyandot and Wendat Hahsęndaseh, 'He has a new name' and was used for Jesuit Father Jerome Lalemant who was the Father Superior of the Wendat mission, and of New France at different times. the local Jesuit Father Superior[95]. The -d- here in the Mohawk name is the result of Jesuits writing the name as if it were Wendat, which was not unusual at the time..

A Mohawk military leader in the American Revolution was Captain David Hill (1745–1790). His Mohawk name was Karonghyontye, which has been interpreted on the internet without a declared reference as 'Flying Sky'. This appears to be cognate[96] with the Wyandot name Harǫyǫkyes,[97] which can be interpreted as 'he continues to move in the sky'.

The Mohawk name usually written as Oronhyatekha 'Burning Sky', which was given to Dr. Peter Martin (1841–1907), one of the first Indigenous doctors in

---

94. JR1:30, 57:145–7. 58:171–5, 59:237–9, 60:177–9, and 61:173–9.

95. JR16:239, 22:151, 24:109, 41:121, 43:163, 169, 173, 185 and 277, 44:107 and 113, 43:3, 169, 173, and 185.

96. The pronominal prefix appears to be different with the -ka- being the equivalent of the Wyandot -ya- .the feminine-zoic singular agent 'she or it'. The Wyandot term takes -ha-, which is the masculine singular agent –'he'.

97. Another difference is that the Wyandot term has the -s- marking the habitual aspect, while the Mohawk term has the -e- of the purposive aspect.

Canada. It appears to be a shared name with the Wyandot Harǫnyateka and Wendat Harǫnyatexa, 'He burns the sky'.

Oneida (Onyota'a:taka 'People of the Standing Stone')

There is one shared sachem name with the Oneida, cognate with the Wyandot Tsunǫšes, 'It is a very long house.' The Oneida name is presented by Hale as Sonohse:s of the Turtle clan, a name which he says means 'his long house,' or 'he has a long house.' (Hale 1883:157).

Another name connection is also significant. In a *Jesuit Relation* written in 1658 this name is given as the Oneida version of Onnontio (the French governor's Wendat name), representing the French generally. In this presentation of gifts in Onnontio's name the French gift-giver/speaker says: "I remove The irons from the Onneiout [Oneida], and send back one of them with You, that Garontagwann may know that I am a better Father than he is a child" (JR44:129).

Writing in the 19th century, Horatio Hale says about an Oneida self-naming:

> The name of the Oneida nation in the Council was *Nihati[98]rontakowa*...usually rendered the 'Great-Tree People,' – literally, 'those of the great log.'...in the singular it becomes *Niharontakowah*, which would be understood to mean 'He is an Oneida' (Hale 1883:157).

Hale suspected but did not know whether this was connected to the white pine that the Peacemaker established as the 'Tree of Peace'.

With Wyandot we have two names that relate to the Oneida name. One takes a feminine-zoic singular agent - Yarǫtuwaneh 'She or it is a large tree' (female Bear clan), and the other the masculine singular agent - Harǫtuwaneh 'He is a large tree'.

There is one more potential sharing of a name between the Oneida and the Wyandot. The name Oskennontonha appears twice in Potier's writing, when a man was baptized in 1730 (Toupin 1996:828) and when a child of his was baptized in 1732 (Toupin 1996:832). I have analysed it as follows:

Uskęnǫtǫha	Little Deer
u-	feminine-zoic singular patient – it
-skęnǫtǫ	be a deer + stative aspect
-ha	diminutive aspect suffix

What is particularly interesting about this name is a possible link to that of the famous Oneida war chief Skenandoah or Shenendoah (c. 1706–1816) who would have been of the same generation. This name has recently been written in a number of sources in a reconstructed Oskanondonha (see for example "Oneida Chief Skenandoah" in the Native Heritage Project, https://nativeheritageproject.com/2012/05/29/oneida-chief-skenandoah/).

---

98. The -hati- is the masculine plural agent term referred to in an earlier footnote concerning the Mohawk equivalent.

The word for 'deer' in Oneida in a modern dictionary is oskanu·tú· or oskʌnu·tú· (Michelson and Doxtator 2002:959[99]), cognate with the Wyandot word. My experience with Wyandot and Wendat written in the 17th, 18th and 19th centuries shows that names and other words that have a vowel written before an -s- might not be recorded. This may have happened with early writing of Oneida as well.

An alternative translation for the Oneida chief's name has been built on the Oneida noun root for 'evergreen' (as in Wyandot) -hnéht- (Michelson and Doxtator 2002:983, noun "ohnéhta²").[100] From this has been constructed Skanętowah meaning 'It is a very large evergreen.'[101] The verb root for 'be large' is seen in the previously presented Oneida name Niharontakowah 'He is a large tree. He is Oneida.' with the verb form being -kowah- (as also seen in the Mohawk Korahkowah). This translation could draw upon such a form.

This interpretation could relate in part to Shenendoah once saying late in life that he was "an aged hemlock". He was well over six feet tall and this may have been a nickname that related to his height. The noun for hemlock in Oneida is kanʌ²tú·sa² (Michelson and Doxtator 2002:1126), but this does not mean that this interpretation of the name is wrong.

The name was not passed on among the Oneida nor the Wyandot, so it appears not to have been a clan name, but a nickname. The arguments for both sides as to its meaning are as yet not completely airtight.

Onondaga ('People of the Hills')

With the Onondaga we have three apparent shared names. One is the sachem name Sganawadih of the Turtle clan of those people, which has a cognate in Wyandot Skandawati 'It is one the other side of the river' (Barbeau 1915:61), a mythical character (see chapter eight).

The Onondaga cognate of this name is recorded in the *Jesuit Relation* of 1648 as Scandouati (JR33:120–1 and 124–5), with a contemporary reference as Sganawadih (www.haudenosauneeconfederacy.com/government/current-clan-mothers-and-chiefs/).

Another is the traditional name of the head chief, which according to Hale's informants, was the name of the Onondaga people in council. He wrote that "the head-chief of the Onondagas was often known by the title of *Sakosennakehte,* 'the Name-carrier'" (Hale 1883:78). It would be more literally translated as 'he carries their names'.

In the *Jesuit Relation* of 1656 we see the name as Agochiendaguehté (JR42:88-9), most likely misspelled as Agochiendaguesé (JR42:94–5, 114–5, 116–7, and 190–1), in 1657 as Agochiendagueté (JR43:173). I would interpret these names as 'they (indefinite)' bear names.' Then there is Sagochiendagehte (JR41:69–71, 43:277, 45:89, 47:77), which I would interpret as 'he bears their (indefinite) names.' In both cases a Wendat version of the name was recorded. This is seen by the presence of the -d-,

---

99. The ʌ represents a nasal -e- or -ę-.

100. Eight Wyandot names in this collection involve this noun root, seven of them female.

101. Thanks to Rebekah Ingram, a linguist of the Mohawk language, for suggesting this to me.

which is the standard Wendat and Wyandot form. What could be the Wyandot version of the name is Huhšęndayehte[102] 'He bears a name' (male Bear).

An important Onondaga leader in the second half of the 17th century was Otrewa'ti[103] (JR45:89, 47:71, 95 and 277[104]). The Wyandot versions of the name are, for a male Snake clan member Hatrewatih 'He is opposing, resisting, criticizing it', and for a female (clan unknown) Utrewatih 'She is opposing, resisting, criticizing it'. The latter is closer to the Onondaga name, represented in the Jesuit Relations as "Otre8a'-ti" (JR45:88) and "Ot8re8ati" (JR47:276) in terms of pronominal prefix, but the initial -h- may have been dropped in the early Onondaga word, which happened often with French recording of Indigenous names at that time.

Interestingly, he had the nickname of "la grande Gueule" or 'big mouth' (Grassman). What makes this interesting is that it was a male nickname in Wyandot as well, as Yašwanęh 'it is a large mouth', used for a French commandant of the 18th century (see next chapter).

Cayuga (Guyohkohnyo or Gayogohó:no, 'People of the Great Swamp')

I have found no Wyandot names shared with the Cayuga. Their lack of mention in the *Jesuit Relations* is a major factor contributing to that.[105] I would be very surprised if there were no sharing of names between the two peoples. In a very short list of Cayuga names from 1879 in the Smithsonian Online Virtual Archives (https://sova.si.edu/record/NAA.MS1690), James Jamieson had the name Déonondokenn 'A depression between hills'; the Wyandot version would be Teǫnǫduyę, using a noun root and a verb root[106] that are used several times in Wyandot names. Mrs. Julie Ann Jamieson had the name Kaiakon 'She is cutting', which would be Kayakǫ in Wyandot, using the verb root -yay- 'cut, break', used several times used in Wyandot names.[107]

Seneca (Onondowagah 'Great Hill People')

Two Seneca sachem names are shared with the Wyandot. One I write in Wyandot Šateyarǫnyes 'It is as tall, as long as the sky. Half the height of the sky', which belongs to the Large Turtle clan. Hale records the Seneca name as Shadekaronyes meaning 'skies of equal length' (Hale 1883:162).

A second is in its Wyandot form Shayę'tsuwat 'He has a very big forehead', of the Large Turtle clan. Hale recorded it as a Seneca term: "Shakenjowane ... 'large

---

102. Barbeau has what appears to be this name as belonging to the Large Turtle clan (Barbeau 1915:x)

103. For his biography see Grassman.

104. In this last case, he is identified as an "Iroquois", and the name is spelled as "Otourewati."

105. They are only mentioned twice, which contrasts with 13 for the Mohawk and Oneida and 12 for the Onondaga.

106. See, for example "Teyarǫtuyęh 'It is between two logs': 'Between the Logs'" for the verb root.

107. See, for example, Shǫnǫkyakǫ' 'He breaks a mountain or hill into very many pieces.'

forehead'"(Hale 1883:162–3), and recently Bardeau 2019:334 "Shogĕjo:wa:nĕh ... 'he of the large forehead'" (Bardeau 2019:334), who belonged to the Hawk clan. What complicates this discussion is that in a Wyandot story recorded in 1911 by Marius Barbeau, entitled "The Wyandot at War With the Seneca," the war leader of the Wyandot leading them into victory was Shayę?tsuwat (Barbeau 1915:271–5 and 1960:51–3 and 291–300). There is a story here that I want to know.

Barbeau presents a cognate with Skandawati in Wyandot (and Onondaga) in Seneca "*Sku˙nnawundi*, 'beyond the ripples or rapids'", citing A. C. Parker (Barbeau 1915:61 fn 1).

In an 1867 Treaty involving the Seneca, Wyandot, and several other tribes, the first name of the Seneca signatories is John Whitetree.(https://www.wyandotte-nation.org/culture/treaties/treaty-of-1867/). There is recorded in 1747 a male Wyandot named saronta,enrat.(Toupin 1996:212), which I have analysed as Sharǫtayęraht[108] 'he is a very white tree'.

Tuscarora (Skarù:rę?, said to mean either 'Hemp Gatherers' or 'Shirt-Wearing People')

I have too few names to choose from in the sources I have access to. No Tuscarora names are mentioned in the *Jesuit Relations*. Again, that does not mean that they did not share names.

List: Wyandot Names Shared with the Haudenosaunee

Wyandot Name	Translation	Clan	Haudenosaunee Language
Teyarihuyęh	A matter divided	Striped Turtle	Mohawk (sachem)
Šateyarihwate	Two equal matters	---	Mohawk (sachem)
Kwiyǫteh	It lives two ways.	Large Turtle	Mohawk (sachem)
Ustamęšrǫt	It has a turtle shell rattle attached, rattlesnake.	Snake (?)	Mohawk (sachem)
Hahšęndaseh	He has a new name.	---	Mohawk
Harǫnyǫkyes	He often leaves the sky.	---	Mohawk
Hurǫnyateka	His sky often burns.	---	Mohawk
Tsunǫšes	It is a very long house.	---	Oneida (sachem)
Harǫtuwanęh	He is a large, great tree.	---	Oneida
Uskęnǫtǫha	Little Deer	Deer	Oneida
(Yarǫntuwanęh	She/it is a big, large tree.	female	Bear)
Skandawati	It is on the other side of the river.	---	Onondaga
Huhšęndayehte	He bears a name.	Bear	Onondaga
Hatrewatih	He opposes, resists, it.	Snake	Onondaga
(Utrewatih	She opposes, resists it.	--- (female))	
Šateyarǫnyes	It is as tall, as long as the sky.	Large Turtle	Seneca (sachem)
Shayę?tsuwat	He has a very big forehead.	Large Turtle	Seneca (sachem)
Skandawati	It is on the other side of the river.	---	Seneca
Sharǫtayęrah	He is a very white tree.	---	Seneca

---

108. Toupin 1996:212 has saronta,enrat. White is a spiritual colour to the traditional Wyandot. There is a story in which a woman has a succession of visions of white animals (partridge, bear, beaver, deer, and turkey; Barbeau 1915:97–8 and 1960:77–91), as well as a story about a spiritual white otter (Barbeau 1915:65–72 and 1960:106–7).

CHAPTER SEVEN
Naming the Incomers

There is an extensive record of Wyandot naming the French incomers they encountered in the Detroit area during much of the 18th century. This record is based on the detailed writings of Jesuit Father Pierre Potier and a few of his colleagues. Different strategies applied to different groups of Frenchmen. Unsurprisingly and unfortunately, any names the Wyandot gave to French women are not in that record.

The importance of this chapter is that it allows the voice of the people to speak through their language. It tells you what they thought of the newcomers.

A Bear Clan Name is Given to Bishops and a Methodist Missionary

The name was translated in Father Pierre Potier's dictionary of the mid-18th century as follows: "harih8a8a,i…il a l'affaire en main, il en a le maniement" [He has the affair in hand, he is handling it] (Potier 1920:223). My analysis is as follows:

Hariwawayi	He holds, grasps the matter. (male Bear)
ha-	masculine singular agent – he
-riw-	noun root – matter, law
-a-	joiner vowel
-way-	verb root – take, hold
-i	stative aspect

The name was first recorded in the *Jesuit Relations* in 1659, when the Wendat met the newly-arriving François de Montmorency Laval (1623–1708). In that *Relation* we read that:

> Hariouaouagui[1]… is the name they give Monseigneur, and which signifies in their language 'the man of the great work' ["l'homme du grand affaire" JR45:40] (JR45:41).

The name was recorded in the same text as "Rarionaouagni"[2] (JR45:42), and in 1664 as "hari ouaouagui" (JR49:88). In 1674 he became the first bishop of New France. This name was after Laval given to whomever held the position of bishop. It became a title. In an unpublished Wendat dictionary of 1697 we have: " Evéque [bishop] harih8a8a,i. Evéché [bishop's palace, house] harih8a8a,i hondaon [he has it as his home] (FH1697:71).

Among the Wyandot of the mid-18th century the name used by the Wendat for bishops was held by two young men in succession, one named François in the 1747 census (Toupin 1996:214), having a child baptized and being named a godfather in 1752 (Toupin 1996:863-4), with a new name (Sonnonkiaxon) in 1753 (865), and

---

1. Also JR45:88.

2. Sometimes the masculine singular agent pronominal prefix begins with an -r- instead of an -h-.

dying in 1755 (926). Then the name reappears with a man involved with a baptism ceremony in 1758 (878) and giving a gift in a mortuary ceremony (949).

In 1782, the Wyandot referred to Bishop Jean-François Hubert with the name (Toupin 1996:236). He officiated at Wyandot baptisms from 1781 to 1783, recording Wyandot names badly as he did so.

In the next century in a Wyandot community a little south of Lake Erie in what is now Ohio, the name reappears for an incomer, but one belonging to a different sort of Christianity. In 1821, Rev. James B. Finley was assigned by the Ohio Annual Conference the task of establishing a Methodist mission among the Wyandot of Upper Sandusky. He was adopted into the Bear clan and given the name he recorded in 1840 as Re-wah-wah-ah (Finley 1840:38). Connelley in 1900 wrote that the missionary's name was "Rēh'-wäh-wih'-ih. Means, Has hold of the law. In his books Finley does not write his name properly" (Connelley 1900:112). Neither of them did.

The Augmentative Clitic in Wyandot Names

In an earlier chapter I described the augmentative clitic -ywę which comes at the end of words, and which, in my experience of the language, is used almost exclusively with names or titles. In her excellent grammar of the related language of Onondaga, Hanni Woodbury describes its effect: "With nominals [nouns]: referent is large for its kind. With verb: indicates increased effort or effect" (Woodbury 2018:85). It is used in eight recorded Wyandot names:

Name	Translation	Gender	Clan
Handareywę	He lives large, puts a lot into life.	male	Wolf
Hutrǫnywę	He is a great, expansive sky.	male	Prairie Turtle
Ǫmašrutǫywę	Our large number of great axes	male	---
Ǫtareywę	It is a very big lake.	male	Deer
Tihšǫywę	Large star	female	Striped Turtle
Ukwišriwę	She is a great force.	female	---
Wętaywę	It is a great, a large stick.	none stated	---
Yawinǫywę	She is a very beautiful young woman.	female	Snake

Titles: Popes, Kings and Generals

A BISHOP'S TITLE IS AUGMENTED TO THAT OF THE POPE

In the Wendat dictionary earlier mentioned, we see that the name for pope was built by adding to the term for bishop: "Pape. Hari8a8a,i,8anne le grand Evéque…" (FH1697:138). In Wyandot that would have been composed with the augmentative clitic -ywę.

FROM GOVERNOR TO KING OF FRANCE

The first governor (1636–48) of New France was Charles Jacques Huault de Montmagny (c. 1583-99–1657). The Wendat translated his last name as Onnontio 'It is a large or great mountain' (ǫnǫtižu in Wyandot). It became the name used for every governor of New France afterwards. The Wyandot took the same term, adding the augmentative clitic produced Onnontïo-ï8oin, and used it to refer to the king of France in 1747 (Toupin 1996:233 and 265). I would write it in Wyandot as Ǫnǫtižuywę 'It is the largest great mountain'. In chapter eight you will see that this clitic is also used to refer to the king of a different country.

Long Knife: A Title for a General

In 1747, the governor of "la caroline" was called Asareï8oin in Wyandot (Toupin 1996:233). Under "Places aux anglois," we find "asareï8oin v. asaregoa Le grand couteau" (Toupin 1996:233). The term literally means 'it is a large blade'. In Potier 1920:154, there is added "i8ennenchr8annen [It is a large knife]" and at the end of that entry "ou Sabre". It is the Wyandot version of the 'Long Knives' Indigenous term for Americans: Asareywę 'It is a great, large blade'.

In the same year it was also a title for Ayawas 'It took it by force' of the Bear clan, recorded along with his name (Toupin 1996:209 and 924). In Potier's list of the male and female members of the elders council in 1747, the word "general" was written after his name, which was first on the male list for his clan (Toupin 1996:228). After that was written the Wyandot phrase "ha8endio d'hotiskenra,et". These words can be analysed as follows:

ha8endio		He is great in voice, word in authority.[3]
	ha-	masculine singular agent – he
	-8end-	noun root – word, voice
	-io	verb root – be great + stative aspect
	d'	who

hotiskenra,et		They (m) bear war, are warriors.
	hoti-	masculine plural patient – they (masculine)
	-skenr-	noun root – war
	-a-	joiner vowel
	-,et[e]	verb root – bear + stative aspect

He is authority over those who are warriors.

He would appear to be the war chief of the time, at least for his clan.

Naming the Jesuits

The Jesuit missionaries who lived with the Wendat and Wyandot from early in the 17th century to late in the 18th century were named in a generally different way than most of their fellow Frenchmen. In five cases, this involved giving them names that had been held by their predecessors, names that belonged to clans with Wyandot having the names too at various times.

---

3. Taken by itself, this is the term for God, Hamędižu in 19th-century Wyandot.

Jesuit Missionaries to the Wyandot[4]

The name Ǫndešrawasti 'It is a beautiful country' was given to Father Armand de La Richardie (1686–1758), the first priest to live with the Wyandot in the Detroit area. He arrived in 1728 and left in 1751. The name comes from a Jesuit description of heaven (Steckley 2014:77). It would later be used, with the alternate word for 'land' -ǫmets- in a Wyandot story entitled "The Land of Bliss" (Barbeau 1915:233–9, and 1960:44–7 and 255–72, see 255 #39), a story told by a Deer clan woman. He was adopted by Marie Nendaentons, a Deer clan elder, who was described by Potier as Richardie's sister (Toupin 1996:225 and 258; see Steckley 2014:78). His name was not passed on to anyone else after he left.

The Wolf clan name Hurǫnyayete 'He bears the sky' was given to Potier shortly after he arrived in the Wyandot community in 1744 (Toupin 1996:236 and 261). By 1747, a Wolf clan member of the elders council had relinquished the name so that the newly-adopted Potier could receive it. The elder took on the name Tandarei8oin[5] (Steckley 2014:90-1). Potier was not the first Jesuit to receive the name. Father Pierre Chaumonot bore the Wendat version of the name before Brébeuf died in 1649. He resuscitated Brébeuf's name Hechon a short time afterwards. In 1677, Father Claude Chauchetiere had the name when he lived with the Wendat (FH1697:241). He died in 1709.

Father Nicholas de Gonnor arrived in the Wyandot community in 1743, only staying for a year. He did, however, receive the much respected Wyandot/Wendat shared name Sharęhes 'He is very tall treetops' (Toupin 1996:235 and 261). No other Jesuit ever bore that name. In the 1747 census of 1747, two male Wyandot were recorded as having the name, eight year old François, of the Prairie Turtle clan (Toupin 1996:175, 206 and 244), and Pierre, an adult of the Striped Turtle clan, had the name in 1751 (Toupin 1996:208 and 860). In 1753, the name was held by a four- or five-year-old boy named Jacques who was buried that year (Toupin 1996:924).

Jesuit Father Jean Baptiste de Salleneuve (1708–1764) worked at the Wyandot mission from 1743 to 1761 (JR70:310 and 71:77). He had the Snake clan name, Hatrewatih – 'He opposes, resists, criticizes, is opposing, resisting, criticizing it' (written as Otrewati, Toupin 1996:236). He performed several baptisms from 1756 to 1758 (873, 874, and 877). Several different Wyandot had the name in 1747, 1760 and in the 1770s (Toupin 1996:884,897, 903, 908, and 948).

Jesuit Brother, Frère Pierre Gournay received the name Utęrut 'It is a standing palisade' by 1747 (Toupin 1996:234 and 261). It was translated into French as 'la tour' or 'the tower' (Toupin 1996:234). No one else was recorded as having this name. It could be a nickname.

Jesuit Missionaries Who Did Not Work with the Wyandot

The name Hęšrǫ (Hechon with the Wendat) initially represented a Wendat attempt to pronounce the first name of Father Jean de Brébeuf, adding the pronominal prefix

---

4. For a discussion of these individuals see Steckley 2014:76–94.

5. See Handareywę at the beginning of this chapter and in Translations. The initial -t- written here may have been a mistake.

marker -h- to make the word masculine. After Brébeuf's death in 1649, the name was passed on to worthy successors: Fathers Pierre Chaumonot (1611–1697), and Daniel Richer (Toupin 1996:235 and 261), the latter being a missionary to the Wendat (from 1715 to 1760) with whom the Wyandot were familiar. The Wyandot made the word conform to their dialect by adding the -r- after the -š-. With the name being passed down or resuscitated as it was, there is reason to suspect that the name belonged to a clan. Brébeuf would have definitely been adopted by the Wendat. I just have never been able to discover the clan. It is important to me as, at a language learning session in Wendake, they named me Hechon. It is a name that I proudly identify with.

Four Jesuits who would bear the Ondesonk or Hawk name used both by the Wyandot and the Wendat would be involved with the missions to the Mohawk and the Onondaga. The first Jesuit to bear this name was Father Isaac Jogues ((1607–1646; JR26:186–7 – 1643, JR31:88–9, 132–5 – 1647 and JR32:244–5 – 1648)

The second was Father Simon Le Moyne (1604–1665; JR41:96–7 – 1654; JR43:194–5, 200–1, 214–5, 217 – 1657, JR44:90–1, 96–99, 128–9, 198–9, 202–3, 206–7, 210–1, 212–3, 216–7 – 1658; JR45:84–5, 88–9 – 1659; JR46:238–9 – 1661; JR50:128–9 –1666).

The third Jesuit to receive the name was Father Thierry Beschefer (1630–1711; JR50:170–1 –1666). Finally, there was Father Jacques de Lamberville (1641–1710; FH1697:241).

Teharǫnyayandra? 'He often looks at the sky,' like Father Richardie's name one appropriate for a missionary, was a name given by the Wendat and later by the Wyandot to a Jesuit who did missionary work with the Haudenosaunee (see Steckley 2007:239 for a more complete story). It might have originated among one of those people, possibly the Onondaga. I have found six Jesuits who bore the name. The first was Father François Joseph Le Mercier, who arrived in New France in 1635, shortly to live with the Wendat, who first called him Chaose, like Hechon, an attempt to pronounce a first name. He appears to have gained this new name when he went to live with the Onondaga in 1656. The second was Father Pierre Millet, who lived with the Onondaga from 1668 to 1672. Following him was Father Sebastian Rale who arrived in New France in 1689 (FH1697:241). Father Jean Baptiste Tournois spent 1741–51 in New France, working with the Kahnawake Mohawk (Toupin 1996:261). Then there was Father Pierre René Floquet (Toupin 1996:236) who had the name in the mid-18th century. Lastly there was Father Joseph Marcoux, who had the name in the 19th century. The -d- in the name in Potier's naming of Tournois and Floquet shows that the Wyandot knew the name and spoke it in their dialect. No Wyandot seems to have ever had the name.

Jesuit Father Jacques de la Bretonnière (1689–1754) served the Kahnawake Mohawk community by the St. Lawrence River from 1721 to c.1752. He received the name Ta,orhensere 'Day is dawning' (Toupin 1996:236 and 261), possibly given to him by the Mohawk.[6] The first Jesuit to bear this name was Father Jean de Lamberville (Jacques' brother), who worked with the Onondaga from 1669 and died in 1716 (FH1697:241). For the Wendat, it is also a name of chiefs from the Picard family (Vincent 1984:72,

---

6. The Wendat version would not have the -r- (Steckley 2014:241).

83, 87, 179, 324, 433 and 461, and JR17:145). I did not find the name recorded for any 18th-century Wyandot but found it among the Striped Turtle of the early 20th century as Taurhęšre' with Isaiah Walker (Barbeau 1911:44, 1915:x and Connelley 1900:111).

Summary Chart

French Name	Wyandot Name	Translation	Clan
Missionaries Living/Working with the Wyandot			
Richardie	Ǫndešrawasti	It is a beautiful country.	Deer
Potier	Hurǫnyayete	He bears the sky.	Wolf
De Gonnor	Sharęhes	He is tall treetops.	Striped/ Prairie Turtle
de Salleneuve	Hatrewatih	He is opposing, resisting, criticizing it.	Snake
Gournay	Utęrut	It is a standing palisade.	---
Hubert	Hariwawayi	He holds, grasps the matter.	Bear
Missionaries Not Living with the Wyandot (but known to them)			
Richer	Hęšrǫ	---	?
Tournois	Teharonyayandra'	He often looks at the sky.	?
de la Bretonnière	Ta,orhensere	Day is dawning	Striped Turtle
Jogues, Le Moyne, Beschefer, de Lamberville	Ondesonk	Hawk	?

Commandants of Fort Pontchartrain

Unlike the Jesuit missionaries, the French commandants of Fort Pontchartrain did not live with the Wyandot, so were unlikely to be adopted with names that would carry on through a succession of name-holders. Each name appears to be unique to each commandant. Further, for the first few commandants, there would be no one to record the names these individuals would be given. Father Richardie did not live with the Wyandot until 1728.

Antoine Laumet de la Mothe, Sieur de Cadillac (1658–1730) was the first French official the Wyandot had contact within the Detroit area. I am not sure what the people called him.

In 1712, the same year that the Wyandot helped drive the enemy Fox tribe from the fort, François de la Foret became the commandant. Like Cadillac, he appears to have no recorded Wyandot name. But his name became attached to a Wyandot family. In 1747, we find that Margaret Atsironde, a Porcupine clan elder having "la la foret" appear after her name in the census (Toupin 1996:202 and 240).

The next commandant (1715–7), Jacques Charles Sabrevois, likewise does not seem to have any recorded Wyandot name. He served again from 1749 to 1751.

His successor, Pierre Alphonse de Tonty (1717–1727), whom the Wyandot successfully petitioned to have removed, likewise did not receive a Wyandot name. The people just used Tonti (Toupin 1996:234), a word easily pronounced in their language. It looks and sounds like a Wyandot word.

During the years 1727–8, François Marie Picote, Sieur de Belestre was acting commandant, and again in 1758–60 (Lajeunesse 1960:310). As he was the first commandant to be there when Father Richardie was in residence, we have a Wyandot name recorded for him. He seems to have been known indirectly by his father's name: Shandetsi h8ena (Toupin 1996:234 and 262), meaning 'He who has a very long arrow has him as his son':

Shandetsi		He has a very long arrow
	s-	repetitive – very
	-ha-	masculine singular agent – he
	-nd-	noun root – arrow
	-ets-	verb root – be long
	-i	stative aspect
Huena		He has him as child, his son
	hu-	masculine singular agent and masculine singular patient – he – him
	-en-	verb root – have as child + stative aspect
	-a	diminutive aspect suffix

I have seen no instance in which the father's name has been used for a Wyandot.

Next there was Jean Baptiste de St. Ours, Sieur de Chaillons, who was commandant in 1728–9. He was called Tsokeniasθa. This does not appear elsewhere as the name for a Wyandot. It is probably a nickname, with the second translation alternative (i.e., 'very little') the more likely one.

Tsokeniasθa[7]		One does very much or very little
	ts-	repetitive – very
	-o-	feminine-zoic singular patient – it
	-k-	semi-reflexive voice
	-ęny-	verb root – surpass
	-ast-	causative-instrumental root suffix
	-a	habitual aspect

Louis Henry Deschamps, Sieur de Boishebert served as commandant from 1728 to 1729. His name, which has no equivalent in any name held by a Wyandot, was 8ngnacta8asti (Toupin 1996:234) or 8'tacta8asti (Toupin 1996:262). The latter reference includes a translation into French of his name "belle buche" [good or beautiful log] which plays on the "bois" [wood] in his name.

Uhtahtawastih		It is a beautiful, good piece of wood.
	u-	feminine-zoic singular patient – it
	-htaht-	noun root – wood, piece of wood

7. The verb I have chosen takes the causative -t- and not the causative-instrumental -st- (Potier 1920:246).

-a-	joiner vowel
-wast-	verb root – be good, beautiful
-ih	stative aspect

From 1733–6 there was Ives Jacques Hugues Pean, Sieur de Livaudiere. His Wyandot name was Osta8oinchront (Toupin 1996:234 and 262). The name can be analysed as follows:

Ustamęšrǫt	It has a turtle shell rattle attached, rattlesnake,
u-	feminine-zoic singular patient – it
-stamęšr-	noun root – turtle shell rattle
-ǫt	verb root – attach, be attached + stative aspect

A Wyandot man had this name recorded in baptisms from 1743 to 1751 (Toupin 1996:851, 855 and 861) and in the census of 1747 (Toupin 1996:223). It was probably a Snake clan name. As we saw in an earlier chapter, it was a name shared with a Mohawk sachem.

The next commandant was Nicholas Joseph de Noyelles, who held the position from 1736–1739. His Wyandot name was Handetanion 'He is arriving, has arrived in the pines' (Toupin 1996:234 and 262 as endetanion). No Wyandot is recorded as having that name.

In 1739, commandant Pierre Jacques Payan de Noyan, Sieur de Charv(o)is received the name T'a8ista8is (Toupin 1996: 234) or Ta8ista8i (262). It does not seem to fit well into any construction I can put together.[8] It does, however, look a lot like the Mohawk and Onondaga words for snipe "tawistawis" (Michelson 1973:175), being the name of the clan in the latter language: dahwisdahwis (Woodbury 2003:13540. This is before the Wyandot had a Snipe clan. And this was not their name for 'snipe'.[9] I am reasonably certain that this name was not borne at any time by any Wyandot of the 18th century.

In 1742, the new commandant was Pierre Joseph Céleron. His Wyandot name was written as ,aronhia,e 'in the sky' (Toupin 1996:234 and 262). I wonder if some of the Wyandot knowing French heard the -cel- in the name and thought it related to the French word 'ciel' 'sky'. Again, no Wyandot seems to have been recorded as having this name.

In one of the entries (Toupin 1996:262), there is another name for him put in brackets, a very complimentary nickname: hondi,onra8asti. It does not appear as a name for a Wyandot.

Hǫndiyǫrawasti	He has a good, beautiful mind.
hǫ-	masculine singular patient – he
-ndiyǫr-	noun root – mind

8. I tried Tawistawi 'His metal is not rotten', but it does not work.

9. The Wyandot word for 'snipe is tsandehšenyǫhka'.

-a-		joiner vowel
-wast-		verb root – be good, beautiful
-i		stative aspect

Paul Joseph Lemoyne, Chevalier de Longueuil was the next commandant, serving from 1744 to 1749. His was a powerful family, two being deemed "Baron de Longueuil." Paul Joseph was given a Wyandot name written variously as Tatak8isere, ak8iechre (Toupin 1996:234) or Tatak8ichere (261). In 1771, it appears that he was involved with a Wyandot mortuary ceremony, as one of the major participants was called Paul tak8isere (Toupin 1996:974). A very tentative presentation of what the word might be is hatakwišre. I suspect that the noun root -hwišr- 'force' is involved, but I cannot be sure.

Another son of the baron, "Le fils du baron de longueuil," was called 'ok8esen h8ena' (Toupin 1996:234). The first word 'okwesen' refers to 'chicken' in Wyandot. The second can be analysed as follows:

huwę̨ʔah		He has him as child; his son.
	huw-	masculine singular agent + masculine singular patient – he - him
	-ę̨-	verb root – have as child
	-ʔ-	stative aspect
	-ah	diminutive aspect suffix

The combination looks like 'He is the child, the son of a chicken'.

The next commandant, Jacques Charles de Sabrevois, Chevalier de St. Louis, was returning to the post, serving this time between 1749–51. Again, no Wyandot name is given for him. He was followed by another repeat commandant, Céloron, from 1751 to 1754.

There is a Pajot (likely Jean-Thomas) listed under the "Commandans au Detroit" as ',achi8a-inen' and ',achi8annen' (Toupin 1996:234 and 262). The Pajot in the Toupin collection was active from 1767 (1028) to 1781 (1158), with no mention of being a commandant or having a connection with the fort. In 1754 there was a baptism with the name of ',achi8annen' as the father (Toupin 1996:867). The name, looking to be a nickname, is 'Yašiwanęh' 'it is a big mouth'.

So what do we have in sum? We have 14 names of commandants, only one with a possible clan connection, and that is one held also by a Wyandot. None seem to be passed on to a successor. They seem to be treated as nicknames. Here is the chart:

SUMMARY CHART

French Name	Name	Meaning	Clan
Cadillac	de la Mothe	---	no
Dubuisson	Uskwiratayi	dense branches	no
de la Foret	la Foret	---	no
Sabrevois	---	---	no

Tonty	tonti	---	no
Belestre	Shandetsi	He has a very long arrow.	no
Chaillons,	Tsokeniasθa	One does very much/ little.	no
Boishebert	Uhtahtawastih	It is a good piece of wood.	no
Pean	Ustamęhšrǫt	It has rattles attached.	Snake
Noyelles	Handetanyǫ	He has arrived in the pines.	no
Payan	Tawistawi	?	no
Céleron	Yarǫnyaʼye	In the sky	no
Longueuil	Tatak8ichere	?	no
Pajot	Yašiwanęh	It is a big mouth.	no

Other Officers

One officer, with the last name of Demuisseau, received a name shared with two Wyandot (one male and one female), the name for otter 'ota8indet' (Toupin 1996:234) and the more usual term 'ta8indet' (Toupin 1996:261) under "François du Detroit." It does not seem to be associated with any particular clan. Potier wrote that "Demuisseau aux aguets partout" (348) 'Demuisseau is on the lookout everywhere'. It would be easy to picture an otter in that way; a Wyandot name-giver might have done likewise.

Another Demuisseau, probably a brother, and possibly a soldier (the entry has "com" after it, likely short for "commandant") was called ta8achro8annen or to8achro8annen in Wyandot (Toupin 1996:234 and 261). In one reference he is called "Menton". While this looks like a possible nickname, as 'menton' means 'chin', the noun root for that in Wyandot is -yǫhęh-. My analysis has it as:

Tawašruwanęh	Where there is a large axe.
taw-	cislocative
-ašr-	noun root – axe
-uwanę-	verb root – be large
-h	stative aspect

A name given to an "officier" at Fort Pontchartrain, likely a high-ranking soldier, is presented as Hachiend8annen (Toupin 1996:233) and Hochiend8annen (Toupin 1996:265). The latter is a bit more likely to be the right form. Potier gives a name in 1762 as hachrend8annen (Toupin 1996:884). As there is no noun root -chrend- this might involve him adding a Wyandot feature where none existed. I have analysed the name as follows:

Hušęduwanęh	He has a great name.
hu-	masculine singular patient – he
-šęd-	noun root – name
-uwanę-	verb root – be great
-h	stative aspect

Potier translates this noun and verb root combination as:

,achiend8annen avoir un grand nom, une grande reputation; etre d'une grande considerable [to have a great name, a great reputation; to be a greatly considerable person] (Potier 1920:254)

Occupational Names

A good number of French tradesmen were referred to by a Wyandot word for their occupation: blacksmiths, woodworkers, masons, and doctors.

BLACKSMITHS

There are two men with an occupational name that indicates that they are blacksmiths. One has the last name of Chauvin, with an entry of 'choïn ok8istonniak' (Toupin 1996:235 and 262), the first word being his name as pronounced by the Wyandot. The other has the last name of Martin, bearing the more accurate 'hok8istonngiak' in one entry (Toupin 1996:235) and another, adding the word "haotsindachra" (Toupin 1996:261), which is a noun meaning 'he (is an) old man'. The occupational name for a blacksmith then is:

Hukwistǫngyaʔ	He often makes metal.
hu-	masculine singular patient – he
-k-	semi-reflexive voice
-wist-	noun root – metal
-ǫngy-	verb root – make
-aʔ	habitual aspect

WORKERS IN WOOD

The Wyandot name given for Pierre Meloche was written as Hannonchianngiak (Toupin 1996:235) He was very much involved with house building (Lajeunesse 1960:30). The vowel after -chi- should be written as -o-. With that change we have the following:

Hanǫšǫngyaʔ	He often builds, makes houses.
ha-	masculine singular agent – he
-nǫš-	noun root – house
-ǫngy-	verb root – make
-aʔ	habitual aspect

A Frenchman named Parent was referred to in Wyandot as Ha8oin,aronniak (Toupin 1996:235). The occupation name appears again with a man named Gervais (Toupin 1996:955). There was a Louis Gervais who owned a sawmill in 1749 (LeJeunesse 1960:44). Their occupation name can be analysed as:

Hahmęyarǫngyaʔ	He often makes, works with boards, worked wood.
ha-	masculine singular agent – he
-hmęyar-	noun root – worked wood

-ǫngy-	verb root – make
-aʔ	habitual aspect

Another kind of worker in wood is found in the "François du detroit 1752", with the entry "handakonniak … barrois" (Toupin 1996:235 and 262 with "Barois"). The French name could relate to the English word 'barrel'. The Wyandot word definitely does:

Handakǫngyaʔ	He often makes barrels, is a barrel maker.
ha-	masculine singular agent – he
-ndak-	noun root – barrel, drum
-ǫngy-	verb root – make
-aʔ	habitual aspect

Another name that qualifies as being a description of someone working in wood is "haentonngia…jacob s. martin" (Toupin 1996:235). It can be analysed as follows:

Haętǫngyaʔ	He often makes, works with sticks[10].
ha-	masculine singular agent – he
-ęt-	noun root – stick
-ǫngy-	verb root – make
-aʔ	habitual aspect

A Mason

Nicholas François Janis worked as a mason in Detroit (Lajeunesse 1960:30). His Wyandot name was written as Hong8atonngiak (Toupin 1996:235), which can be analysed as:

Hǫngwatǫnyaʔ	He often makes, works with white clay.
hǫ-	masculine singular patient - he
-ngwat-	noun root – white clay
-ǫngy-	verb root – make
-aʔ	habitual aspect

There are two references to this name in mortuary ceremonies of 1760, one to the person bearing the name (Toupin 1996:948), another to the wife of such a person (the name followed by H8nda 'She is spouse to him' (Toupin 1996:952)). It is likely that it is the Frenchman, and not a Wyandot.

---

10. In the baptismal record of 1743, there is a father of the baptized named 'haentondi', which has the same noun and verb root, but takes the stative aspect, with the meaning of 'He is making, working with sticks.' It is probably not the same person and might not be an occupational name (Toupin 1996:851).

A Shoemaker

There are three different spellings for another tradesman, named Goyau, making potential translation difficult: honniak, hakenniak (Toupin 1996:235) and xondgiak (Toupin 1996:261). Fortunately, in the latter entry there is the French translation of "facteur de soulier," that is shoemaker. So what we have here is a word that would be analysed as follows:

Hakǫngya'	He often makes shoes.
h-	masculine singular agent – he
-ak[11]-	noun root – shoe, shoes
-ǫngy-	verb root – make
-a'	habitual aspect

After this name is that of the shoemaker's son Baptiste. His name is presented as Xondiak anien. Added to the 'he makes shoes' is a term meaning 'my child'.

Doctors

We see the occupational name for doctors, healers, Hatetsens and atetsens (Toupin 1996:235 and 262) in the "François au Detroit 1752", with a Frenchman named Chapoton: This is different from the Wyandot name based on the same verb Shutetsęnskǫh[12] 'He is quite frequently a healer, curer'. Potier presents it simply as: "hatetsens il est medecin [He is a doctor.]" (Potier 1920:369).

Hatetsęs	He often heals, cures, is a doctor.
h-	masculine singular agent – he
-ate-	semi-reflexive voice
-tsę-	verb root – heal, doctor
-s	habitual aspect

Summary Chart

Name	Translation	Occupation
Hukwistǫngya'	He often makes metal.	Blacksmith
Hanǫšǫngya'	He often makes houses.	Builder
Hahmęyarǫngya'	He often works with boards.	Carpenter
Handakǫngya'	He often makes barrels.	Barrel-maker
Haętǫngya'	He often works with sticks.	Carpenter
Hǫngwatǫngya'	He often works with white clay.	Mason
Hahkǫngya'	He often makes shoes.	Shoemaker
Hatetsęs	He often heals, cures.	Doctor

Nicknames with Body Parts

There are three nicknames for Frenchmen that relate to body parts being long. One is a

---

11. The usual form this noun root takes is -akw-, but with the -ǫ- following, the -w- is dropped.

12. Toupin 1996:221; Barbeau 1911:7 and 44.

man with the French name of Bondi, whose Wyandot name appears twice: hondgietsi and aiongietsi[13] (Toupin 1996:234 and 261), the latter reference with the French "(Long nez)[14]."

Huyǫngyetsi	He has a long nose.
hu-	masculine singular patient – he
-yǫngy-	noun root – nose
-ets-	verb root – be long
-i	stative aspect

In another nickname, one of two references has a translation into French: haskonchietsi Les grandes dents [large teeth]" (Toupin 1996:262). The other just gives the name (Toupin 1996:235). My analysis of the name is:

Haskǫšetsi	He has long teeth.
ha-	masculine singular agent - he
-skǫš-	noun root – tooth
-ets-	verb root – be long
-i	stative aspect

A third nickname with the verb root -e(t)s- 'be long' involves the nickname of a man with the occupational name of 'barrel-maker'. This nickname is presented as "handeretsi" and "anderetsi" (Toupin 1996:235 and 262). It can be analysed as:

Handeretsi	He has a long waist, torso
ha-	masculine singular agent – he
-nder-	noun root – waist, torso
-ets-	verb root – be long
-i	stative aspect

Another nickname describing the physical nature of a Frenchman is of a man with the surname of Douville. The Wyandot name is written as "and8store" (Toupin 1996:234 and 262). I have analysed it as follows:

Handusture	He is covered with scabs, calluses
ha-	masculine singular agent – he
-ndust-	noun root – scabs, calluses
-ure	verb root – cover, be covered + stative aspect

13. The -g- in these names represents the Wyandot dialect form added by Potier as a superscript. The -d- is Wendat.

14. The Wyandot name as presented looks more like the noun root is -ngy- 'finger', but here I am using the French translation to guide my analysis.

Summary

We have seen that there were several different ways in which the Wyandot named Frenchmen. There were what I call "titles" for people of high authority: bishops, popes, governors, and kings. Then we have the Jesuits, who were generally adopted and had names, some clan-based, that were passed down. Although this distinguishes them from most other French, a few others fit this pattern. A man named Courtmanche had the Porcupine clan name "ts8trates" 'It has long quills' (Toupin 1996:235, Shutraʔtes in Translations). Robert Navarre received the Deer clan name "hahiatonk" 'He often marks, writes' (Toupin 1996:235).

The commandants of Fort Pontchartrain usually had names that seem unique to them, some of them nicknames, and not names that linked with clans. The various tradesmen typically had names with the verb root meaning 'to make' and the habitual aspect, referring to something often done. And finally, there were nicknames, relating to parts of the body, usually describing them as 'long'.

CHAPTER EIGHT
Names in the Narratives

In 1911–2, Marius Barbeau obtained 40 stories or narratives in Wyandot from some of the last fluent speakers of the language. Despite the diminished status of the language, he was able to find a strong and dedicated team of storytellers and interpreters. These stories were published in English and Wyandot in 1960, but, as mentioned in the introductory chapter, little constructive analysis had been done by Barbeau since the time they were first recorded. However, along with the narratives collected in English at the same time, and published by Barbeau in 1915, the stories did supply some names of characters in stories. These names would have been familiar for centuries to Wyandot children and adults alike from their experiences listening to stories.

Kurahkuwah: A King Appears in the Narratives

The name Kurahkuwah appears in two Narratives (Narrative 26, "The Steer and the Ill-Treated Stepson," and Narrative 28, "The Land of Bliss"). It is the name of a rich, prominent man who gets outsmarted by a Wyandot trickster. Barbeau gives the word as meaning "the important or wealthy person" (Barbeau 1915:222 fn 1). When I was first translating these stories, I wondered what the name really meant. It did not appear to be a Wyandot name, although it did not violate any of the rules of Wyandot pronunciation. It sounded Wyandot, but I could not break it down into morphemes or meaningful pieces.

Eventually, with a little research, I discovered that the name was the result of a double borrowing. Korah was the Mohawk version of the last name of Arent van Corlaer (1619–1667), the founder of Schenectady, New York. The language did not have an -l-, so speakers substituted the nearest sound: -r-. Governors of New York and at least one elsewhere were thereafter called Korah. In 1747, Potier wrote "Kora ... gouverneur de baston [Boston]" (Toupin 1996:233).

Attaching the -*kowah* suffix 'be great' (cognate with Wyandot -yuwaṇe- and the augmentative clitic) made the individual of even higher authority: King of England. The Wyandot of the informants had -u- where Mohawk had -o-, so the name was converted to Kurahkuwah. I wonder how many listeners to stories mentioning the name Kurahkuwah knew the history of the title. Children listening to the story might have just thought of him as a rich and powerful white man that one of their people could easily trick. The elders would know better.

Yaaʔtayęhtsih – She Is an Old Person.

Yaaʔtayęhtsih is an important mythic figure in traditional stories of the Wyandot and Wendat people. In the Wendat origin story, she fell from the sky and became the first woman on earth. She was the grandmother of the twins (see below). That story is told in the Narratives, but the woman is not named. In four of the Narratives, she was given the character of a 'witch': "Two Giants and the Old Witch" (Barbeau 1960:77–91), "The Trickster and the Old Witch" (Barbeau 1960:158–69), "Tatenri'a" (Barbeau

1960:169–83); and "Tawidiʔa and His Uncle" (Barbeau 1960:235–55). And in the second named story there are references to "awaʔtayętsih," variously translated as "we ... are old women," "we are old" and "our bodies are old" (Barbeau 1960:162 #21, 163 #20 and 166 #46), a group of fellow old women that the character wants to impress.

It has long been frustrating for me to translate fully the meaning of the name. Barbeau translated it as follows:

"her body old (old woman)"   1960:77#37
"her-body is old"   1960:90 #7, 160 #20, 163 #14, 165 #50, and 167 #12
"she-body is old"   1960:86 #53, 87 #52, 88 #32, 89 #46, 161 #19, and 166 #35
"she body old (woman)"   1960:158 #34
"she body old"   1960:158 #47
"body is old"   1960:91 #9

In an English version of the first story mentioned above, Barbeau presents another attempt at translation, which is more implication than literal translation: "*her-body-is-wise*, the old woman, or old witch" (Barbeau 1915:65 fn 6).

The noun root -aʔt- 'body' is clearly Wyandot, and it appears in many names. My initial problem with the verb identified in the translation was that there were no Wendat dictionaries, including Potier's, that had -yęts(i)- as a verb root. And the verb did not appear in the Narratives with any other noun root. So it did not seem to be a Wyandot verb root. Checking dictionaries I found that this verb root exists in Seneca and Cayuga.

In Wallace Chafe's excellent English-Seneca dictionary of 2012, we see the verb root "-gegëhjih- old in body" with the verb root by itself, and -yaʔtakëhtsi- when the noun root for 'body' shared with Wyandot and Wendat is incorporated into the verb (Chafe 2012:115). In Froman et al.'s Cayuga dictionary of 2002, we see "be an old person -gęhjih", also appearing with the -aʔt- noun root (2002:217 and 450). The -g- in the two languages corresponds to -y- in Wyandot, the -j- corresponds to Wyandot -ts-. Both the Seneca and Cayuga verbs make reference only to humans. The verb root with a corresponding meaning in Wyandot, -aʔtǫ- appears in the Narratives, but is not a cognate.

As the Seneca-Cayuga Nation in Oklahoma have for some time been neighbours of the Wyandotte Nation of Oklahoma, and as one of Barbeau's main informants was Smith Nichols, whose father was Cayuga, it seems reasonable to say that someone's knowledge of the closely related languages of Seneca and Cayuga informed the translation found in the Narratives.

The Twins

The names of the twins that were the first human males born on earth, the grandchildren of Yaaʔtayęhtsih, were not mentioned by name in the Narratives, although their stories were told. Fortunately, these names can be found in other, earlier sources, republished in Barbeau's *Huron and Wyandot Mythology* (1915), in which the stories are told, often by the same informants that provided stories in Wyandot in the Narratives.

The Good Twin: Tižaskeha

Name	Reference
Te-zha-ska-haw	Clarke 1870:150 (referred to as the "God of Nature")
Tijuskeha	Hale 1888 (Barbeau 1915:301)
Tijaiha	Hale 1889 (Barbeau 1915:344–7)
Tsēh'-stäh	Connelley 1889b (Barbeau 1915
Tsɛ''sta?	B.N.O. Walker 1911 (Barbeau 1915:45–6)

To establish a kind of consensus form for this name, I have considered both the names given above, and the 17th-century Wendat forms republished in Barbeau's 1915 work. The latter include "Youskeha" originally published in Recollect Brother Gabriel Sagard's work of 1632 (Barbeau 1915:289-90), "Jouskeha" (the -j- representing an -i- sound) in Father Jean de Brébeuf's *Jesuit Relation* of 1635 (JR8 and Barbeau 1915:291), and "Iouskeha" in his *Jesuit Relation* of 1636 (JR10, and Barbeau 1915:293-4). From these versions of the name, we can say that the word can be represented as Tižaskeha.

There were two failed attempts to translate the word. The worst of the two was as follows. I do not know whether it came from Hale or Barbeau:

This name, Tijuskeha (the Joskeha of the French missionaries) may be a derivative from the root *io* (*iio, iyo*) or *iju*, which signifies both 'great' and 'good'. This root forms the concluding portion of the name *Hamendiju* (Huron), *Rawenniio* (Iroquois) applied to the chief divinity, and signifying 'the great good master' (Barbeau 1915:301).

The Wendat verb root referred to, -ižu- in Wyandot, does not make up part of this name. It belongs at or near the end of the word, as the two illustrating examples show, not as part of the first syllable.

Connelley's attempt was little better. He claimed that it meant "Made of Fire, or the Man who was made of Fire" (Barbeau 1915:306). He would seem to believe that the noun root -tsist- 'fire' is part of the word. This does not fit with earlier representations of the name, both in Wyandot and in Wendat, plus there would need to be a pronominal prefix before the noun root. Unfortunately, I have not yet been able to put together a reasonable translation of this name.

The Bad Twin: Tawiskarǫ

The names presented for the 'bad twin' are easier to deal with. The connection with flint, the noun root for which is -atawihskar-, is obvious.

Name	Translation given	Source
Tawiskarong	"flinty, or flint like"	Hale 1888 in Barbeau 1915:301
Täh'-wĕh-skä-rĕh	"Made of Flint, or the Man Who Was Made of Flint"	Connelley 1889b in Barbeau 1915:306–11
Taˇwɛ'skaˇrɛ	---	B.N.O Walker 1911 in Barbeau 1915:45–6

Brébeuf recorded the name in Wendat in 1635 as "Tawiskaron", and he told the story of how the Bad Twin's blood became flint (JR10 in Barbeau 1915:293). From this presentation of the name and Hale's, I reckon that the name should be written as Tawiskarǫ, with the verb root and the pronominal prefix being as yet not determined.

Names in "The Old Bear and the Nephew"

In the narrative "The Old Bear and the Nephew" (Barbeau 1960:197–210), the hero of the story, the nephew, is pursued by one of his uncles, a bear (who has no name mentioned), while a spirit and three other uncles are there to help him escape that evil uncle. Their names are provided.

HE WHOSE CHEST IS AFFIXED – A HELPFUL SPIRIT

The helpful spirit is called He Whose Chest is Affixed. Barbeau described this spirit as "The-one-with-bare-loins-and-without-lower-limbs" (Barbeau 1960:33), "his loins are bare," "his loins (are) struck up" and "his loins rests on (has no lower extremities)" (Barbeau 1960:199 #46, 204 #1 and 210 #29 respectively). The noun root meaning 'loin(s)' in Wyandot, -ikar-, is not used in this name but is part of the human name Ndikaratase 'They two (f) have twisted loins, flanks.'

The first description/translation relates to the following phrase of three words:

huʔtuhšruskǫʔ	His chest is naked.
hu-	masculine singular patient – his
-ʔtuhšr-	noun root – chest
-uskǫ-	verb root – be naked
-ʔ	stative aspect
ąʔątaʔ	not
tehaʔnǫtǫht	He does not have legs.
te-	negative
-ha-	masculine singular agent – he
-ʔnǫt-	noun root – leg, legs
-ǫht	verb root – be attached + stative aspect

The word that is repeated more often and is more like a name is the following. Barbeau translated it as "his loins (are) stuck up", "his loins (shirt) is up" and "his loins rest on (has no lower extremities)" (Barbeau 1960:199 #46, 204 #1, and 210 #29 respectively). I have translated and analysed it as follows:

Huʔtušruraʔ[1]	His chest is affixed.
hu-	masculine singular patient – he
-ʔtušr-	noun root – chest
-ura	verb root – affix
-ʔ	stative aspect

1. Barbeau 1960:199 #46, 204 #1, and 210 #29.

Three Helpful Uncles

While the nephew is not named, three uncles are. They are spirits as well as being uncles.

He Has Fringes alongside his Leggings

Tehunyęʔnhažuʔkyeʔ	He has fringes alongside his leggings
te-	dualic
-hu-	masculine singular patient – he
-nyęʔnhaž-	noun root – fringe, fringes on leggings
-uʔkye-	verb root – be alongside, continue
-ʔ	stative aspect

In an English version of the story, with the original translation "revised with Allen Johnson" (Barbeau 1915:210 fn 4), the translation for this name is explained in the following way: " 'his-double-fringes-in-the-water-float', a manitou[2] [spirit, uki in Wyandot], apparently a monster living in the water, and with long hair along his legs" (Barbeau 1915:215, fn 4).

He Sleeps Often

HutaʔwiʔaH	He sleeps frequently, often.
hu-	masculine singular patient – he
-taʔ-	verb root – sleep
-wi-	transitional root suffix
-ʔah	habitual aspect

Barbeau translates it as "he is sleepy ever" (Barbeau 1960:207 #52). In the 1915 English version with revisions by Allen Johnson the name is translated as "Sleepy Head" (1915:214), and, in footnote 2 Barbeau states that the translation is *"he sleeps habitually.* This was an uki [spirit]. Allen Johnson thought that this might refer to the groundhog[3]" (Barbeau 1915:214 fn 2).

He Often Penetrates Flowers

Hutsiʔtsuʔyaʔtaʔ	He often penetrates flowers.
hu-	masculine singular patient – he
-tsiʔts-	noun root – flower
-uʔya-	verb root – penetrate
-ʔt-	causative root suffix
-aʔ	habitual aspect

I have added the pronominal prefix hu- to what Barbeau recorded. Dropping the

---

2. This is the main word used for 'spirit' in the Anishinaabe language, a member of the Algonquian language family.

3. The usual Wyandot name for groundhog or woodchuck is ǫndaʔyęhk, but this does not mean that Allen Johnson was wrong.

pronominal prefix sometimes happens in the writing of names with a -tsi- after that prefix. There is no translation in the Narratives, just "Ts. n[ame]" (Barbeau 1960:208 #25, 31, and 59). In English texts in Barbeau 1960:35 and 1915:214 it is translated as "He-who-sucks-the-flowers," "probably the wasp or the bee according to Allen Johnson"[4] (Barbeau 1960:214 fn 3).[5]

Yuhšaharęht

Yuhšaharęht[6] is the young male hero giant of "The Two Giant Cousins and the Old Witch" (Barbeau 1915:65–72 and 1960:77–91)). The 'old witch' is Yaaʔtayęhtsih. The name is mistranslated, as was He Whose Chest is Affixed, with the noun root for 'loin.' Barbeau wrote that the word was "a proper name, probably meaning 'it-loin-is hollow'" (Barbeau 1915:66 fn 1).

Yuhšaharęht	One has a hole in its mouth
y-	partitive – such
-u-	feminine-zoic singular patient – she, it, one
-hš-	noun root – mouth
-a-	joiner vowel
-haręht	verb root – have a hole + stative aspect

This is an appropriate name, as he was a cannibal (Barbeau 1915:65).

Tawidiʔa

There are two stories in the Narratives in which the main character is Tawidiʔa, a short form for Tunyʔętawindiʔah: "Tawidiʔa and His Uncle" (Barbeau_1915:224–33, 1960:40–4, 235–55) and "The Land of Bliss" (Barbeau 1915:233–9; 1960:44–7, 255–72). In the first one he makes foolish misinterpretations of his uncle's instructions, in the latter he fools Kurahkuwah. My interpretation of the name is as follows:

Thunyętawindiʔa	His little shins are rotting or girded.
t-	dualic
-hu-	masculine singular patient – he, his
-nyęt-	noun root – front of the leg, shins
-a-	joiner vowel
-awi-	verb root – rot or gird (two different possible verb roots)
-nd-	dative root suffix
-iʔ-	stative aspect
-a	diminutive aspect suffix

4. When the 'bad uncle' arrives in this uncle's house he was "badly stung" (Barbeau 1915:215).

5. The usual name for bee or wasp is ǫndahkǫt, which I have tentatively translated as 'it stings'.

6. Barbeau 1960:78 #20, 79 #4 and 14, 80 #1, 30 and 39, 81 #32, 82 #20, 84 #10, 33 and 49, 85 #24, 31 and 39, and 86 #20 and 45).

I am not sure which of the two potential verb roots 'rot' or 'gird' is the better one. Both fit equally well in the morphology or structure of the name.

Tatęri²a

In "Tatęri²a" (Barbeau 1960:169–83) or "The Two Wizards and the Witch" (Barbeau 1915:175–80) there are two brothers. The older one is unnamed, the younger one is called Tatęri²a. The older brother goes out hunting, while the younger one stays at home. On the English side of the text are the translations: "the one left at home" (Barbeau 1960:169 #15, 170 #44, 172 #8, 173 #12), "the one left" (Barbeau 1960:174 #2, 175 #42, 177 #4, 179 #12, 180 #7, 34, 181 #35, 182 #3 and 183 #3 and 10) or "one left" (Barbeau 1960:177 #47). I translate it as:

T[h]atęri²a	He is (the little/younger one) left behind.
t-	dualic
-h-	masculine singular agent – he
-at-	semi-reflexive voice
-ęri-	verb root – omit or leave behind
-²-	stative aspect
-a	diminutive aspect suffix

Two Joking Names

In a very short story, "Bear and the Rabbit," told in English by Mary Kelley, there are two names presented in jest by the two cousins. Bear says that his name is ya'ta˘ma''ka'' (Barbeau 1915:209 fn 2), the translation of which is given as "Thin-hide." It can be analysed as:

Yaa²tamahkah	It has a small body.
ya-	feminine-zoic singular agent – it
-a²t-	noun root – body
-mahka-	verb root – be small
-h	stative aspect

The rabbit, when asked for his name, gives it as "ya²di˘hatę''tsi'',"[7] translated as "Thick-hide":

Yandihatętsih[8]	It has a thick hide.
ya-	feminine-zoic singular agent – it
-ndih-	noun root – hide
-a-	joiner vowel
-tętsi-	verb root – be thick
-h	stative aspect

---

7. Barbeau 1915:209 fn 3. Barbeau wrote a superscript -n- before the -t-.

8. Barbeau 1915:209 fn 4.

Tsižutǫʔ: The Sun Shower

In "Origin of the Sun Shower" (Barbeau 1960:63–74), the son of a Wyandot woman and a Thunderer becomes the sun shower. His name is tsĩjˀútǫʔǫ (Barbeau 1960:74). Unfortunately, Barbeau puts on the English side just "Ts. (n.)" with no translation. The same is true in the English version of the story (Barbeau 1915:56). The initial -tsi- can be the repetitive prefix meaning 'very, again' or it could be part of a noun or verb root that follows a pronominal prefix that has been dropped. I cannot come up with a translation of the rest of the word that makes sense. Perhaps Barbeau's informants found themselves in a similar situation.

Skandawati

In the story known as "Skadawati and the Giant" (Barbeau 1915:60–2), provided to him in Wyandot by his main storyteller Catherine Johnson, but published only in English, there is a man called Skandawati, whose name can be translated and analysed as follows:

Skandawati[10]   It is on the other side of the river.
[skan-dah-wah-tee]
    s-   repetitive – other
    -ka-   feminine-zoic singular agent – it
    -ndaw-   noun root – river
    -a-   joiner vowel
    -ti   verb root – be on a side + stative aspect

He was called this, as, when a female Strędu?[11], or flinty cannibal giant, was chasing after him, three times he waded across a river, escaping to the other side. We have seen in an earlier chapter that Skandawati is cognate with the Onondaga sachem name Sganawadih.

Hąndaʔwaʔ – He (is) Soft

It was earlier mentioned that there is the humorous story "The Deer and the Owl," in which both the owl and the deer have the same name and are competing for the daughters of Yaaʔtayęhtsih. It is given as the noun hąndaʔwaʔ. The noun root refers to soft objects such as cotton, down, feathers, wool, and the coat of a fawn (see Steckley 2007a:140). Barbeau translated it as "he is cotton-like" (1960:187 #59, 188 #8, 32, 189 #16, 32, 190 #21, 34, 45, 191 #34, 192 #46. 193 #22, 37 and194 #9) "he is soft (cotton-like)" (183:3), "cotton-like" (184 #20, 36 and 64). In the solely English telling of the story, the name was given as "the Woolly-one" (Barbeau 1915:203–7). There is always the definite article, either as "ne" or "de" coming before this word, adding the meaning of "the" or "who."

9. The -j- here represents the same sound as -ž-.

10. Barbeau 1915:61. He presents the translation as "always on the other side of the river."

11. I have no translation for this word. With the reference to its being 'flinty', it could include the noun root -ręnd- 'rock or stone.'

Qtarayęrat – It is a White Lake

While this name isn't in the Narratives, it does represent a sharing a of Wyandot names with mythology, so it is included in this chapter. In 1735, Mathias Ontara,onra was baptized as an adult (Toupin 1996:839). This may be the same man whose name is given as "tara,onra" the father of a baptized eight year old girl in 1731 (Toupin 1996:829). Names identical to this representation of a Wyandot name were recorded for two boys named Jacques (Toupin 1996:196, 224, baptized as newborns in 1741, 849) and Herman or Armand (Toupin 1996:205, baptized as a newborn in 1743, 851). Their names deceptively appear to take the noun root -tar- 'clay, mud'.

Mathias' name matches a Wendat mythic character discussed by Father Jean de Brébeuf in 1636, when he was talking about healing taking place at feasts or ceremonies.

> They ascribe their origin to a certain meeting of Wolves and of the Owl, in which that nocturnal creature predicted for them the coming of *Ontarraoura*, a beast allied to the Lion, by its tail. This *Ontarraoura*, resuscitated, they say, I know what good Hunter, a firm friend of the Wolves, in the midst of a great feast. From this they conclude that feasts must be capable of healing the sick, since they even restore life to the dead. (JR10:177)

No verb takes the form -yǫra-. I write and analyse the name as follows:

Qtarayęrat	It is a white lake.
qtar-	feminine-zoic singular agent – it + noun root - lake
-a-	joiner vowel
-yęrat	verb root – be white + stative aspect

CHAPTER NINE
Wyandot Names in the 19th Century

Introduction

In the 18th century, when Potier wrote down two names for an individual, the first was the Christian name, the second the person's current Wyandot clan-derived name. The latter was not a surname or family name. In the 19th century that changed. Most of the Wyandot acquired surnames as they came into closer contact with and experienced greater influence by mainstream North American society. For some, that was a male clan-derived name, for more it was a translation of such a name. For others, a name was created or borrowed in English.

Of course, this kind of forced name changing was not unique to the Wyandot. It was part of a colonial project run by federal governments to bully Indigenous cultures into conforming with the patriarchal family pattern followed by mainstream American and Canadian society (see Scott, Tehranian and Mathias 2002 and 2004). The following passage from an essay written in 1897 by Frank Terry, the superintendent of the U.S. Boarding School for Crow Indians in Montana, illustrates the uncompromising prejudicial attitude towards Native American naming and their cultures generally:

> The Indian Department has continually urged this matter upon its agents, superintendents, and other workers "in the field." The command to give names to the Indians and to establish the same as far as possible by continuous use has been a part of the "Rules and Regulations" for years past.... In this thing, as in nearly all others, the Indians do not know what is best for them. They can't see that our system has an advantages over their own, and they have fought stubbornly against the innovation (Terry 1897).

In keeping with the patrilineal nature of mainstream North American society, it appears that every surname based on a Wyandot word comes from a male name.

There are many repeated references in this chapter to sources that are found on the Wyandotte Nation of Oklahoma website. So, to simplify references written in the text, please see that website's section of the References Cited that follow chapter 10. And for the Missionary Society of Upper Sandusky in 1828 and 1832, see the Wyandot of Kansas website references.

The Big Names

The verb root -(y)(u)wane- 'be large, big, great', appears in 24 Wyandot names, the greatest number of any verb root. Eight are recorded in the 19th century, and six became surnames.[1]

---

1. In the land grant section of the Treaty of 1817, there is a reference to "Toworordu or Big Ears." The only aspect of this word that fits with the English translation is the dualic t- at the beginning. The Wyandot word for 'he has two big ears' would be Tehahǫtawanę?s, with -hǫt- meaning 'ear'.

BIGARMS

In 1770 a man with the Wyandot name of te[2] haïachi8annen and his wife had their two-year-old daughter baptized (Toupin 1996:894). In 1772, the name now written with the addition of the plural aspect suffix -s, the baptism of their son was recorded (Toupin 1996:896). The name is structured and analyzed as follows:

Tehažahšuwanę's	He has two large arms.
te-	dualic – two
-ha-	masculine singular agent – he
-žahš-	noun root – arm
-uwanę-	verb root – be large
-'-	stative aspect
-s	plural aspect suffix

In the Treaty of 1814, the name of one of the signatories was presented as "Zashuona – Big Arm". This is just a bad representation of the name. In the land division that was part of the Treaty of 1817, the name Bigarms is first mentioned.

During the 19th century that surname was often recorded, frequently with the first name "John." In 1848, one signed a Wyandot letter to Congress (Divine 2019:244). John Bigarms was listed in the 1857 payments[3] and the 1870 Muster Roll. In the second source there was a reference to a Martin Bigarms. In 1888 a John Bigarms was the landholder of two plots of land in Oklahoma (Divine 2019:292–3). In the Huron Cemetery in Kansas there is an Ethan Bigarms. Barbeau recorded Tähäjyăcúwanę'ęs as the Wyandot name for John Bigarms (Barbeau 1911:46).

BIG FOOT

In 1782, a large Wyandot man known as Big Foot was murdered by two "Indian fighter" brothers (Finley 1840:254-5 and Divine 2019:141–4). He was a brother to "Scotosh' (i.e., Haskutaše) so he was Porcupine clan. Unfortunately, his name does not appear in any other source I have consulted. I have translated the name into Wyandot as follows, using the dualic and the plural aspect suffix as that is more likely than the singular recorded in English:

Tehašitawanęs	He has two big feet.
te-	dualic
-h-	masculine singular agent – he
-ašit-	noun root – foot
-a-	joiner vowel
-wanę-	verb root – be large + stative aspect
-s	plural aspect suffix

As I have found no one before or after who had this name, and as he was a big man,

2. Potier regularly separated the -te- of the dualic and the negative from the word it was part of.

3. https://sites.rootsweb.com/~kswyanhp/history/1857aprwyantribeincompetents.html

I believe that this was a nickname based on his size, not a surname or a clan name.

Big Neck

While, as we have seen, the Rev. James B. Finley (1781–1856) had a much respected Bear clan name, he also had a nickname that Connelley recorded as "Hah-gyĕhh'-rĕh-wah'-nĕh. Means, Big Neck, because the Wyandots say, he had the neck of a bull" (Connelley 1900:111). I present it as follows:

Hangyaruwanęh	He has a large neck.
ha-	masculine singular agent – he
-ngyar-	noun root – neck
-uwanę-	verb root – be large
-h	stative aspect

Big River

The Wyandot name meaning 'Big River' first appeared in 1755 as handa8io[4] 'he is a large or big river' (Toupin 1996:869) and yanda8io 'it is a large river' (Toupin 1996:871). The man, who had the letters "fr." before his name, possibly François, died in 1759 (Toupin 1996:929).

Handawižuʔ	He is a large river.
ha-	masculine singular agent – he
-ndaw-	noun root – river
-ižu-	verb root – be large, great
-ʔ	stative aspect

The first recordings of the name as an English surname were as Big River, Mrs. Big Rivers, and Wm. Big River, in the membership of the Missionary Society in Upper Sandusky, Ohio in 1828 for the first two and 1832 for the last. Then William Big River was a landholder in the Grand Reserve in Ohio (Divine 2019:210). Finley recorded the name as "An-da-wiz-u" (Finley 1840:427). William Big River is buried in the Huron Cemetery in Kansas.

Big Sinew

The surname Big Sinew is listed without a first name in the map of the Grand Reserve in Ohio (Divine 2019:210). It is found as Samuel Bigsinew in the 1855 Kansas Allotments (Divine 2019:265). A John Bigsinew is in the Huron Cemetery in Kansas. As I have seen no Wyandot language version, I have created the following likely word:

Hatsiʔnǫnyąhtawanęh	He has a big sinew.
ha-	masculine singular agent – he

---

4. Two later references had the spelling handa8ïo (Toupin 1996:878 and 974), and one in 1759 had honda8io (Toupin 1996:944). As elsewhere, the -8- represents a -w- before a vowel.

-tsi'nǫnyaht-	noun root – sinew[5]
-a-	joiner vowel
-wanę-	verb root – be large
-h	stative aspect

BIG TOWN

The surname 'Big Town' first appears as a signatory on a letter sent to Congress in 1848 (Divine 2019:244). The name can be written as.

Yandatawanęh	It is a large camp, village, town.
ya-	feminine-zoic singular agent – it
-ndat-	noun root – camp, village, town
-a-	joiner vowel
-wanę-	verb root – be large
-h	stative aspect

In the Kansas Allotments of 1855 we have Baptiste, Sallie, and William B. Bigtown (Divine 2019:265). In the payments of 1857, the two men are mentioned. All three names appear in the Huron Cemetery in Kansas. The last appearance of the Wyandot name is in Barbeau's pronominal prefix divested "Dătawānĕ'" = 'a big camp' (Barbeau 1911:24).

BIG TREE

The first occurrence of this name I have found is of the father of a two-year-old child baptized in 1767. The name was given as "haront8annen" (Toupin 1996:889). I write it as:

Harǫtwanęh	He is a large tree.
ha-	masculine singular agent – he
-rǫt-	noun root – tree, pole, log
-wanę-	verb root – be large
-h	stative aspect

Big Tree or Bigtree was commonly found as a surname in the 19th century, with James Bigtree being prominently featured. He was recorded as being a member of the Missionary Society in 1828 and 1832. In the Grand Reserve in Ohio, we find it simply presented as "Bigtree" with no first names (Divine 2019:210). In the Ohio Muster Roll we again have James Big Tree. He signed the treaty of 1843.

His name also appears as a signatory in the letter sent in 1848 to Congress (Divine 2019:244). There are six people with the surname Bigtree as landholders in the Kansas Allotments of 1855: four women—Catherine, Eliza, Mary, and Sarah—and two men, James, and John (Divine 2019: 264-5.

---

5. This noun root can also be used to refer to arteries, veins, and nerves: "otsinnonhiacta... veine...artere...nerf" (Potier 1920:454)

In the Muster Roll of 1870, we have both Sarah and Eliza. In the Huron Cemetery, we have James (1796–1856), John (1827–1857) and Mary (1830–1860).

In his 1911 collection of names, Barbeau makes reference to Sara L. Big Tree. He presents her surname in Wyandot as yarŏntŭwaṇĕ' (Barbeau 1911:17), using the feminine-zoic singular agent instead of the masculine. I do not believe it reflects that a woman had the name.

Big Voice

One of the great names of the Striped Turtle clan and of the Wyandot generally is Shumęduwat. In keeping with the rest of the names on the list of Big Names, I have called it 'Big Voice'. No translation is available in the literature. Here is how I have interpreted it.

Shumęduwat	He is very large, great in word, voice, authority.
s-	repetitive – very
-hu-	masculine singular patient – he
-męd-	noun root – word, voice
-uwat	verb root – be large + stative aspect

During the 18th and 19th centuries the name was spelled in many ways. For the father of a newly-baptized child in 1731, it was Tso8end8ann (Toupin 1996:828). In the census of 1747, it was spelled Sa8oind8aʽt (244) Sa8oind8at (945), and Sa8end8at (209 and 229). Two men were recorded as having the name, the first, Martin, a Striped Turtle member of the elders council in 1747. When he changed his name (209), a man named Nicholas took it up (945).

The 19th-century pronunciation and spelling of his name was different. The first -w- (represented by an -8- in the names presented above) changed to an -m- because of the following nasal vowel. Summunduwat[6] (1799-1840) was elected as the Principal Chief of the Wyandot of Upper Sandusky in 1835 (Buser 1989). I have seen no reference to a first name. In the map of the Grand Reserve in Ohio, his name is listed as Summendewat (Divine 2019:210). He and his wife were murdered in 1840 (Andrews), the settler culprits were caught, later to escape.

The name carried on as a surname. In the Kansas Allotments of 1855, there is a landholder named Mary Summonduwat (Divine 2019:264). In Kansas City, Kansas, there is a Summunduwat Lodge of the Order of Odd Fellows.

Lineages

There appear to be three male-based names involving the verb root -yękyu- 'be a lineage', which, with the instrumental nominalizer becomes the noun stem -yękyukw-. In other Iroquoian languages this noun stem is presented as just a simple noun root,

---

6. Written as Summundowot and Summendowot in the Missionary Society lists of 1828 and 1832.

without reference to a verb root (for Mohawk, Michelson 1973:64 -ityohkw-), and it is used to mean 'group'.

HIS LINEAGE, GROUP

In his unpublished work of 1911, Barbeau records a male Deer clan name as "húkyuʼkwaʼ = a crowd" (Barbeau 1911:12). That can be analyzed as follows:

Hukyuhkwaʼ	His group, his crowd, his lineage.
hu-	masculine singular patient – his
-kyu-	verb root – be a matrilineage, clan
-kw-	instrumental nominalizer
-aʼ	noun suffix

There are names found in the early part of the 19th century that appear to be the same name (see next section). However, these are more likely shortened versions of the longer name presented next. It is rare for a noun by itself to be a name.

HIS VERY LONG LINEAGE

The written record of this name begins with Ignatius Sentiok8es, a godfather in a 1729 baptism (Toupin 1996:826). A land grant receiver named Cuqua with the 1817 Treaty, and Quouqua who signed the September 17, 1818 Treaty were the father and grandfather of the next two people who bore the name.[7] In the Ohio Muster Roll of 1843 we see a Caty Cuqueh (1806-1876 (the two names written in other sources as Catherine or Katie Quo Qua or Quoqua (Steckley 1999:199). In 1911, Barbeau wrote the name "Kitty Sekyúʻkweš" and Sekyuʼkwis.(Barbeau 1911:17 and 45). She married Thomas McKee and was the mother of Mary McKee. In 1915, Barbeau wrote down a shortened version of the name, as Kyuʼʼkwe (Barbeau 1915:xi). I analyze the long version of the name as follows:

Shękyukwes	He has a very long lineage.
s-	repetitive – very
-h-	masculine singular agent – he
-ękyu-	verb root – be a lineage
-kw-	instrumental nominalizer
-es	verb root – be long + habitual aspect[8]

HIS VALUABLE LINEAGE

Hukyukwanduroʼ	He is of a valuable lineage, his valuable group.
hu-	masculine singular patient – he
-kyu-	verb root – be a lineage, clan

7. See Andrews, "Catherine Quoqua McKee Clark, www.wyandotte-nation.org/culture/history/biographies/catherine-quoqua-mckee-clark/.

8. This is another case, like those in earlier chapters, of what appears to be a habitual form of the verb root -es- 'be long, tall' having a stative meaning.

-kw-	instrumental nominalizer
-a-	joiner vowel
-nduro̧-	verb root – be valuable, difficult
-ʔ	stative aspect

This Striped Turtle name was well represented in the 18th century in a variety of spellings (see Translations), ending with the aged eulogizer of Father Pierre Potier in 1781, his name written as Tiockouanohon and Tiokouoanhoron. (Lajeunesse 1960:124 and 126).[9]

The name persisted into the 19th century with a recipient of a land grant through the Treaty of 1817, spelled as -cuquawdorow, and in the Missionary Society in Upper Sandusky Ohio in 1828 and 1832 as Hoocuhquondooroo, and does not seem to appear after that.

Log Names

There are three names of the 19th century that include 'logs' in their translation and can be easily confused. I am presenting them together so that the differences can be seen, especially with the slight difference between the verb roots used for Between-the-Logs and Splitlog.

BETWEEN-THE-LOGS

The first Between-the-Logs recorded in writing was a Wyandot leader who lived between 1780 and 1827 and had a Seneca father and a Wyandot Bear clan mother. He signed treaties representing the Wyandot of Upper Sandusky. His name in Wyandot can be presented as:

Teyaro̧tuyȩh	It is between two logs, Between the Logs.
te-	dualic – two
ya-	feminine-zoic singular agent – it
-ro̧t-	noun root – tree, log, pole
-uyȩ-	verb root – be at the meeting, merging point, the divide
-h	stative aspect

In the treaties, the writing of his name varied:

Tearroneauou	1814
T. Aruntue	1817
Tauyaurontoyou,	1817 (in the land division list)
Tuayaraurontoyou	1818 (September 17)
Taruntne	1818 (September 20)
Tayarrontoyea,	1836 (land division)

Both flawed and comical is the mistake made in the spelling/interpretation of the name

---

9. www.wyandot.org/1828us.htm.

in English in the first two treaties: Between the Legs. The noun root for 'leg' is -'nǫht-. I imagine that some Wyandot in the know had a good laugh when they read the treaty.

Useful information about the name came in 1840 when James B. Finley reported what he was told that the name was Bear clan, and that it was "denoting the manner in which the bear crouches, or sleeps" (Finley 1840:31). Connelley wrote the name as Tēh'-äh-rōhn'-tōōh'-yĕh,. (Connelley 1900:113). Barbeau wrote the name both in Wyandot "Teyarõntuyę'" and in English "between the logs" and identified the name with Irwin Long (Barbeau 1911:16, 46 and 48). Both writers agreed with the Bear clan identification. Between-the-Logs did not become a surname, possibly because it was too long.

Chop-the-Log

The Wyandot word for Chop-the-Log (also Choplog and Chop the Logs) does not appear in the records. I believe that the word would be something like this:

Harǫtaru'	He is chopping down a tree, log.
ha-	masculine singular agent – he
-rǫt-	noun root – tree, log
-a-	joiner vowel
-ru-	verb root – chop (down)
-'	stative aspect

The earliest references I have found are in the Grand Reserve with "Tall Solomon or Chop-the-Log" (Divine 2019:210), and the Ohio Muster Roll with a simple Chop-the-Log. Then there is the Wyandot letter to Congress in 1848, upon which John Chop the Logs signed his name (Divine 2019:244). Later references are to Russia Chop the Log (1870), who, according to the 1874 Voters List, belonged to the Striped Turtle clan.[10] In a report of Wyandot men who fought in the Civil War, Rusha Chaploy was mentioned.[11]

Splitlog

The earliest recording of a man bearing this name occurs in a baptism in 1737, in which a Joseph named Teotrontoren was recorded as being the godfather of a newborn boy baptized as Joseph (Toupin 1996:842). Two years later a Pierre with the name written Taotonoren was a godfather of a boy baptised as Pierre (Toupin 1996:846). A baptism of July 21, 1743 was of a daughter to a T'aotrontoren (Toupin 1996:851). In 1777 the baptism of a boy named Mathias, involved a Te otrontoren as godfather, probably named Mathias himself (Toupin 1996:902).

Here is the name and analysis of component parts of the name Splitlog.

---

10. www.wyandotte-nation.org/culture/history/historic-rolls/wyandot-voter-list-by-clan/.

11. www.wyandot.org/civilwar.htm.

Tehutrǫturęh	He splits the log in two.
te-	dualic
-hu-	masculine singular patient – he
-ront-	noun root – log, tree
-uren	verb root – split in two
-h	stative aspect

The name stayed among the Detroit-area Wyandot, where there was a Splitlog as leader, the brother of Bark-Carrier, therefore Porcupine clan. He was a leading figure there until 1835 (Buser 1989). The surname Splitlog continues today in the Anderdon community.

A later Splitlog, named Mathias (1812-1897), was born to French and Cayuga parents, but he was sent to live with the Wyandot of Ohio. He was successful as a "mechanical genius."[12] In the 1870 Muster Roll, with the surname of Splitthelogs, he was listed along with his wife and seven children. He was listed as Snake clan in the 1874 Voters by Clan, as was a James Splitlog, but that would not necessarily apply to most other Splitlogs at the time.

Charles Split-the-Log was at the Ohio Grand Reserve (Divine 2019:210), and in the Ohio Muster Roll. His name was registered as Charles Splitlog, a landholder in the Detroit River community in 1836. He was buried in the Huron Cemetery in Kansas.

Lucinda Splitlog was a landholder in the 1855 Kansas Allotments (Divine 2019: 265), and with her six children was recorded in the Muster Roll of 1870.

Standing Names

As noted in an earlier chapter, there are 12 names that involve the verb root -ut- and six -t-, both meaning 'to stand'. The former incorporates noun roots, the latter does not. At least three, maybe four of the 19th-century names use a verb root meaning to stand.

STANDING IN WATER

The earliest reference to this name that I have seen is Mayeatohot in the Treaty of 1817. Later we get English translations with Standing-in-the-Water in 1828 and William Standing Water in 1832 as members of the Missionary Society in Upper Sandusky. Stand-in-the-Water appears as a landholder's name in the Grand Reserve in Ohio (Divine 2019:210), as it does in the Ohio Muster Roll. Finley in 1840 records it as May-yat-ta-hat (Finley 1840:429). In 1900, Connelley explains the name's Deer clan connotations: "Mah'-yĕh-tĕh'-hah't 'Stand in the water.' Refers to the habit of the deer, which stands in summer to get rid of the annoyance of flies" (Connelley 1900:113).

---

12. http://grandlakenewsonline.com/matthias-splitlog-the-indian-millionaire-p336-126.htm. *History of Wyandotte Country Kansas and its People*, 1911, edited and compiled by Perl W. Morgan, Chicago: The Lewis Publishing Company, chapter VII, "Come to their Promised Land." http://genealogytrails.com/kan/wyandotte/history7.html#:~:text=Splitlog%20was%20a%20mechanical%20genius,he%20was%20his%20own%20engineer.

Ameye[13] Tehat		He is standing in the water.
Ameye		In the water.
	am-	feminine-zoic singular patient – it
	-e-	noun root – water
	=yeh	external locative clitic
Tehat		He is standing.
	te-	dualic
	-ha-	masculine singular agent – he
	-t	verb root – stand + stative aspect

STANDINGSTONE

The earliest recorded person with the Wyandot name for Standingstone, horend8t, was a Mathias, who was baptized as an adult in 1737 (Toupin 1995:843) and was in the census of 1747 (Toupin 1996:223 as oreend8t). This name can be represented as:

Hurendut		He is a standing stone.
	hu-	masculine singular patient – he
	-rend-	noun root – rock, stone
	-ut	verb root – stand + stative aspect

In the Grand Reserve of Ohio, the name was recorded for John P., John H., and T. Standingstone (Divine 2019:211) in the Ohio Muster Roll for John, J.P., and Thomas. In the 1857 payments list there is John H. Standingstone. In the Huron Cemetery there are John H., John Peter, his wife, just plain Standingstone and the anything-but-plain One-Hundred-Snakes Standingstone (see discussion that follows).

STANDING TREETOPS

In the Missionary Society of Upper Sandusky there were two members who had a surname amusingly written as Harryhoot, James and William (1828 and 1832). The name appears again in Barbeau's writing as noted Oklahoma storyteller Ha`rehut (Barbeau 1915:4). In an article about Smith Nichols, Jeremy Turner gives the name of Nichols' maternal grandfather as "HarEhu`t (There He Stops Up a Hole)"[14]. That is not a literal translation. Maybe there were such connotations in a now-forgotten and never-recorded story that involved a standing treetop blocking a hole. A literal translation of the name is as follows:

Harenhut		He is or has a standing treetop or branch.
	ha-	masculine singular agent – he
	-renh-	noun root – treetops, branch
	-ut	verb root – stand + stative aspect

13. The first word, Ameye 'in or on the water', also in Walk in the Water, is found in another name, as the first word in the name for John Barret in 1837: Myme Hamkee (Buser). I haven't yet been able to translate the second word.

14. https://www.wyandotte-nation.org/traditions/biographical-panels/smith-nichols/.

Stand

In addition to the surnames that include the English translation "Standing," there is the name Henry Stand, found in the 1888 Oklahoma Allotments (Divine 2019:292), and discussed by Barbeau as one of his informants (Barbeau 1915:xi). This name may be linked to that of a nine year old boy, Baptiste, referred to in the 1747 census as "te hatat" (Toupin 1996:208). I have this name as:

Tehaaʔtat	He stands, his body is standing.
te-	dualic
-ha-	masculine singular agent – he
-aʔt-	noun root – body
-a-	joiner vowel
-t	verb root – stand + stative aspect

Walk-in-the-Water

The spelling of his name in Wyandot is widely varied. In the treaties he signed representing the Wyandot of the Detroit River area, we have Awmeyeeray (1795), Miere (1805, 1807, and 1808) and Myecrah (1815). As he signed at least once with the drawing of a turtle, he must have belonged to a Turtle clan (Large Turtle, Striped Turtle or, less likely, Prairie Turtle). P.D. Clarke gives the name as "Walk-in-water (whose name in Wyandot was Mey-re-ra)" (Clarke 1870:102). My representation of the name is of two words, not one:

Amęnye ire	On water he walks.
amęn-	feminine-zoic singular patient – it + verb root – be water + stative aspect
=ye	external locative clitic
i-	partitive
-r-	masculine singular agent – he
-e	verb root – come, go, walk + stative aspect

Wyandot leader Walk-in-the-Water (c.1748–1817) was a contemporary of Tarhe (1742–1816). There is a story that Tarhe had a daughter named Myeerah, with the same translation into English, who married Isaac Zane, who had been adopted by Tarhe.[15] This is unlikely for three reasons. For one, that would mean that two people had the same Wyandot name at the same time. Secondly, that would have males and females with the same name, which is rare. Thirdly, the name is male, as indicated by the -r- in the second word.

Zane Grey (1872–1939), the popular writer of adventure novels, was a descendent of the Zanes. His first novel was *Betty Zane* (1903), a fictionalized account of the life of Isaac Zane's sister. He named a daughter Betty Zane. I suspect that the female Myeerah as Walk-in-the-Water story may have come from him.

15. http://www.myeerah.com/story.htm.

Remaining Names that Became Surnames
ARMS

There are several people who have the English surname of Arms. There was John Arms, who was on the Ohio Muster Roll, and was one of the men who signed the letter to Congress in 1848, and who died in 1856 (HC). In addition, there was his wife, and an Eliza or Elizabeth, and a Schofield, her son (OMR). It is difficult to know what the name would be in Wyandot. Was it an offshoot of Big Arms? If it is a separate name, and means 'He has two arms,' it might look something like this, but I cannot be sure:

Tehažahšęh	He has two arms.
te-	dualic
-ha-	masculine singular agent – he
-žahš-	noun root – arm
-ę-	verb root – have
-h	stative aspect

BEARSKIN

The name Bearskin is best known to Wyandot today for Chief Leaford Bearskin (1921–2012), a decorated war veteran who was a long-standing chief (1983–2011). I have seen no source in which the noun 'bearskin' is presented in Wyandot as a name. There is one, however, that includes the noun stem (like a noun root but with a verb root plus a nominalizer) for bearskin: -nyǫnyęt-. This noun stem is presented twice in Potier's written work in the name Pierre annionentase (Toupin 1996:190 and 196) of the Bear clan in 1747, which I present as:

Anyǫnyętase	It is new bearskin. (male)
a-	feminine-zoic singular agent – it
-nyǫnyę-	verb root – be a bear
-t-	nominalizer
-ase	verb root – be new + stative aspect

Bearskin itself would be:

Anyǫnyęta'	Bearskin
-a-	feminine-zoic singular agent – it
-nyǫnyę-	verb root – be a bear
-t-	nominalizer
-a'	noun suffix

Is New Bearskin a different name, or one that got shortened into 'Bearskin'? I'm not sure. I am also not clear whether there should be a -y- at the beginning of this word, as it belongs to the consonant conjugation, or whether it was dropped as eventually happened in the name for 'bear' itself - anyǫnyę.

Burning

The name otsitsate,en appears in the baptismal record for 1732 as a godfather for a baptized boy named 'Joseph', so he was probably a Joseph too (Toupin 1996:832). I have analyzed it as:

Utsistateyęh	It is a burning fire.
u-	feminine-zoic singular patient – it
-tsist-	noun root – fire
-atey-	verb root – burn
-ęh	stative aspect

Although several names use the verb root -atey- 'to burn', this name makes the most sense to me as one that connects with the surname 'Burning' in the 19th century as the others involve burning something (e.g., scalp or tongue). In the 1870 Muster Roll, there is an Amelia Burning and her husband Nicholas Burning. Amelia Burning appears in the Oklahoma Allotments of 1888 (Divine 2019:292–3) as the landholder for three plots of land.

Corn

In the Kansas Allotments of 1855, there is a Francis Corn (Divine 2019:265), the only time I have encountered 'corn' as a surname. As stated earlier, there are 10 names that contain the noun root -nęh- 'corn', eight of them male. No one of them seems most likely to be the name from which this name would be formed.

Cornstalk

From 1757 to 1767 (Toupin 1996:874, 883, 887 and 889), Potier recorded in several ways a male name that I represent as:

Kyuherasa	It is where there are small stalks of corn.
-ky-	cislocative – where
-u-	feminine-zoic singular patient – it
-her-	noun root – cornstalk
-a-	verb root – be a size + stative aspect
-s-	plural aspect suffix
-a	diminutive aspect suffix

Barbeau wrote the name as Ižuhera'sah which would mean 'small stalks of corn' (Barbeau 1911:14 and 33). I believe this could be the same name, and the one represented in the Wyandot surname Cornstalk. In the Kansas Allotments of 1855, we have a James P. Cornstalk (Divine 2019:265), and in the Huron Cemetery there are buried a John B. and a Sarah Cornstalk.

Fighter

During the period 1747 to 1775 (Toupin 1996:223, 256, 873, 900, 928 and 962) there were two individuals who had the male name I am representing as:

Shutrižuskǫ^ʔ	He very frequently fights, kills.
s-	repetitive – very
-hu-	masculine singular patient – he
-t-	semi-reflexive voice
-rižu-	verb root – fight, kill
-skǫ-	frequentative root suffix
-ʔ	stative aspect

In the land division of the Treaty of 1817, a Sootreeshuskoh was mentioned. This Wyandot name seems to fit well with the 19th-century surname Fighter, which is found with Tall Fighter in the Grand Reserve in Ohio (Divine 2019:210), Tall Fighter and Harriet Fighter in the Ohio Muster Roll, and Hannah Fighter in the Kansas Allotments of 1855 (Divine 2019:264).

Frost

In the 1730s a man's name appeared in the baptismal record as Franciscus Ochienraen, a father of a child baptized in 1731 (Toupin 1996:828). The second time we have the same spelling of his name for his own baptism in 1736 (Toupin 1996:840). Later that year he appears again as a godfather, with his name written as the male-gendered Hochienraen (Toupin 1996:841). The name can be analysed as follows:

Hušęrąę	He has frost lying on the ground.
hu-	masculine singular patient – he
-šęr-	noun root – frost
-a-	joiner vowel
-ę	verb root – lie + stative aspect

This is the only Wyandot name I have found with the noun root for 'frost' in it. In the 19th century there is a Sally Frost in the Missionary Society in 1832, the Ohio Muster Roll, and referred to as the "Widow Frost" as a landholder on the Grand Reserve in Ohio (Divine 2019:210). She is said to have been married to Tarhe, Between-the-Logs and a man named Frost, outliving all three.[16] This is followed in 1855 by a Michael Frost in the Kansas Allotments of 1855 (Divine 2019:265). In the 1870 Kansas Muster there are three Frost sisters, Eddy, Olive, and Polley, daughters of Michael, buried in 1865 in the Huron Cemetery in Kansas.

Longhouse

This name appears first, as ts8nnonchies, in Potier's writing in 1768 (Toupin 1996:962–

---

16. www.wyandotte-nation.org/culture/history/biographies/tarhe-grand-sachem/

3), then 1772 (896), 1775 (899 and 910), and 1777 (903). This looks like it may be[17] the same name as is found held by a M[onsieu]r de s pierre: "Sonnonchiès (Toupin 1996:234).

This can be analyzed as:

Tsunǫšes	It is a very long house (male).
ts-	repetitive – very
-u-	feminine-zoic singular patient – it
-nǫš-	noun root – house
-es	verb root – be long + habitual aspect

One of the signatories of the Treaty of 1815 has a name presented as "Sanohskee[18] or long house".

In the Kansas Allotments of 1855, we first have the name as a surname, with "Zachariah Longhouse" (Divine 2019:264), the name mentioned again in the payments of April, 1857. He is the second of this name, as seen by the "Jr." after his name in the Huron Cemetery.

LUMPY

In 1746, a man whose name was given as onnonra8eon had a son baptized (Toupin 1996:855). This name can be translated as follows:

Hǫnǫrawęǫt	He has a bump or bulge on his scalp (male Deer).
hǫ-	masculine singular patient – he
-nǫr-	noun root – scalp
-aw-	joiner vowel
-ęǫt	verb root – have a bump or bulge + stative aspect

This name must have continued for at least a few more incarnations. In 1828, a member of the Missionary Society of Upper Sandusky, Ohio was named as Lump-on-the-Head.

In his discussion of Wyandot names in 1840, Finley wrote the following concerning this name: "Lump-on-the head, to the Deer tribe [clan], denoting a buck fawn," which seems to be a reference to the early stage of antler growth (Finley 1840:31). In the Ohio Grand Reserve, a few years earlier, a landholder of two plots of land was the "Widow Lumpy." (Divine 2019:210). She was likely Theresa Lumpy, who was born in 1801 and buried in the Huron Cemetery in Kansas.

---

17. I say "may be" here as the name is followed by "v. tannenhochre" which could indicate an alternative spelling for his name, which would make the word different.

18. The ending looks like what would be the external locative clitic, but that does not work with the presence of the initial -s-, unless the intended meaning was 'at your house', which seems unlikely.

Mudeater

Mudeater is a nickname based on the circumstances in which a very young settler boy became adopted by the Wyandot. A Wyandot war party was in Tennessee as part of the Revolutionary War. As they came across an abandoned settler cabin, they saw a white boy running to escape them. They eventually found him in a muddy stream bed. As written eloquently by Wyandot citizen and author, Lloyd Divine:

> By chance a Wyandot warrior looked under a mass of tangled roots extending over the stream bank where the boy was found pressed deep into the mud. Grabbed by the foot, the you boy was pulled kicking, but not screaming, from the roots where he was hiding. Since he pressed himself deep into the bank of the stream, his mouth was full of mud. From that day onward he was called Mud Eater (Divine 2019:114).

Mudeater was not a clan name, so it was not passed down in the traditional way. However, it was passed down as a surname, one held later by the original Mudeater's grandson, Matthew Mudeater (1812–1878), a landholder in the Detroit River Reserve in 1836, elected as principal chief in 1857, 1859–60 and 1875. He, his wife Nancy, and their six children, were in the 1870 Muster Roll. The 1874 voters list states that he belonged to the Large Turtle clan, while his children, following still the traditional matrilineage way, belonged to the Porcupine clan, as did Matthew's wife. In the Oklahoma Allotments there are five different Mudeaters.

There are Mudeaters in both the Huron Cemetery in Kansas and the Bland Cemetery in Oklahoma, the last one dying in 1891.

Marius Barbeau, in talking about one of his story-telling informants, Henry Stand, stated in 1915 that "He was raised by his uncle John Whitewing, *Tu'ta'ra''s (mud eater)* of the Small Turtle [Striped Turtle] clan of the Wyandots" (Barbeau 1915:xi).

I suspect that instead of a -t-, the initial letter of this name was an -h-, as this verb does not generally take the dualic prefix. So I have analysed the Mudeater's Wyandot origin as follows:

Haʔtaraš		He often eats mud, clay, wet earth (male Striped Turtle).
	ha-	masculine singular agent – he
	-ʔtar-	noun root – mud, clay, wet earth
	-a-	verb root – eat
	-s	habitual aspect

The Mudeater nickname may have an older history than that of the settler boy. Potier presented "I8taras" [ihutaras] in the census of 1747 as the former name of a Large Turtle man then named Matthias Aron-issas (Toupin 1996:205). That part of the story remains a mystery.

The Runner

On August 15, 1682, three Wyandot leaders met for a conference with the French, each one probably representing his phratry and his people. Included in those three was

"Oskoüendeti, the Runner" (NYCD9:181), of the Wolf clan and phratry. The name in full is as follows:

Huskwindehti	He is running with a group (e.g., a pack).
hu-	masculine singular patient – he
-skwinde-	verb root – go running (e.g., with a pack or crowd)
-ht-	causative root suffix
-i-	stative aspect

The name appears next in the written record almost a century later. The name "Osk8indeti" was given for the father of a six-month-old child baptized in 1775 (Toupin 1996:899). There is no other written reference to this individual that I can find.

In the 19th century, the name appears often, but without the pronominal prefix -hu-. Prefixes before -s- are often dropped in the writing of Wyandot by non-speakers. So we have Squindatee in the Treaty of 1817, then Squeendehty as a member of the Missionary Society in 1828 and 1832.

Then it became a surname. A John Squeendehtee was a landholder in the Grand Reserve in Ohio (Divine 2019:210). In his list of Wyandot names, often uniquely spelled, James Finley in 1840 recorded the name "Squindeghty" (Finley 1840:285). Two years later, a signatory to the Treaty of 1842 had his name written Squeendehtee. A John Squendachtee was a landholder in the Kansas Allotments recorded in 1855 (Divine 2019:264). In the Huron Cemetery in Kansas, we find the names John Squeenehtee (1815–1855), and Squeendechtee (1783–1844). Finally, Barbeau in his fieldnotes of 1911 wrote of a person named "skwindě'ti" (Barbeau 1911:44).

Tall

In chapter two I referred to the verb root -es- 'be long, tall' as the second-most common in Wyandot names, with 23 occurrences. That does not include the following, but I believe it is related. In the 1828 Missionary Society of Upper Sandusky, we have both a Tall Man, and another called Willow Tall Man, not a translation of the Wyandot name that goes before it. In the Ohio Grand Reserve, we have three individuals whose name begins with Tall: Tall Charles, Tall Fighter and Tall Solomon (Divine 2019:210). The first two are also found in the Ohio Muster Roll.

In the 1855 Kansas Allotments we have Theresa Tall Charles. In the 1870 Muster Roll there is reference to the widow of Tall Charles, and the orphan child of Teressa [sic] Tall Charles. The Huron Cemetery in Kansas has John Tallcharles or Tall Charles (1801–1856), and a Charlotte Tallman.

This is a different way in which the language and traditional naming impact surnames, but it still belongs in this chapter.

Warpole

Warpole was a significant Wyandot name in the 18th and 19th centuries. The first one recorded was Nicholas, who was politically active in the 1740s. His Porcupine clan name was recorded usually as Orontondi (Toupin 1996:828-9, 831 and 923), twice as Horontondi (Toupin 1996:828 and 829) in Potier's writings. Although both form legitimate words in Wyandot, I have chosen to use the more common Orontondi, even though it was not unusual for initial -h-s in Wyandot to be dropped by French recorders of the language. My representation and analysis of this name is as follows:

Urǫtǫndih	A pole is made; Warpole.
u-	feminine-zoic singular patient – it
-rǫt-	noun root – tree, log, pole
-ǫndi-	verb root – make
-h	stative aspect

An interpretation of the alternative would be:

Hurǫtǫndih	He is making a pole.
u-	feminine-zoic singular patient – it
-rǫt-	noun root – tree, log, pole
-ǫndi-	verb root – make
-h	stative aspect

In the 19th century, we first see a translation in the Treaty of 1818, with "*Rontondu or Warpole.*" Then it is found as a member of the Missionary Society in 1828, as Catharine Warpole in 1832. In the Ohio records of the Grand Reserve (Divine 2019:210) and the Ohio Muster Roll, we have Henry Warpole and Warpole. There is also a Tondee in the latter that might be connected. In the treaties of 1836 and 1842 we have "Rontondee or Warpole" and "Warpole" respectively. In the Kansas Allotments we have Catharine Warpole (Divine 2019:265). In the 1870 Muster Roll we have James, son of John. In the Huron Cemetery are buried Henry and his wife, Jacob, John, Peter, and his wife.

The last mention of the name that I have seen is Rontondi in Barbeau's recordings of 1911: "rontondi" and "rŏntŏnde? = (something about a log)" (Barbeau 1911:42).

It should be pointed out, as Lloyd Divine duly notes in *On the Back of a Turtle*, that Warpole could be used as a name for a war chief (Divine 2019:87-8, 117, 137, 167, 185 and 197). This should not affect the data on Warpole as a surname.

WHITEWING

While I have not seen the name written in Wyandot, my guess is that the name would appear something like the following:

Teha**žay**ę**rat**[19]	He has two white wings.[20]
te-	dualic
-ha-	masculine singular agent – he

19. It could otherwise be yažayęrat 'it is a white wing.'

20. In some versions of the origin myth swans are the ones who rescue the woman who fell from the sky. (Barbeau 1915:38–9 and 1960:59). This could be a reference to them.

-ž-	noun root – wing
-a-	joiner vowel
-yẹrat	verb root – be white + stative aspect

The first reference to Whitewing as a Wyandot surname is in the map of landholders in the Grand Reserve in Ohio. In it "White-Wing" and "White-Wing's Oldest Son" (probably John Sr. and Jr.) are mentioned (Divine 2019:210). In the Ohio Muster Roll a "White-wing" is referred to.

In discussing the metaphorical nature of the Wyandot language, Rev. James B. Findley wrote in 1840 a passage that included a reference to Whitewing as a Wyandot name:

> For instance, the literal meaning of the Wyandott word for a clock, or watch, is, the eye of time;[21] a cow is called, in Wyandott, quo-tus-quo-runt, and the meaning of this is, the oil of milk. And so with their names for their men and women; all have reference to their tribes, or the totem of the tribe. Hence the names of Whitewing, Highskies, Crackskies. These names belong to the Eagle tribe. (Findley 1840:30–31)

Neither of these translations is anywhere near correct. Someone may have been having him on. I do not know any of the sky names that would correspond to "Highskies" or "Crackskies". And there was no Eagle clan. He was probably referring to the Hawk clan.

In the 1855 Kansas Allotments, there are listed a Mary Whitewing (Divine 2019:264) and a John Whitewing Sr. and Jr. (Divine 2019:265). In 1874 Francis Whitewing, who was elected as a councilman that year, was listed as belonging to the Large Turtle clan (1874), although that was most likely the clan of his mother not his father.

Both men named John Whitewing are buried in the Huron Cemetery in Kansas, as well as an Ann and a George.

In Barbeau's unpublished work of 1911, he refers to a Jacob and a Frank Whitewing (Barbeau 1911:20 and 48). In his published work in 1915 he mentions Jacob, John, and Mary (Barbeau 1915:xi), the males belonging to the Striped Turtle clan, and Mary to the Snake clan.

Wind

There was a man whose name was written as ora,e'te, from 1759 to 1772 (Toupin 1996:880, 892, 895, 943–4, 949–50, 952 and 962). I have analysed the name as follows:

Urayehte	It bears air, wind.
u-	feminine-zoic singular patient – it

---

21. There is no word meaning 'time' in Wyandot. The word for 'clock' in the language is uk-wistaʔ, which has a broad range of objects that it refers to, including fish scales, metal, money, and dollar.

-r-		noun root – air, wind
-a-		joiner vowel
-yehte		verb root – bear + stative aspect

I believe that this could be the Wyandot version of the surname of Mary Wind, who was a landholder in the Oklahoma Allotments (Divine 2019:293).

Names Not Yet Translated
GYAMMEE

A difficult name to deal with appears as Gayamma (first name "Jesse") in the Kansas Allotments of 1855 (Divine 2019:265); as Jesse Gyammee and her son and daughter in 1870 and with Jesse in 1863; and as C. Gayamee of the Large Turtle clan and likely her husband James McKee Gayamee of the Striped Turtle clan in the Voters List of 1874. The name could begin with -yangy-, which could be 'finger', but the rest is harder to interpret.

(Hǫ)NDUYEṬET

This is a very frustrating name to deal with. It is spelled many different ways in the written record (and with hǫnduyeṭet I have added my own) and is sometimes conflated with Hǫndawatǫt 'He has a river in his mouth'. I have yet to come up with a translation.

It first appears (1731–1747) with the name Jaques, the son of Urǫtǫndih (Toupin 1996:204, 208, 241, 829, 833, 838, 844, 848, 851 and 854). Then there was Harman (?–1791), recorded from 1760 to 1782 (Toupin 1996:882, 886, 890, 896-7, 899, 901, 905,909 and 949), and who was the Principal Chief in Detroit. In 1785 and 1788 there are references to a Therese with the Wyandot name Doguintette or Nogintette (Toupin 1996:932 and 937), probably Harman's daughter. That it was her father's name and putting her father's name in what for others of the time was a separate Wyandot name seems to be a move towards surnames.

Harman was involved with treaties in the 1780s and 1790 (Buser, Curnoe 1996:218 and Lajeunesse 1960:173). Following him was "Dow-yen-tet the Younger" (Curnoe 1996:28-9), who succeeded Tarhe as Principal Chief in 1820. Before that he signed a treaty in 1817 ("Doouquod, or Half King") and two in 1818 ("Douquod or Half King" and Dunquod, or Half King).

After that, the next reference I have to the name is with Peter Doyentate Clarke (c.1810–c.1892). When he died, his younger brother Thomas took on the name, that Barbeau gave as Duyéntĕt (Barbeau 1911:2). It never became a surname

KAYRAHOO

A Wyandot surname that is a mystery for me is Kayrahoo. It appears by itself in the Missionary Society in 1832 as Kayroohooh. Later references show it with a first name. Solomon Kayrahoo was a landholder in the Grand Reserve in Ohio (Divine 2019:211), and, along with John Kayrahoo, appears in the Muster Roll in Ohio. There is a Milton Kayrahoo listed as a landholder in the 1855 Kansas Allotments, and six people of that last name in the 1870 Muster Roll. In 1874 one John was listed as Porcupine clan, and another, his son, as Bear clan. In the 1888 Oklahoma Allotments there was a Noah Kayarahoo listed. John Kayrahoo Sr. was buried in the Huron Cemetery in Kansas.

The name does not appear to me to be Wyandot in origin. I suspect, but cannot yet solidly prove, that Kayrahoo is connected with Callihoo, found among the Mohawk who moved west to Alberta during the 19th century. In a biography of Louis Callihoo, a Mohawk fur trader and a founding figure of that community, we read that he was baptized Karhiio, the Mohawk -r- changed to a non-Mohawk -l- (www.biographi.ca/en/bio/callihoo_louis_7E.html). Although more research is definitely necessary, I am guessing that it could be translated in the following way, in what would be a Wyandot cognate:

Yarhižuh	It is a large or great forest.
ya-	feminine-zoic singular agent – it
-rh-	noun root – forest
-ižu-	verb root – be large or great
-h	stative aspect

Mononcue

This name was written in a number of different ways: Menoncou (1814 Treaty), Memonkue and Manocue, or Thomas (1817 Treaty), Manoncue (Missionary Society, 1828 and 1832), Monocue (Divine 2019: 210 and 211), Monocue (1836 Treaty), Mononcue (Grand Reserve, Ohio Muster Roll, Divine 2019:244 and 1874 Voters List). It was a surname as in the 1832 membership for the Missionary Society, the person mentioned was "Mrs. Manoncue," a landholder in the Grand Reserve was the "Widow Mononcue" (Divine 2019:211), and as John Monocue, one of the signatories on an anti-slavery letter to Congress in 1848.

Potentially the most useful for translation is Connelley's presentation of the name as James B. Finley's Large Turtle name: "His name should have been written Mäh-nŏŏhn-kyŏŏh. Big Turtle Clan. Meaning of name lost" (Connelley 1900:110). This I would represent as Manǫkyu. I could speculate that the name is imǫnǫkyu, a different version of the name for the French governor typically written as Onnontio 'It is a large mountain', but that does not seem quite right. For me as for Connelley, the meaning of the name is lost.

Tahehyohhrahtseh

Abelard G. Guthrie (1814–1873) was a white settler adopted into the tribe when he married a Wyandot woman, Nancy Brown. He was given a nickname, written out in the following fashion:

Tah-keh-yoh-shrah-tseh (Hancks)
Tah-keh'-yoh-shrah'-tseh,
(www.kckpl.org/wyandot daguerreotype/documents/AbelardGuthrie.pdf)

Both sources translate the name as 'the man with two brains'. Both probably copied from the same document. The writer of that document was probably no speaker of the language and copied another source very badly. The Wyandot word as written does not mean 'two brains'. Here is why I say that. Here are four male Wyandot names that use the two necessary elements when speaking about two of something: the dualic prefix and the verb root -'ye- 'be a number'. Both are bolded in the examples. What comes in between is a pronominal prefix, a noun root, and a joiner vowel -a-:

Name	Translation	Pronominal prefix	Noun root
Teyarota**yeh**	Two trees.	-ya- 'it'	-rot-
Tehahsenda**yeh**	(He has) two names.	-ha- 'he'	-hsend-
Teyawenda**yeh**	Two islands	-ya- 'it'	-wend-
Tewašra**yeh**	Two axes	no sound 'it'	-ašr-

There are two noun roots in the language that can mean 'brain': -nomar- or -nowar- 'brain, head' and -e'set- 'brain'. Neither appears. Even if the initial -t- is the dualic, and the final -e- is some form of the verb root 'be a number', there is no noun root that even comes close to matching the middle part of the word.

Tauromee

This name first appears as Tauromee on the map of the Grand Reserve in Ohio (Divine 2019:210). Then we see the name on the treaties of 1842 (Tauroone and Tauroonee), 1843 (Tan-roo-mie), 1855 (Tan-roo-mee) and 1867 (Tauromee). In none of those cases does a first name appear. In the Huron Cemetery, the name appears "John Hat, or Tauromee" for a man living between 1810 and 1870. So the name does not appear to be transformed into a surname, but as the clan name of one particular individual.

I was hoping that the surname of "hat" would help with the translation, but it does not. The word for 'his hat' in Wyandot is:

hunomarure?	He covers his head with it.
hu-	masculine singular patient – he
-nomar-	noun root – head, brains
-ure-	verb root – cover
-?	stative aspect

This does not fit with how the Wyandot name is presented, which appears to be something like 'Taurumi'.[22] While it could be that the -m- represents the transitional root suffix -m-, and the verb might be 'be in water', a complete translation still eludes me.

Animal Names

There are seven names that make specific reference to animals. I believe that none are clan-names, but were nicknames that became surnames, or were first thought up in English.

---

22. The -o- would be a -u- in standard Wyandot of the early 20th century.

BEAVER

In the Kansas Allotments, one of the landholders was John Beaver (Divine 2019:265). The name is not seen elsewhere, in English or in Wyandot. The Wyandot word for 'beaver' is tsu'tahi which means 'It has very dense, thick fur' (Barbeau 1960:88 #3 and 10, 99 #44, 129 #39, 131 #9 and 190 #56).

BUZZARD

In the 1888 Oklahoma Allotments map the name Rosa Buzzard is recorded (Divine 2019:293). The usual term for buzzard (i.e., vulture) is sętsi'ta'ah, does not appear to my knowledge in any name in Wyandot. It is possible that the source is the name Tsamęhuhiʔ, 'osprey'. It was discussed earlier how the vulture association is strong historically with that word and the name.

COON

When I first noticed that many Wyandot in the 19th century source had the surname Coon, I thought that this might be a translation of the Wyandot name for 'raccoon' 'ętirǫ'. I was wrong. There was no name on record using that Wyandot word as a name. Coon came from the surname Kuhn.

Abraham Kuhn was a boy when he was captured in what Americans call the French and Indian War (1754–1763) and was adopted into the Bear clan and given the name Zhau-Shoo-To (Divine 2019:137) or Tsizutooʔ (www.wyandotte-nation.org/traditions/biographical-panels/catherine-johnson/), which I have yet to translate. His unfamiliar name became Coon, the surname of his descendants.

CRANE

In the 1870 Muster Roll, there appears an Adaline Crane and her husband Frances living in Kansas. The Wyandot word for crane, uhšinguʔt, does not appear as a name anywhere I have searched. There is an off chance that would require research to confirm that there was a connection with Tarhe, whose nickname was 'Crane.'

CUB

This name is presented on the Grand Reserve map, simply as "Cub" (Divine 2019:210), and as "Old Cub" (Divine 2019:211), referring to a previous generation. In the Ohio Muster Roll we have "Cub, Little" and "Cub, Old." In the Treaty of 1815, the entry for one signatory is Outoctutimoh, or Cub", no doubt Old Cub. The Wyandot word used here is not the word for 'bear cub' that I know of in Wyandot. That is tsahkwa'ah. Furthermore, I have not been able to translate the Wyandot word. This name does not appear as a surname.

PORCUPINE

The name Betsey Porcupine appears in the 1855 Kansas Allotments (Divine 2019:264). She (as Betsy) and her son John had that surname reported in the 1870 Muster Roll. The name does not appear elsewhere, in English or Wyandot. And I have not seen the Wyandot word for 'porcupine', tsinę'ka' used as anyone's name.

Wasp

The name John Wasp appears among the landholders in the Ohio Grand Reserve (Divine 2019:211), the Ohio Muster Roll, the Kansas Allotments (Divine 2019:265) and in the Huron Cemetery (1795–?). The Wyandot word for 'wasp' or 'bee' is ǫndaʼkǫt. It was recorded twice as a name. In 1740, we find the name written as Ndakont (Toupin 1996:848) as the father of a baptized child. It also appears in the mid-18th century as ondaʼkon, one of two different names for a Frenchman with the surname Deruisseau who lived in Detroit (Toupin 1996:262), the other being the negative nickname honnonste which means 'he is stingy.' For the Wendat it was recorded in the Jesuit Relations in 1650, 1652 and 1657 (JR35:58–9, 37:108–9 and 43:118–9 respectively).

Names Envisioned in English

I believe that the following were names envisioned as nicknames in English and were not translations of clan names or Wyandot-language-based nicknames.

Blacksheep

This surname with no accompanying first name is encountered in a landholder on the Ohio Grand Reserve (Divine 2019:210), William Blacksheep, and Blacksheep in the 1855 Kansas Allotments (Divine 2019:265). In the Huron Cemetery in Kansas, there is someone referred to as Black Sheep's Wife, who died in 1852. The Wyandot would have encountered sheep in both states.

In Potier's dictionary the term for the entry for 'sheep' involves a verb root that can mean "etre frisé [to be curly]. The word for 'sheep' is "otsinnent8taïa…mouton…a[nim]al dont la poil se passe l'un dans l'autre, se prend l'un à l'autre [sheep…animal whose hairs go one in another, that takes the one in the other]" (Potier 1920:440). In 19th-century Wyandot, that term might be utsinętutaža, the initial -u- possibly dropped as many animal names begin with -tsi-. The word for 'black' is yatsehęstatsih 'it is called charcoal'. The combination with the previous word seems to me to make it too complicated for a name in the Wyandot language. It must have come from English.

The next question is wondering why someone would want to have that name, unless the people put a different, more positive spin on it than existed in mainstream culture.

Canada

In the 1870 Muster Roll, there are references to Rabecca Canada, whose maiden name was Brown before she married Marion Canada. He is also mentioned, as well as their daughter Florinda. She is called Rebecca Canada in Barbeau's unpublished list of names (Barbeau 1911:17). The word 'Canada' meaning 'village' (yandataʔ in Wyandot, as in the word for Big Town) came from the related language of St. Lawrence Iroquoian, first appearing in writing in the 16th century, and disappearing in the 17th century (Steckley 2012). The name may have been used here because Marion may have come from the Canadian side of the Detroit River.

CURLYHEAD

This surname with no accompanying first name is encountered in a landholder on the Ohio Grand Reserve (Divine 2019:211). In a letter sent to Congress in 1848, one of the people that signed it was a John Curleyhead (Divine 2019:244). There was a Nancy Curleyhead in the 1855 Kansas Allotments (Divine 2019:265), a Jacob in the 1870 Muster Roll in Kansas and a Jacob and a Mary buried in the Huron Cemetery. I think that this surname probably began as a nickname. Remember that Crazy Horse was given the name Curly as a nickname by his mother.

GREYEYES

The Greyeyes family was prominent among the 19th-century Wyandot. There was a "Widow Grey-Eyes" and Doctor Grey-Eyes (1795–August 1845) in the landholder map of the Grand Reserve in Ohio (Divine 2019:210–1). The first name 'Doctor' suggests to me that he might have been given the Wyandot name Shutetsęnskǫh 'He is quite frequently a healer, curer' (see Translations). He signed the treaty of 1842. There was also his brother, Lewis 'Squire' or 'Esquire' Greyeyes, an ordained Methodist minister, and John W. Greyeyes, lawyer, and principal chief in 1870,. Doctor and Squire were buried in the Huron Cemetery in Kansas.

In 1836, Matthew Greyeyes was registered as a landholder in the Detroit River reserve.

In the 1888 Oklahoma Allotments two of the landholders had the first names Kattie and Isaac (Divine 2019:293). In the Bland Cemetery in Oklahoma, there is buried a Gracey Whitewing, who lived less than a year.

Probably the first to bear the surname Greyeyes had his name presented as "Tsoondow-enon, the Grey-Eyed man."[23] The color of his eyes may have reflected his partly British genetic heritage. His oldest child was born in 1795, so he was likely born in the 1770s.

The Wyandot name does not translate to mean 'grey-eyed'. It does not have any of the noun roots involved with eyes, and the only verb root relating to grey is -ndra?tę- 'for hair to become grey', which does not appear. The word for 'grey' is u?ęra?atsih 'It is called ash, ashes.' This all points to the surname coming from English. It is more likely a nickname than a clan name. A probable analysis and translation of the name given is:

Tsunduwanęh	It is a very large arrow.[24]
ts-	repetitive – very
-u-	feminine-zoic singular patient – it
su-nd-	noun root – arrow
-uwanę-	verb root – be large
-h	stative aspect

23. "Mary Greyeyes" by Ashley Simmons and Sallie Cotter Andrews www.wyandotte-nation.org/traditions/biographical-panels/mary-greyeyes/).

24. This is similar in structure to the eight names beginning with 'Big.'

Little Chief

This name appears with no accompanying first name as a member of the Missionary Society of Ohio in 1828 and 1832. There is reference to a Mary Little Chief in the Kansas Allotments of 1855 (Divine 2019:264). To say 'Little Chief' in Wyandot would be difficult. The term for 'chief' in the language is verbal and relational, not a simple labelling noun as in English. In the Narratives recorded by Barbeau in 1911–12, the following term was used to refer to a chief:

homayuwaneh	They (masculine/mixed) have him as large; he is chief.
homa-	masculine plural agent + masculine singular patient – they (m) – him
-yuwane-	verb root – be large
-h	stative aspect

While it might be possible to add another relational expression in which two individuals are compared, that would be to my way of thinking difficult and unlikely. No use of such an expression can be found in the 18th century. It would be much easier to say it in English.

One Hundred Snakes

Wyandot names typically have stories associated with them. Unfortunately, this name demands a story, but I haven't found it in the written record. In the Huron Cemetery in Kansas there is a gravestone with the name One-Hundred-Snakes Standingstone on it. While we have seen that his surname is easily expressed in Wyandot, it would not be the case for One-Hundred Snakes. Here is the probable construction:

skat imęgyawe iyaaʔtaye de kyu'ngę'tse	It is one hundred snakes
skat	It is one
imęgyawe	It is such a number of hundreds
iyaaʔtaye	It is such a number of bodies
de	of that which
kyu'ngę'tse	It is a snake.

So it seems fairly certain that this name was created in English. The story behind it would have been fascinating, and I hope that it is one day found.

Pipe

The surname Pipe appeared among 19th-century Wyandot. There is no evidence that yanodame[25] 'it is a pipe' was ever a Wyandot name. The only reference to a pipe in a name in Wyandot is the 18th-century male name Skangyeretsih 'It is a very long pipestone, bird's tail, point of a canoe' (see the chapter on translations). That seems unlikely to generate a surname like 'pipe.'

It seems that the name came to the Wyandot through marriage. There was a Delaware chief who was known as Captain Pipe (c.1725–c.1818) because of his Delaware nickname Hopocan, meaning 'pipe'. He and his family had a close relationship to the

---

25. At some early point in time the -m- would have been a -w-.

Wyandot. His son, also known as Captain Pipe, married a Wyandot woman, and the name became a Wyandot family name through their descendants (Hancks, n.d. and Morgan 1911).

The earliest reference to a surname "Pipe" with the Wyandot is to Nancy Pipe as a member of the Missionary Society in 1832. Then in the 1855 Kansas Allotments, we have John and Thomas Pipe (Divine 2019:264). The 1870 Muster Roll includes several Pipe families and 12 names. In the 1874 Voters List by Clan there is an Eli that belonged to the Striped Turtle clan. In the Huron Cemetery there is a Nancy Rankin Pipe, while in the Bland Cemetery there is Eli.

White Crow

The first occurrence of this English name appears for someone simply called "Whitecrow" as a landholder in the Grand Reserve in Ohio (Divine 2019:210). In the second incidence, it was the name of a signatory of a Wyandot letter to Congress, likewise without a first name (Divine 2019:244). The third and last incidence is with the name Polley Whitecrow, a landholder in the Oklahoma Allotments of 1888 (Divine 2019:292).

Crows can be albinos. And 'white' is a colour of cultural significance to the Wyandot for animals (see Barbeau 1915:97–8 and 1960:77–91). The fact that there is no evidence for a combination of the onomatopoetic word for 'crow' yahka'a with another word which would involve the verb root -yęrat 'be white' plus the noun root for 'feather' -hǫr- or 'body' -a?t-suggests that this surname originated in English.

The Future of Wyandot Names

As you can see, names and naming changed for the Wyandot in the 19th century, not following a single path but several. Most of these paths came to an end by the 20th century. But that is not the end of the story of Wyandot names, the end that some outsiders might feel was inevitable. The Wyandot people have a growing interest in their heritage, including that of names. In August 2020 I received an e-mail message concerning a name connected with the family that a few still knew something about, but wanted to know more. They knew roughly how to say it, Tayanonka. Family members differed in whether it was Large Turtle or Deer clan. The man who contacted me had been told that it meant 'flying arrow' . I looked up -taya- in the names list and found Taya?nǫkye? 'An arrow is continuing on its way (this way)' (male Deer). Barbeau recorded it in 1911 as the Wyandot name of Smith Nichols, one of his story informants.

New names are being created, something that I saw in growing numbers when I was tribal linguist of the Wyandotte Nation of Oklahoma from 2015 to 2020. Wyandot are asking for names in their language, for themselves, for family members and friends. This names are often given in sacred ceremony in the annual gathering in September in numbers that increase every year.

Chapter Ten
Translations

In this collection of Wyandot names, there are 602 names. For some of these names a clan identity has been found: Deer 38, Snake 21, Bear 44, Large Turtle 46, Striped Turtle 33, Porcupine 31, Prairie Turtle 10 , Wolf 26, Hawk 2, Sturgeon 1, Beaver 1 and Snipe 1, possibly 2. That comes to 242 of the names, or less than half.

Names in Alphabetical Order

Ahandaturęha[1]
[ah-han-dah-tooh-ren-ha]

	He has found a village. (male Hawk)
a-	factual
-ha-	masculine singular agent – he
-ndat-	noun root – village, community
-urę-	verb root – find
-ha	inchoative root suffix + punctual aspect

Ahanęhutaha[2]
[ah-ha-nen-hoo-taha]

	He planted, stood up the corn. (male)
a-	factual
-ha-	masculine singular agent – he
-nęh-	noun root – corn
-ut-	verb root – stand
-aha	inchoative root suffix + punctual aspect

Ahanęnratęndi[3]
[ah-han-nen-rah-ten-dee]

	He changed groups. (male Snake)
a-	factual
-ha-	masculine singular agent – he
-nęnr-	noun root – group
-a-	joiner vowel
-tęndi	verb root – change + punctual aspect

---

1. This is presented as "hondatorenha and andatorenha (Toupin 1996:176, 874, 194, 210, 220, 227, 229, 254, 260, 824, 828, 832, 837, 841, 847, 850, 861 and 874. It is the name of the leader of that clan (Toupin 1996:260).

2. Toupin 1996:224, 257, 866, and 873.

3. This name was recorded as hannenratendi and ennenratendi (Toupin 1996: 185, 187, 207, 211, 228, 243, 245, 826, 853, 859, 865–6, 870, 924–5, and 927). His French nickname was "l'etourneau" meaning 'the starling'. 'He changed groups' may refer to an aremed group.

Ahatrǫtamęrat[4]   He got over a log. (male Wolf)
[ah-hah-tron-tah-men-raht]

    a-   factual
    -h-   masculine singular agent – he
    -at-   semi-reflexive voice
    -rǫt-   noun root – tree, log
    -amęrat-   verb root – pass over + punctual aspect

Ahatsihstare[5]   He moved the fire around, put coals on top. (male)
[ah-hah-tseeh-stah-reh]

    a-   factual
    -ha-   masculine singular agent – he
    -tsihst-   noun root – fire
    -a-   joiner vowel
    -re   verb root – move + punctual aspect

Ahętǫnya[6]   He made a day. (male)
[ah-hen-ton-yah]

    -a-   factual
    -h-   masculine singular agent – he
    -ęt-   noun root – day
    -ǫny-   verb root – make
    -a   punctual aspect

Ahurędayęnyat[7]   He surpassed him regarding[8] a rock. (male)
[ah-hoo-ren-dah-yen-nyat]

    -a-   factual
    -hu-   masculine singular agent + masculine singular patient – he – him
    -ręd-   noun root – rock
    -a-   joiner vowel
    -yeny-   verb root – surpass
    -at   causative root suffix + punctual aspect

---

4. Barbeau 1911:30.

5. Toupin 1996:868. This was also a name for a great Wendat warrior of the 17th century (Steckley 1992:19–25). See chapter five.

6. Toupin 1996:855. It is possible that there is an -a- before the -e-, as that combination happens several times with other aspects. That would give the meaning 'he worked with sticks'.

7. Toupin 1996:847 horendaienat, and 852 arenda,ennion. As the former seems more specific, I chose it. And as the punctual form is used I added an initial a- depicting the factual, the most likely of the modals to be missed.

8. This could be interpreted as 'on a rock' or even 'with a rock'.

Ahuręwa⁹   He floated. (male)
[ah-hoo-ren-wah]
    a-   factual
    -hu-   masculine singular patient – he
    -rę-   verb root – be stable
    -wa   undoer root suffix + punctual aspect

Akwęndihata?¹⁰   She often shouts out, raises her voice. (female Porcupine)
[ah-wen-dee-hah-tah-ah]
    akwęndihat-   feminine-zoic singular agent – she + verb root – shout
    -a?   habitual aspect

Amęye Tehat¹¹   He is standing in the water (male Deer)
Amęye   In the water.
[ah-men-yeh]
    am-   feminine-zoic singular patient – it
    -ę-   noun root – water
    =yeh   external locative clitic
Tehat   He is standing (male)
[teh-haht]
    te-   dualic
    -ha-   masculine singular agent – he
    -t   verb root – stand + stative aspect

Amęteha¹²   She came to know. (female Deer)
[ah-men-teh-hah]
    a-   factual
    -m-   feminine-zoic singular patient – she
    -ęte-   verb root – know
    -ha   inchoative root suffix + punctual aspect

Amęnye ire¹³   He is walking on water. (male, one of the Turtle clans)
Amęnye
[ah-men-yeh]

9. Toupin 1996:926.

10. Barbeau 1911:10. This word may contain the noun root -męnd-/-węnd- 'voice, word', which may be preceded by the semi-reflexive voice.

11. Finley 1840:429 and Connelley 1900:113.

12. Toupin 1996:929-30, 943, 946-7, 950 and 956.

13. Sallie Cotter Andrews, https://www.wyandotte-nation.org/culture/history/biographies/walk-in-the-water/. P.D. Clarke gives the name as "Walk-in-water (whose name in Wyandot was Mey-re-ra" (Clarke 1870:102). See discussion in chapter nine.

	amęn-	feminine-zoic singular patient – it + verb root -be water + stative aspect
	=ye	external locative clitic
ire		
[ee-reh]		
	i-	partitive
	-r-	masculine singular agent – he
	-e	verb root – walk + stative aspect: he walks

Amęseskwa[14]
[ah-men-seh-skwah]

    am-   feminine-zoic singular patient – she
    -ęse-   verb root – value, cherish, esteem
    -s-   habitual aspect
    -kwa   past aspect suffix

Anyǫnyęta?[15]
[an-yon-nyen-tah-ah]   Bearskin (male Bear)

    a-   feminine-zoic singular agent – it
    -nyǫnyę-   verb root – be a bear
    -t-   nominalizer
    -a?   noun suffix

---

14. Toupin 1996:211 and 850.

15. See discussion in the ninth chapter. Just as a noun, not a name, it was recorded in several 17th-century Wendat dictionaries (see Steckley 2007:195).

Anyǫnyętase[16]		It is new bearskin. (male Bear)
[an-nyon-nyen-ta-seh]		
	a-	feminine-zoic singular agent – it
	-nyǫnyę-	verb root – be a bear
	-t-	nominalizer
	-ase	verb root – be new + stative aspect

Aǫmętsisatih[17]		It is the corner of the country. (female)
[ah-on-men-tsee-sah-tee]		
	a-	feminine-zoic singular patient – she or it
	-ǫmęts-	noun root – land, earth
	-is-	verb root – press against
	-at-	causative root suffix
	-ih	stative aspect

Aǫndatǫti[18]		She abandoned, left her village. (female Snake)
[ah-on-dah-ton-tee]		
	a-	factual
	-ǫ-	feminine-zoic singular patient - she
	-ndat-	noun root – village, community
	-ǫti-	verb root – abandon, quit + punctual aspect

Aǫnęta[19]		She often falls. (female)
[ah-on-nen-tah]		
	-a-	feminine-zoic singular patient – she
	-ǫnęt-	verb root – fall
	-a	habitual aspect

Aǫwe[20]		She is human. (female)
[ah-on-weh]		
	-a-	feminine-zoic singular patient
	-ǫwe	verb root – be human + stative aspect

16. Toupin 1996:190, 196 and 976 Pierre annionentase. In 1759 a man named Pierre ,anientase is recorded as a godfather at a baptism (Toupin 1996:879), probably the same name and person.

17. Toupin 1996:900.

18. Connelley 1900:117–8 as quoted in Barbeau 1915:341. For the clan significance of this name see chapter four: Clan Naming

19. Toupin 1996:927 aonnenta and 971 haonnenta. There is also the possibility that this could mean 'she often swallows' as that verb root takes the same forms.

20. Toupin 1996:876, 884 and 929 as aon8e, 950 as aon8a and 956 as haon8e. It could also be making reference to her being Indigenous.

Araskwahǫ[21]	She leaves many times. (female Bear)
[ah-rah-skwah-hon]	
arahskwa-	feminine-zoic singular agent – she + verb root – leave
-hǫ	distributive root suffix + stative aspect
Asareywę[22]	It is a great, large blade, a sword. (male, military title)
[ah-sah-reh-ywen]	
asar-	feminine-zoic singular agent – it + noun root – blade
-e-	verb root - ?[23] + stative aspect
=ywę	augmentative clitic
Asęra'ye haǫ[24]	She comes from the south. (female Bear)
[ah-sen-rah-ah-yeh]	
asęr-	feminine-zoic singular agent + noun root – south, noon
-a'	noun suffix
=ye	external locative clitic
haǫ	particle – comes from
Ateyašǫtata'[25]	Her heart often shakes. (female)
[ah-teh-yah-son-tah-tah-ah]	
at-	feminine-zoic singular agent – her + semi-reflexive voice
-eyaš-	noun root – heart
-ǫtat-	verb root – shake
-a'	habitual aspect
Atęruwat[26]	It is a large palisade. (no gender indicated)
[ah-ten-ru-wat]	
atęr-	feminine-zoic singular agent – it + noun root – palisade
-uwat	verb root – be large + stative aspect

21. Toupin 1996:190, 215, 249, 825, 837, 855, 858, 872, 878, 924 and 976.

22. Toupin 1996:209 and 904.

23. The same verb root appears in the Mohawk cognate (Michelson 1973:41).

24. Toupin 1996:190, 214, 228, 846, 852, 959, 962-3 and 976.

25. This only appears once in what I believe is its full form (Toupin 1996:222), but three times we see the woman whose name is written as te ,achiontata has the same husband as the name written in full (849, 854 and 864) where the name of the spouse is provided. The same recording also appears elsewhere (867, 882, 927, 929 and 947). The name is also recorded as te ,achiatontata(k) (949, 951 and 954), as te ,achiatonta (952) and te ,achiontaθa (860). Only the name presented in this list has a meaning that makes good sense.

26. Toupin 1996:889, 961, and 966 as atonr8at. An -on is sometimes written in names when there should be -en-. There is no noun root -atonr-. It is unusual for a noun root appearing with -uwat- not to begin with a ts-, the repetitive, indicating 'very'.

Atrakyaskwa[27] She used to cut, break apart dry leaves. (female Porcupine)
[ah-trah-kyah-skwah]

- at- — feminine-zoic singular agent + semi-reflexive voice
- -rak- — noun root – dry leaves
- -ya- — verb root – cut
- -s- — habitual aspect
- -kwa — past aspect suffix

Atsirǫnde[28] She is going to go about on all fours. (female Porcupine)
[ah-tsee-ron-deh]

- atsirǫn- — feminine-zoic singular agent - she + verb root – go about on all fours
- -de — purposive aspect

Athuehtes[29] Every one of his nails is often long. He often has long claws. (male Bear)
[at-hu-eht-es]

- -a- — translocative
- -t- — dualic
- -hu- — masculine singular patient – he
- -eht- — noun root – claw
- -es — verb root – be long + habitual aspect

Autsistęha[30] She fell into the fire. (female)
[ah-oo-tsee-sten-ha]

- -a- — factual
- -u- — feminine-zoic singular patient – she
- -tsist- — noun root – fire
- -ę- — verb root – fall
- -ha — inchoative root suffix + punctual aspect

Auwas[31] It was short for her. (male Wolf – nickname)
[ah-oo-was]

- -a- — factual
- -u- — feminine-zoic singular patient – her
- -wa- — verb root – be short
- -s — dative root suffix + punctual aspect

27. Toupin 1996:203

28. Toupin 1996:173, 182, 186, 200, 202, 229, 238, 240, and 932.

29. Powell 1881:60: A-tu-e-tĕs *(Long Claws)*.

30. Toupin 1996:889 and 893 otsistenha, 899 and 968 otsistena, 899 tsiena, and 903 and 965 tsistenha.

31. Connelley 1900:113. See discussion in chapter six.

Awenyǫhakye⁷³² She is going to pass by many times. (female Snake)
[ah-wen-nyon-hah-kyeh-eh]
    aw- feminine-zoic singular patient
    -e- verb root – go, come, walk
    -nyǫ- distributive root suffix + stative aspect
    -haky- progressive root suffix
    -e⁷ purposive aspect

Ayandatǫgyah³³ She has made a community, village. (female Large Turtle)
[ah-yan-dah-ton-gyah]
    a- factual
    -ya- feminine-zoic singular agent – she
    -ndat- noun root – community, village
    -ǫgy- verb root – make
    -ah punctual aspect

Ayanyęmiha³⁴ She learned how to do it; she knows how. (female Large Turtle)
[ah-yan-yen-mee-ha]
    a- factual
    -ya- feminine-zoic singular agent – she
    -nyę- verb root – have skill, ability
    -mi- transitional root suffix
    -ha inchoative root suffix + punctual aspect

Ayarǫyiet³⁵ She scraped the sky. (female Porcupine)
[ya-ron-nyee-eht]
    -a- factual
    -ya- feminine-zoic singular agent – she or it
    -rǫy- noun root – sky
    -iet- verb root – scrape + punctual aspect

Ayatsitsarawa⁷³⁶ She took flowers off (of a bush). (female Wolf)
[ah-yah-tsee-tsah-rah-wah-ah]
    a- factual
    -ya- feminine-zoic singular agent – she
    -tsits- noun root – flower, blossom
    -a- joiner vowel

32. Barbeau 1911:49

33. Barbeau 1915:xi.

34. Barbeau 1915:xi. Connelley 1900:111 #48 Nyĕh'-mĕh-ah, Toupin 1996:211 as anienh8iha.

35. Toupin 1996:206, 229, 242,860, 867, 871, 878, 891, 900, 926, 928–9, 942, and 953–4.

36. Barbeau 1911:7.

-ra-	verb root – put on top
-wa-	undoer root suffix
-ʔ	punctual aspect

Ayatsitsęmah³⁷
[ah-yah-tsee-ten-mah]

a-	factual
-ya-	feminine-zoic singular agent – she
-tsits-	noun root – flowers, blossoms
-ęma-	verb root – bring, carry
-h	punctual aspect

Ayawas³⁸
[ah-yah-wahs]

-a-	factual
-ya-	feminine-zoic singular agent – she, it
-wa-	verb root – take
-s	(inchoative root suffix) + punctual aspect

Ayiatǫhǫk³⁹
[ah-yee-ah-ton-honk]

ayi-	1st-person dual exclusive agent – we two
-atǫ-	verb root – say, speak
-hǫ-	habitual aspect
-k	past aspect suffix

Ayižatǫ⁴⁰
[ah-yee-zhah-ton]

We two (excluding the listener(s)) are marking, writing, (female).⁴¹

ayi-	1st-person dual exclusive agent - we two (exclusive)
-žatǫ	verb root – mark, write + stative aspect

---

37. Barbeau 1911:7.

38. Toupin 1996: 209–11, 219–20, 226, 228, 829 and 841.

39. Toupin 1996:879 a,iatonhonk and 903 aïatonhonk.

40. Toupin 1996:960.

41. The reason for identifying the name as female is that the individual is recorded as a participant in the mortuary ceremony known as Testaments et Anniversaires. Women are the primary participants in all 76 of these ceremonies.

Ayǫmętsižu[42]	She is a large earth, land. (female Striped Turtle)
[ah-on-men-tsee-zhoo]	
ay	feminine-zoic singular patient – she, it
-ǫmęts-	noun root – land, earth
-ižu	verb root – be large + stative aspect

De Hehnyateh[43]	It is a rainbow. (male Deer)
[deh-hen-nyah-teh]	
de	the
he-	?
-nhy-	noun root – rainbow
-a-	joiner vowel
-te-	verb root – exist (?)
-h	stative aspect

Ehamęnǫ[44]	She is going away from him. (female)
[eh-hah-men-non]	
e-	translocative – away
-ham-	feminine-zoic singular agent – masculine singular patient – he
-ę-	verb root – go, come, walk
-nǫ	stative aspect

Ehędihaǫ[45]	They (m) will say, speak. (female)
[eh-hen-dee-hah-on]	
e-	future
-hęd-	masculine plural agent – they (m)
-iha-	verb root – say
-ǫ	punctual aspect

Ekyayumęndata[46]	It is at the end of one's or their word, voice. (male Porcupine)
[eh-kyah-yoo-wen-ah-tah]	
eky-	cislocative
-ayu-	indefinite patient – one's, their
-męnd-	noun root – word, voice
-a-	joiner vowel
-ta	verb root – be at the end + stative aspect

42. Barbeau 1911:36 and Toupin 1996:204, 208, and 217.

43. Connelley 1899a:124 as Deh'-hehn-yihn'-teh and 1899b:9 as "Dēh-hĕhn-yahn-teh".

44. This is a composite of a Wyandot example Toupin 1996:840 ha8ennond and a Wendat example JR37:93 – Ehawennon.

45. Toupin 1996:834.

46. Toupin 1996:204 tio8endata, 241 tion8oindata, 827 tiaon8endata, 833 etiao8endata, 837–8, 840, 846, 852 and 855, tiao8endata, and 863 tia8endata.

Ekyǫnętat[47]
[eh-kyon-nen-tat]   Where an evergreen stands, or evergreens stand. (female)

    eky- cislocative – where
    -ǫ- feminine-zoic singular patient – it
    -nęt- noun root – evergreen
    -a- joiner vowel
    -t verb root – stand + stative aspect

Etsuskwa[48]
[eh-tsoo-skwah]   She will be able to smell again. (female Striped Turtle)

    e- future
    -ts- repetitive – again
    -u- feminine-zoic singular patient – she
    -skwa verb root – smell (something) + punctual aspect

Ędeǫskwara[49]
[en-deh-on-skwah-rah]   One is with the sweat lodge. (male)

    ędeǫ- feminine-zoic singular agent – she, one, it + verb root – hold a sweat[50]
    -skw- nominalizer[51]
    -a- joiner vowel
    -ra verb root – be with + stative aspect

Haaʔtayetak[52]
[hah-ah-tah-yeh-tak]   He used to bear her body. (female)

    ha- masculine singular agent – he + female singular patient
    -aʔt- noun root – body
    -a- joiner vowel
    -yet- verb root – bear
    -a- habitual aspect
    -k past aspect suffix

---

47. Toupin 1996:901 and 933. See introductory chapter for discussion.

48. Toupin 1996:208 ts8sk8a, 868 ts88skwa, and 870 and 872 ets8skwa.

49. Toupin 1996:848 and 884.

50. See Steckley 1989 for a linguistic background of this verb.

51. This is an unusual construction for a nominalizer, which is usually -šr- or the instrumental -kw-.

52. Toupin 1996:212 ata,etak and 838 haata,eta. My choice of using a masculine pronominal prefix for a female name might be wrong, but I believe that the -h- would not be there if it were not supposed to be.

Haetondi[53]
[hah-en-ton-dee]
    ha-   masculine singular agent – he
    -et-   noun root – stick, sticks
    -ondi   verb root – make + stative aspect

He is making, working with sticks. (male)

Haetongya'[54]
[hah-en-ton-gyah-ah]
    ha-   masculine singular agent – he
    -et-   noun root – stick, sticks
    -ongy-   verb root – make
    -a'   habitual aspect

He makes, works with sticks. (occupational name for Frenchman]

Haheto'[55]
[ha-hen-ton-on]
    ha-   masculine singular agent – he
    -het-   verb root – lead
    -o'   stative aspect

He is leading. (male Striped Turtle)

Hahkeya'ah[56]
[hah-ken-yah-ah-ah]
    ha-   masculine singular agent – he
    -hkey-   verb root – be small, a baby, infant
    -a'-   stative aspect
    -ah   diminutive aspect suffix

He is a baby, an infant, small. (male Large Turtle)

Hakongya'[57]
[hah-kon-gyah-ah]
    h-   masculine singular agent – he
    -ak[58]-   noun root – shoe, shoes
    -ongy-   verb root – make
    -a'   habitual aspect

He makes shoes. (male occupational name)

---

53. Toupin 1996:851. I believe that this is not a nickname, but could be a clan name.

54. Toupin 1996:235.

55. This name was given to B.N.O. Walker (Barbeau 1915:x, 181, fn7 and 190 fn 1, even though he earlier had a Large Turtle name (Barbeau 1911:2). Name also given in Connelley 1900:112.

56. Barbeau 1911:31.

57. Toupin 1996:235 and 261.

58. The usual form this noun root takes is -akw-, but with the -o- following, the -w- is dropped.

Hakyędase[59]
[hah-kyen-dah-seh]
    h-   masculine singular agent – he
    -aky-   semi-reflexive voice
    -ęd-   noun root – bow
    -ase   verb root – be new + stative aspect

He has a new bow. (male Wolf)

Hamęndandinyǫt[60] His word, voice is hanging, suspended. (male Wolf)
[hah-men-dan-deen-yont]
    ha-   masculine singular agent – he
    -męnd-   noun root – word, voice
    -a-   joiner vowel
    -ndinyǫt   verb root – hang, be suspended + stative aspect

Hamęndarakyes[61]
[hah-men-dah-rah-kyes]
    ha-   masculine singular agent – he
    -męnd-   noun root – word, voice
    -a-   joiner vowel
    -ra-   verb root – be with + stative aspect
    -kye-   progressive root suffix
    -s   habitual aspect

He often goes about talking. (male Bear)

Hamęndašen[62]
[ha-men-dah-sen]
    ha-   masculine singular agent – he
    -męnd-   noun root – voice, word
    -a-   joiner vowel
    -šęn   verb root – be bad + stative aspect

His voice is, his words are bad. (male)

59. Toupin 1996:822 and 826 akiendase, 861, 866 and 876 atiendase, 865 hatiendase. While this looks like the hati- form used for the masculine plural agent, there are no other examples of that pronominal prefix in any other name

60. Toupin 1996:218, 251, 821 and 826 and Barbeau 1915:65 fn 4, 194 fn 1 (Joseph Williams) and 215 fn 5. The Wendat version of this name is "a8a8endadiont Sa voix est suspendue aux lèvres [His voice is suspended on the lips] (Vincent 1984:461).

61. Toupin 1996:196, 205, 851 and 976.

62. Toupin 1996:902.

Hamętaweti[63]
[hah-men-tah-weh-tee]

ham-	masculine singular patient – he
-ęt-	noun root – day
-a-	joiner vowel
-we-	verb root – be together
-t-	causative root suffix
-i	stative aspect

He has all the days. (male)

Hahmęyarǫngya?[64]
[hah-men-yah-ron-yah-ah]

He often makes, works with boards, worked wood. (male occupational name)

ha-	masculine singular agent – he
-hmęyar-	noun root – worked wood
-ǫngy-	verb root – make
-a?	habitual aspect

Handakǫngya?[65]
[han-dah-kon-ngyah-ah]

He often makes barrels, is a barrel maker. (male occupational name)

ha-	masculine singular agent – he
-ndak-	noun root – barrel, drum
-ǫngy-	verb root – make
-a?	habitual aspect

Handareywę[66]

He is living large, putting a lot into life. (male Wolf)

ha-	masculine singular agent – he
-ndare-	verb root – dwell, live, exist + stative aspect
=ywę	augmentative clitic

Handawižu?[67]
[han-dah-wee-zhoo-oo]

He is a large river. (male)

ha-	masculine singular agent – he
-ndaw-	noun root – river
-ižu-	verb root – be large, great
-?	stative aspect

63. Toupin 1996:896, as ha8ointa8eti. The noun root could also be -hwęt- 'small fish', but it is less likely. There is also a man's name ha8oinsa8eti, which could be a miswriting of the same name (Toupin 1996:903).

64. Toupin 1996:235 and 955.

65. Toupin 1996:235 and 262.

66. Toupin 1996:220 and 865 as "andareï8oin".

67. Finley 1840:428, Toupin 1996:867, 869, 871, 878, 929, 944 and 947.

Handataes[68]	He often hits, strikes a village (male Porcupine)
[han-dah-tah-ehs]	
ha-	masculine singular agent – he
-ndat-	noun root – village
-ae-	verb root – hit, strike
-s	habitual aspect

Handataroyẹh[69]	He hears or is listening to a village. (male)
[han-dah-tah-ron-yenh]	
ha-	masculine singular agent – he
-ndat-	noun root – village, community
-aroy-	verb root – listen, hear
-ẹh	stative aspect

Handaʔarẹnhaoh[70]	He is bringing, carrying antlers, horns. (male)
[han-dah-ah-ren-hah-onh]	
ha-	masculine singular agent – he
-ndaʔar-	noun root – antler(s), horn(s)
-ẹnhao	verb root – carry
-h	stative aspect

(i)Handehwatiri[71]	He is supported by pelts. (male Deer[72])
[han-deh-wah-tee-ree]	
-(i)-	partitive
ha-	masculine singular agent – he
-ndehw-	noun root – pelt
-atiri	verb root – support + stative aspect

Handeretsi[73]	He has a long waist, torso. (nickname for Frenchman)
[han-deh-reh-tsee]	
ha-	masculine singular agent – he
-nder-	noun root – waist, torso
-ets-	verb root – be long
-i	stative aspect

68. Barbeau 1915:x, 127 fn1 and 175 fn1 and Toupin 1996:184, 185, 205, 207, 242–3, 834–5, 839, 841, 845, 849, 851, 854 and 856.

69. Toupin 1996:888

70. Barbeau 1911:10.

71. Toupin 1996:836, 894, 949, 963 and 966 as nde8atiri and 955 as ihande8atiri. It is shared by the Wendat.

72. Connelley 1881:60 has a male Deer name as "De-wa-tí-re *(Lean Deer)*."

73. Toupin 1996:235 and 262).

Handetanyǫ[74] He is arriving in the pines. (male)
[han-deh-tah-nyon]
    ha- masculine singular agent – he
    -ndet- noun root – pine
    -a- joiner vowel
    -nyǫ verb root – arrive + stative aspect

Handutǫ[75] He is standing up many arrows (quills). (male Porcupine)
[han-doo-ton]
    ha- masculine singular agent – he
    -nd- noun root – arrow
    -ut- verb root – stand
    -ǫ distributive root suffix + stative aspect

Handišayęžat[76] He is at the top of the ice. (male)
[han-dee-shah-yen-zhat]
    ha- masculine singular agent – he
    -ndiš- noun root – ice
    -a- joiner vowel
    -yęžat verb root – be at the top + stative aspect

Handurǫh[77] He is valuable, difficult. (male)
[han-doo-ronh]
    ha- masculine singular agent – he
    -ndurǫ- verb root – be valuable, difficult
    -h stative aspect.

Handusture[78] He is covered with scabs, calluses. (nickname for Frenchman)
[han-doo-stoo-reh]
    ha- masculine singular agent – he
    -ndust- noun root – scabs, calluses
    -ure verb root – cover, be covered + stative aspect

74. Toupin 1996:234 as handetanion and 262 as endetanion). See Chapter seven.

75. Powell 1881:60 "Ha-dú-tu *(The one who puts up Quills)*". Toupin 1996:847, and 868–9. This may be the male Porcupine clan name presented in Connelley 1900:110 as "Ohn-dŏŏh'-tŏŏh".

76. Toupin 1996:900.

77. This is presented in the Treaty of 1818 as "Hawdoro, or Matthews."

78. Toupin 1996:234 and 262.

Handušrara[279]	He has a shell on top. (male Striped Turtle)
[ha-ndoo-shrah-rah-ah]	
ha-	masculine singular agent – he
-ndušr-	noun root – shell
-a-	joiner vowel
-ra-	verb root – be on top
-ʔ	stative aspect
Handutǫk[80]	He often tells, recounts a story. (male)
[han-doo-tonk]	
ha-	masculine singular agent – he
-ndutǫ[81]-	verb root – tell, recount a story
-k	habitual aspect
Hanęhasa[82]	He has little corn. (male Prairie Turtle)
[ha-nen-hah-sah]	
ha-	masculine singular agent – he
-nęh-	noun root – corn
-a-	verb root – be a size
-sa	stative aspect + diminutive aspect suffix
Hanęhanyǫ[783]	Corn often arrives for him. (male)
[ha-nen-hah-nyon-on]	
ha-	masculine singular agent – him
-nęh-	noun root – corn
-a-	joiner vowel
-nyǫ-	verb root – arrive
-ʔ	habitual aspect

79. Barbeau 1911:4 and 30.

80. Toupin 1996:896 as and8ton and hand8tonk.

81. Potier wrote that the -ǫ- only appears when the verb root incorporates a noun root, but that seems to be contradicted here (Potier 1920:297).

82. Toupin 1996:185, 190–1, 207, 215–6, 229, 238, 243, 250 and 907. His name was also given in French. He could be the speaker at the Grand Council in Detroit with William Johnson, September 9, 1761, the name written as Anáiásá (Curnoe 1996:5). He was a clan elder in 1747, the first one mentioned (Toupin 1996:229).

83. Toupin 1996:891.

Hąnęhurak[84]
[han-nen-hoo-rak]

    yą-

He is intact or whole corn. (male)

    yą-   masculine singular agent – he
    -nęh-   noun root – corn
    -urak   verb root – be entire, intact + stative aspect

Hanękinyǫndih[85]
[ha-nen-kee-nyon-deeh]

He is an evergreen sticking out. (male)

    ha-   masculine singular agent – he
    -nęk-   noun root – evergreen
    -inyǫndi-   verb root – stick out
    -h   stative aspect

Hanęraęha'[86]
[ha-nen-rah-en-hah-ah]

He used to put a group in a place. (male)

    ha-   masculine singular agent – he
    -nęr-   noun root – group
    -a-   joiner vowel
    -ę-   verb root – put, place
    -ha-   habitual aspect
    -'   past aspect suffix

Hanęrayęžat[87]
[ha-nen-rah-en-zhat]

He is at the top of the group. (male)

    ha-   masculine singular agent – he
    -nęr-   noun root – group
    -a-   joiner vowel
    -yęžat   verb root – be at the top + stative aspect

Hangyarutah[88]
[han-gyah-roo-tah]

His tail repeatedly stands. (male Deer)

    ha-   masculine singular aspect – he, his
    -ngyar-   noun root – tail
    -ut-   verb root – stand
    -ah   habitual aspect – often

---

84. Toupin 1996:858.

85. Toupin 1996:868. In the first half of the 17th century it was a name held by a leading figure of the Bear nation of the Wendat (JR10:230–1, 280–1, and 13:168–9).

86. Toupin 1996:840.

87. Toupin 1996:800, 887, 947, 949 and 954.

88. Connelley 1900:109.

Hangyayẹhwi[89]
[han-gyah-yen-hwee]
    ha-   masculine singular agent – he
    -ngy-   noun root – finger, fingers
    -a-   joiner vowel
    -yenhw-   verb root – clean off
    -i   stative aspect

He is cleaning off his fingers. (male Striped Turtle)

Hangyaruwanẹh[90]
[han-gyeh-roo-wan-nenh]
    ha-   masculine singular agent – he
    -ngyar-   noun root – neck
    -uwanẹ-   verb root – be large
    -h   stative aspect

He has a large neck. (male nickname)

Hannariskwa[91]
[han-naah-ree-skwah]
    ha-   masculine singular agent - he
    -nna-   noun root – bone(s)
    -a-   joiner vowel
    -ri-   verb root – chew
    -s-   habitual aspect
    -kwa   past aspect suffix

He is a wolf (he often used to chew bones). (male Wolf)

Hanẹranyọ[92]
[hah-nen-rah-nyon]
    ha-   masculine singular agent – he
    -nẹr-   noun root – group, raiding party
    -a-   joiner vowel
    -nyọ   verb root – arrive + stative aspect

He is arriving in a group. (male)

Hanọngyahak[93]
[ha-non-gyah-hak]
    ha-   masculine singular agent – he
    -n-   noun root – arrow
    -ọngy-   verb root – make
    -a-   habitual aspect
    -hak   past aspect suffix

He used to make arrows. (male)

89. Toupin 1996:244, 837, 839, 868, 884, 922 and 926

90. Connelley 1900:111. This refers to the Rev. James B. Findley.

91. Toupin 1996:881 as hannâriskwa and 907 and 932 as narisk8a. Frenchmen named La Mothe and Blondeau were given this name (Toupin 1996:235).

92. Toupin 1996:901.

93. Toupin 1996:865 as hannonngiak and 875 as hannonngiahak.

Hanǫšanǫ[794]
[ha-non-sha-non-on]
    ha-   masculine singular agent – he
    -nǫš-   noun root – house
    -a-   joiner vowel
    -nǫ-   verb root – guard, protect
    -ʔ   habitual aspect

He guards the house (male)

Hanǫšǫngya[795]
[ha-non-shon-gyah-ah]
    ha-   masculine singular agent – he
    -nǫš-   noun root – house
    -ǫngy-   verb root – make
    -aʔ   habitual aspect

He often makes, builds houses. (male occupational name)

Hanyędase[96]
[ha-nyen-dah-seh]
    ha-   masculine singular agent – he
    -nyęd-   noun root – skill, ability, way of doing things.
    -ase   verb root – be new + stative aspect

He has a new skill, ability, a new way of doing things. (male)

Haǫdešǫkye[97]
[ha-on-deh-shron-kyee]
    ha-   masculine singular patient – he
    -ǫde-   verb root – have as country
    -š-   nominalizer
    -ǫnky   verb root – abandon
    -e   purposive aspect

He is going to abandon the country. (male Deer)

94. Toupin 1996:211 and 224 (beginning with o-), 842–3 (beginning with e-) and 862 and 943 (beginning with h-).

95. The Wyandot name for Frenchman Pierre Meloche (Toupin 1996:235), who built houses (Lajeunesse 1960:30).

96. Toupin 1996:851 haiendase.

97. Toupin 1996:213 hondechonti, 247 and 253 dechonti 655, 930, and 954 haondechonti, 823, 826, 831, 840–1, and 850 ondechonti, 849 aondechontie, 865 desontkie, 872 desontie, and 929 hondesontie.

Haǫmętsayarha[98]
[hah-on-men-tsah-yar-hah]
    ha-   He often makes noise in the land. (male Bear)

ha-	masculine singular patient - he
-ǫmęts-	noun root – earth, land
-a-	joiner vowel
-yar-	verb root – make noise
-ha	habitual aspect

Haǫmętsiayih[99]
[ha-on-hwen-tsee-ah-yeeh]   He is cutting across the earth, land. (male)

ha-	masculine singular patient – he
-ǫmęts-	noun root – earth, land
-iay-	verb root – cut
-ih	stative aspect

Haǫmętsižuh[100]
[hah-on-men-tsee-zhooh]   He is or has a large land, country. (male)

ha-	masculine singular patient – he
-ǫmęts-	noun root – land
-ižu-	verb root – be large, great
-h	stative aspect

Haręhaęžat[101]
[hah-ren-hah-en-zhat]   He is at the top of the treetops. (male)

ha-	masculine singular agent – he
-ręh-	noun root – treetops
-a-	joiner vowel
-ęžhat	verb root – be at the top of + stative aspect

Haręhatase'[102]
[ha-ren-hah-tah-seh-eh]   He is going around a branch. (male Large Turtle).

ha-	masculine singular agent – he
-ręh-	noun root – branch, treetops
-a-	joiner vowel
-tase-	verb root – twist, turn
-'	stative aspect

---

98. Toupin 1966:196, 865, 872, 876, 928, 944 and 976.

99. Toupin 1996:872, 942, 949, 952–4.

100. Toupin 1996:220 and 887.

101. Toupin 1996:960.

102. Barbeau 1911:3 and 49 and Toupin 1996:974.

Haręnhut[103]	He is or has a standing treetop or branch. (male)
[hah-ren-hoot]	
ha-	masculine singular agent – he
-ręnh-	noun root – treetops, branch
-ut	verb root – stand + stative aspect

Haręhutǫn[104]	He is many standing treetops, branches. (male Large Turtle)
[ha-ren-hoo-ton]	
ha-	masculine singular agent – he
-ręh-	noun root – treetops
-ǫn	distributive root suffix + stative aspect

Haręhužah[105]	He moves, shakes the treetops. (male Porcupine)
[hah-ren-hoo-zhah]	
ha-	masculine singular agent – he
-ręh-	noun root – treetops, branches
-už-	verb root – move, shake
-ah	habitual aspect

Harihǫtawan[106]	He is deposing her, it of a position, status. (male)
[hah-ree-hon-tah-wan]	
ha-	masculine singular agent – he + feminine-zoic singular patient – she, it
-rih-	noun root – matter
-ǫt-	verb root – attached, be attached
-awa-	undoer root suffix
-n	stative aspect

Harihužah[107]	He stirs up matters (e.g., is quarrelsome) (male Striped Turtle)
[hah-ree-hoo-zhah]	
ha-	masculine singular agent – he
-rih-	noun root – matter, affair, news
-už-	verb root – stir up
-ah	habitual aspect

103. Barbeau 1915:4, and Jeremy Turner (https://www.wyandotte-nation.org/traditions/biographical-panels/smith-nichols/).

104. Toupin 1996:193, 218, 251, 847, 944, 958 and 960.

105. Connelley 1900:110 fn. 12. He refers to it as relating to the porcupine pulling down branches and nipping at the buds and bark.

106. Toupin 1996:898 as harihonton8a. The second -on- does not seem possible to me.

107. Barbeau 1911:5.

Hariwae[108]
[hah-ree-wah-eh]
- ha- — masculine singular agent – he
- -riw- — noun root – matter, affair
- -ae — verb root – hit, strike + stative aspect

He is hitting striking a matter. (male)

Hariwaerǫ[109]
[hah-ree-wah-eh-ron]
- ha- — masculine singular agent – he
- -riw- — noun root – matter, affair
- -erǫ — verb root – trick, do wrong + stative aspect

He is tricking in a matter. (male)

Hariwakyǫditi[110]
[hah-ree-wah-kyon-dee-tee]
- ha- — masculine singular agent – he
- -riw- — noun root – matter, news, affair
- -akyondit- — verb root – take something away
- -i — stative aspect

He is saying or doing something surprising. (male)

Hariwandinyǫtak[111]
[hah-ree-wan-deen-yon-tak]
- ha- — masculine singular agent – he
- -riw- — noun root – matter, affair, news
- -ndinyǫt- — verb root – suspend, hang
- -a- — habitual aspect
- -k — past aspect suffix

He used to suspend matters. (male Striped Turtle)

Hariwandutǫ[112]
[hah-ree-wan-doo-ton]
- ha- — masculine singular agent - he
- -riw- — noun root – matter, affair
- -a- — joiner vowel
- -ndutǫ — verb root – to tell + stative aspect

He is telling about a matter, affair. (male)

---

108. Toupin 1996:894.

109. Toupin 1996:872, 878, 887 and 892. Barbeau 1915:139 fn 2 presents the name for James Armstrong as "hariwakyǫnde?." In another reference (Barbeau 1915:152 fn 1, he has it end with an -i-.

110. This appears as "harih8ationdi" in Toupin 1996:827, 830, 836, 925 and 926, but as ,arih8atkiondi on 909, reflecting Potier's added -ky- Wyandot form.

111. Toupin 1996:189, 201, 214, 229, 239, 832, 837, 841. 843, 855 and 858.

112. Toupin 1996:885, 894, 896-7, 934, 942, 947, 954, 962, 970, 973-5.

Hariwawayi[113] He holds, grasps the matter. (male Bear)
[hah-ree-wah-wah-yee]

    ha- masculine singular agent – he
    -riw- noun root – matter, law
    -a- joiner vowel
    -way- verb root – take, hold
    -i stative aspect

Harǫtwanęh[114] He is a large tree. (male)
[hah-ront-wah-nenh]

    ha- masculine singular agent – he
    -rǫt- noun root – tree, pole, log
    -wanę- verb root – be large
    -h stative aspect

Harǫyateka[115] He often burns the sky. (male possible Deer)
[hah-ron-yah-teh-kah]

    ha- masculine singular agent – he
    -rǫy- noun root – sky
    -atek- verb root – burn
    -a habitual aspect

Harǫyayęs[116] He often goes out of the sky. (male)
[hah-ron-yah-yens]

    ha- masculine singular agent - he
    -rǫy- noun root – sky
    -ayę- verb root – go out + inchoative root suffix
    -s habitual aspect

---

113. Toupin 1996:214 and 248, Connelley 1900:111, 44 and Finley 1840:38. See discussion in chapter seven.

114. Toupin 1996:889. This is cognate with an Oneida term for an individual Oneida.

115. This name first appears in 1701 with the "chef du sault", referring to the Michilimackinac area where the Wyandot were living (Havard 2001:117 and 214 and Vincent 1984:141). He signed the agreement of the Great Peace of 1701 with what looks like a deer (217). It is next found in the 1730s with someone called Martin, baptized in 1734 and the father of a baptized child in 1736 and 1739 (Toupin 1996:836, 841 and 846). This name is shared with the Wendat and the Mohawk. See chapter six.

116. Toupin 1996:886.

Haroya'es[117]   He often strikes the sky. (male Large Turtle)
[ha-ron-nyah-ah-es]

- ha- — masculine singular agent - he
- -roy- — noun root – sky
- -a'e- — verb root – strike, hit
- -s — habitual

Haroyaweyih[118]   He is closing the sky. (probably male)
[hah-ron-nyah-weh-yeeh]

- ha- — masculine singular agent – he
- -roy- — noun root – sky
- -a- — joiner vowel
- -wey- — verb root – close
- -ih — stative aspect

Haroyieht[119]   He scrapes or scratches the sky. (male).
[hah-ron-yee-eht]

- ha- — masculine singular agent – he
- -roy- — noun root – sky
- -ieht — verb root – scrape + stative aspect

Haroyokyes[120]   He often leaves, abandons the sky. (male)
[hah-ron-nyon-kyes]

- ha- — masculine singular agent – he
- -roy- — noun root – sky
- -oky- — verb root – abandon, quit
- -es — habitual aspect

Haroyu'[121]   He is sky in the water, on top of the water. (male Wolf)

- ha- — masculine singular agent – he
- -roy- — noun root – sky
- -u- — verb root – be in water
- -' — stative aspect

117. Sallie Cotter Andrews, "Nicholas Cotter." He was born in the Detroit/Windsor area (1822–1887), and became chief. His name was written as Rhon-yan-ness in Finley 1840:41 and as Ron-nyan-es in. (https://www.wyandotte-nation.org/culture/history/biographies/nicholas-cotter/)

118. Toupin 1996:886. In his name index on page 1248, Toupin claimed that the individual was the "marraine" or godmother, but that was not true.

119. Toupin 1996:901.

120. Toupin 1996:878. Of the nearly identical verb roots 'to abandon' and 'to continue' I chose the former as it takes the right habitual, and because the latter often involves the dualic (Potier 1920:424–5).

121. Barbeau 1911:31, 1915:x. Connelley 1900:113 said that the meaning was lost. Powell 1881:60 said that it meant "One who goes about in the Dark; a Prowler)."

Haskǫšetsi[122]
[hah-skon-sheh-tsee]
    ha-   masculine singular agent – he
    -skǫš-   noun root – tooth
    -ets-   verb root – be long
    -i   stative aspect

He has long teeth. (a nickname for a particular Frenchman)

Haskutaše[123]
[hah-skoo-tash-eh]
    ha-   masculine singular agent – he
    -skut-   noun root – skull
    -a-   verb root – be a size
    -š-   dislocative root suffix
    -e   purposive aspect

He is going to have a skull of such a size. (male Porcupine)

Hahšęndaseh[124]
[hah-shen-dah-she]
    ha-   masculine singular agent – he
    -hšęnd-   noun root – name
    -ase-   verb root – be new
    -h   stative aspect

He has a new name. (male)

Hašęnduwanęh[125]
[hah-shen-oo-wah-nenh]
    ha-   masculine singular agent – he
    -šęnd-   noun root – name
    -uwanę-   verb root – be large, great
    -h   stative aspect

He has a great name, is a notable (male)

Hahšitrah[126]
    h-   masculine singular agent – his
    -ahšit--   noun root – foot
    -ra-   verb root – represent
    -h   stative aspect

He has a footprint, paw print. (male Wolf)

122. Toupin 1996:235 and 262.

123. Barbeau 1911:44 for William Driver Jr., Buser 1989, Clarke 1870:55 fn, Finley 1840:99, NYCD9:274 and 293, 10:156-7. Toupin 1996:173, 183–4, 200, 204, 238, 241, 824, 833, 838, 844–5, 850, 853, 857 as "sk8tache", 939 (as sCoutaChe), and 941 (as sCoutak). The baptisms 1539 and 1540 cannot be found. In Barbeau 1915:x he has the one with the name as Allen Johnson—Catherine Johnson's husband and a Large Turtle.

124. Toupin 1996:832 in 1732 and 973 in 1771. This name is shared with the Wendat, Mohawk and with the Jesuits.

125. Toupin 1996:233 and possibly 884. See discussion in chapter seven.

126. Barbeau 1915:271 fn 3. Connelley 1900:35 and 110.

Hašras	He often spills, overflows[127]. (male Large Turtle)
[hash-rahs]	
ha-	masculine singular agent – he
-šra-	verb root – overflow, leak, spill
-s	habitual aspect

Hašrayetak[128]	He used to bear an axe (on a strap). (male)
[hah-shra-yeh-tak]	
h-	masculine singular agent – he
-ašr-	noun root – axe
-a-	joiner vowel
-yet-	verb root – bear on a strap
-a-	habitual aspect
-k	past aspect suffix

Hašręhaǫh[129]	He is carrying an axe. (male Snake)
[hah-shren-hah-onh]	
h-	masculine singular agent – he
-ašr-	noun root – axe
-ęhaǫ-	verb root – carry
-h	stative aspect

Hašrǫnęta[130]	He often drops an axe. (male)
[ha-shron-nentah]	
h-	masculine singular agent – he
-ašr-	noun root – axe
-ǫnęt-	verb root – drop
-a	habitual aspect

Hatetsęs[131]	He heals, cures, is a doctor. (male name for a doctor)
[hah-teh-tsens]	
h-	masculine singular agent – he
-ate-	semi-reflexive voice
-tsę-	verb root – heal, doctor
-s	habitual aspect

127. Connelley presents this as "Hah-shah'-rehs", said by him to mean "overfull," and referring to a stream "overflowing its banks at flood" (Connelley 1900:36 and 111). This may well be a nickname for Governor William Walker, as he had another name, and Barbeau 1911:1 has euʔris as "spilling (something)."

128. Toupin 1996: 830, 882, 888, 890 and 893

129. Potier 1920:148, and Toupin 1996:203

130. Toupin 1996:893

131. Toupin 1996:235 and 262.

Hatirǫta[132]   He draws, attracts. (male Deer)
[hah-tee-ron-tah]
    h-   masculine singular agent – he
    -atirǫta-   verb root – draw, attract, pull out + stative aspect

Hatrewatih[133]   He opposes, resists, criticizes it. (male Snake)
[hah-treh-wah-teeh]
    h-   masculine singular agent – he
    -at-   semi-reflexive voice
    -rewat-   verb root – act, speak against
    -ih   stative aspect

Hatsihęstayęrǫh[134]   He has little or bad charcoal, or gunpowder (male)
[hah-tsee-hen-stah-yen-ronh]
    ha-   masculine singular agent – he
    -tsihęst-   noun root – charcoal, gun powder
    -a-   joiner vowel
    -yęrǫ-   verb root – be mediocre, insufficient
    -h   stative aspect

Hatsistayęrǫh[135]   He is or has an insignificant, mediocre fire (male)
[ha-tsee-stah-yen-ronh]
    ha-   masculine singular agent – he
    -tsist-   noun root – fire
    -yęrǫ   verb root – be insignificant
    -h   stative aspect

132. Toupin 1996:182, 195, 221, 225, 254, 258, 833, 849, 851, 854, 859, 862, 873, 923, 925, 928, 936 (as thironta) ,940, 942, and 978.

133. Toupin 1996:206 and 868 as hatre8ati, 211 and 859 as atre8ati, and 855 and 863 as otre8ati (in the father's position in the baptismal record). A French Jesuit priest by the name of Salleneuve shared this name (Toupin 1996:236). So did an Onondaga chief Houtreouati (usually written as Oretouti) of the second half of the 17th century (Grassman http://www.biographi.ca/en/bio/otreouti_1E.html).

134. Toupin 1996:889 and 898. It is tempting to say that this is a nickname, but I cannot be sure if it is.

135. Toupin 1996:891.

Hawęndayehte?[136]	He bears an island. (male Large Turtle)
[ha-wen-dah-yeh-teh-eh]	
ha-	masculine singular agent – he
-węnd-	noun root – island
-a-	joiner vowel
-yehte-	verb root – bear on a strap around the neck, shoulder
-ʔ	stative aspect

Hažatǫh[137]	He marks, writes. (male Deer)
[hah-zhah-tonh]	
ha-	masculine singular agent – he
-žatǫ-	verb root – mark, write
-h	habitual aspect – often

Hętaras[138]	He lays down often. (male)
[hen-tah-ras]	
h-	masculine singular agent – he
-ętara-	verb root – lay down, go to bed
-s	habitual aspect

Hętarǫmą[139]	Days are disappearing for him. (male Large Turtle)
[en-tah-ron-wan]	
h-	masculine singular agent – he
-ęt-	noun root – day
-a-	joiner vowel
-r-	verb root – be with
-ǫ-	distributive root suffix
-mą	undoer root suffix + stative aspect

Hǫkǫšaę[140]	They (m) are placing, putting their faces. (male)
[hon-kon-shah-en]	
hǫ-	masculine plural agent – they (m)
-k-	semi-reflexive voice

136. Barbeau 1911:3, 10 and 49, and 1915:xii (and Toupin 1996:235(?)—page number is faulty).

137. Barbeau 1915:xi had the name belonging to the "nearly extinct Snipe clan. Connelley 1900:109 fn30: "He marks, i.e., the big buck comes to the mark to meet all comers of his kind of whatever number or size." Potier refers to someone with h8nda 'she is his spouse' after the name (Toupin 1996:963), meaning she was the wife of Hahiatonk, possibly the Frenchman Robert Navarre (Toupin 1996:235). There is a cognate name in Wendat (Vincent 1984;335).

138. Toupin 1996:209.

139. Toupin 1996:207, 243, 869–70, 891, and 922 as entaron8oin, 872 as entaren8an, 910 as entaron8a, 881 as hontaron8oin, 944 as hontaren8oin and 894 as haentaron8oin.

140. Toupin 1996:874.

-ǫš-	noun root – face
-a-	joiner vowel
-ę	verb root – put + stative aspect

Hǫmamęnǫkyǫ[141]
[hon-mah-men-non-kyon]	They are disobeying or rejecting his word. (male)

    hǫma-	masculine plural or feminine-zoic plural agent + masculine singular patient – they – him

    -męn-	noun root – word, voice

    -ǫky-	verb root – abandon

    -ǫ	stative aspect

Hǫmanǫhweh[142]
[hon-ma-non-hweh]	They (masculine or feminine) love, like him. (female)

    hǫma-	masculine plural or feminine-zoic plural agent + masculine singular patient – they (m or f) – him

    -nǫhwe-	verb root – like, love

    -h	stative aspect

Hǫmaskąṭha[143]
[hon-nah-skant-hah]	They (f) often desire him. (male)

    hǫn-	feminine-zoic plural agent + masculine singular patient – they – him

    -askąt-	verb root – desire passionately

    -ha	habitual aspect

Hǫndakǫnya'[144]
[hon-dah-kon-yah-ah]	He makes, works with barrels, drums. (male, nickname)

    hǫ-	masculine singular patient – he

    -ndak-	noun root – barrel, drum

    -ǫny-	verb root – make

    -a'	habitual aspect

---

141. Toupin 1996:882. The verb 'continue' takes the same form here, but 'abandon' is in Potier's dictionary as incorporating this noun and 'continue' does not (Potier 1920:424–50).

142. Toupin 1996:877 three times in 1758, 879 and 952.

143. Toupin 1996:872 as honaskannha. Strangely the one Wyandot example takes a Wendat form. The Wyandot form has the -t- marked as a superscript (Potier 1920:177).

144. Toupin 1996:951 as hondak8oinniak h8nda (referring to his wife), and 952 and 972 hondakonniak. An almost identical name, Handakǫnya' referred to a Frenchman in Detroit in 1752 (Toupin 1996:235 and 262).

Hǫndawatǫt[145]
[hon-dah-wah-tont]
    hǫ-   masculine singular patient – he
    -ndaw-   noun root – river
    -a-   joiner vowel
    -tǫt-   verb root – put in mouth + stative aspect

He has or is putting a river in his mouth. (male Deer)

Hǫnduyarha[146]
[hon-doo-yah-rha]
    hǫ-   masculine singular patient
    -nduyar-   noun root – poplar
    -ha   noun suffix

His poplar (male)

Hǫndeskǫtakwi[147]
[hon-dehs-kon-tah-kwee]
    hǫn-   masculine singular patient – he
    -ndes-   noun root – sand
    -kǫt-   verb root – face
    -akw-   instrumental root suffix
    -i   stative aspect

He is turning to face the sand in such a place. (male)

Hǫndikakǫ[148] ižuh
Hǫndikakǫ
[hon-dee-kah-kon]
    hǫndikakǫ   They (m) were seized by the cold.
    hǫnd-   masculine plural patient – they (m)
    -ikakǫ   verb root – be seized by the cold + stative aspect

It is like they (m) are being seized by the cold.

Ižuh
[ee-zhooh]

It is like

---

145. Toupin 1996:880, 882, 884, 886, 889–90, 892, 906, 922, 945, 961, 966–7, 969, and 972. It appears in the 19th century as Dawatout, or John Hicks in the land grant section of the Treaty of 1817, Hicks again, as Danwawtout in the Treaty of 1836.

146. Toupin 1996:904.

147. Toupin 1996:889 as ondeskontak8i. The -sh- that ends the noun root 'sand' turns to -s- and the -y- of the beginning of the verb root turns to -k- when the two come together. Despite the name beginning with the feminine-zoic singular patient, Toupin notes the individual was a godfather in this baptism.

148. Toupin 1996:966.

Hǫnduyętet[149]	He is … (male – Large Turtle)
[hon-doo-yen-tet]	
hǫ-	masculine singular patient – he
-ndu	??? noun root – ?
-?? ętet	verb root – ? + stative aspect

Hǫnearižu[150]	He is striking, beating a bone. (male)
[hon-neh-ah-ree-zhoo]	
hǫ-	masculine singular patient – he
-ne-	noun root – bone
-a-	joiner vowel
-rižu	verb root – to beat, fight + stative aspect

Hǫnęrawi[151]	He is giving him his group. (male)
[hon-en-rah-wee]	
hǫ-	masculine singular agent + masculine singular patient – he – him
-nęr-	noun root – group, raiding party
-aw-	verb root – give
-i	stative aspect

Hǫngwatǫnyaʔ[152]	He makes, works with white clay. (male occupational name)
[hon-gwah-ton-yah-ah]	
hǫ-	masculine singular patient - he
-ngwat-	noun root – white clay
-ǫngy-	verb root – make
-aʔ	habitual aspect

149. See discussion in chapter nine.

150. There are problems with translating this name. I have seen no other example of this verb root incorporating a noun root. It would make sense if this were 'He is chewing a bone," with the verb root -riy-, which appears in the word for wolf. Of the six instances I have encountered of this name, one (Toupin 1996:834) has a form, "honnearij" which is compatible with such a hypothesis. However, all the other four end with -io-, which becomes -ižu- in 19th-century Wyandot. Toupin 1996:827 as nneario, 834–6, 842 (a possible at annario), and 843–4.

151. Toupin 1996:879. The group could be an armed one. There is also the possibility that the nasal vowel should be -ǫ- rather than -ę- and the noun root means 'scalp'.

152. Lajeuness 1960:30 and Toupin 1996:235. It refers to doing mason work.

Hǫnǫrateyatha[153] He causes scalps to burn. (male)
[hon-on-rah-teh-yah-thah]
    hǫ- masculine singular patient – he
    -nǫr- noun root – scalp
    -atey- verb root – burn
    -at- causative root suffix
    -ha habitual aspect

Hǫnǫraweǫt[154] He had a bump or bulge on his scalp. (male Deer)
[hon-on-rah-weh-ont] (said of a buck fawn)
    hǫ- masculine singular patient – he
    -nǫr- noun root – scalp
    -aw- joiner vowel
    -eǫt verb root – have a bump or bulge + stative aspect

Hǫnǫrẹhawit[155] He is going to carry his scalp. (male)
[hon-non-ren-hah-weet]
    hǫ- masculine singular agent + masculine singular patient – he - his
    -nǫr- noun root – scalp
    -ẹhaw- verb root – carry
    -it purposive aspect

Hǫnǫste[156] He is stingy. (nickname for a Frenchman[157])
[hon-non-steh]
    hǫ- masculine singular patient – he
    -nǫste verb root – be stingy + stative aspect

Hǫnǫšieht[158] He is scraping a house. (male)
[hon-non-shee-eht]
    hǫ- masculine singular patient – he
    -nǫš- noun root – house
    -ieht verb root – scrape, scratch + stative aspect

---

153. Toupin 1996:866, 868, 872, 884 and 960.

154. Toupin 1996:855, Finley 1840:31 states that "Lump-on-the head" is a Deer clan name, "denoting a buck fawn."

155. Toupin 1996:874.

156. Toupin 1996:262.

157. His name was Deruisseau and he lived in Detroit in the mid-18th century.

158. Toupin 1996:882 as Honnonchie′t and p38 as ononchiet.

Hǫnǫtara[159] He is on top of the hill, mountain. (male)
[hon-non-tah-rah]
    hǫ-　　　　　masculine singular patient – he
    -nǫt-　　　　noun root – hill, mountain
    -a-　　　　　joiner vowel
    -ra　　　　　verb root – be on top of + stative aspect

Huaʔtatiri[160] She or it is supporting him, his body. (male)
[hoo-ah-ah-ta-tee-ree]
    hu-　　　　　feminine-zoic singular agent + masculine singular patient – she/it – him
    -aʔt-　　　　noun root – body
    -atiri　　　　verb root – support + stative aspect

Hukwęndisatih[161] His voice is knocking on, pressing against it. (male Striped Turtle)
[hoo-kwen-dee-sah-teeh]
    hu-　　　　　masculine singular patient – he, his
    -k-　　　　　semi-reflexive voice
    -węnd-　　　noun root – voice, word
    -is-　　　　　verb root – be up against
    -at-　　　　　causative root suffix
    -ih　　　　　stative aspect

Hukwistǫngyaʔ[162] He often makes metal. (male occupational name – blacksmith)
[hoo-kwee-ston-yah-ah]
    hu-　　　　　masculine singular patient – he
    -k-　　　　　semi-reflexive voice
    -wist-　　　　noun root – metal
    -ǫngy-　　　　verb root – make
    -aʔ　　　　　habitual aspect

Hukwistontata[163] He shakes metal, rings a bell. (male)
[hoo-kwees-ton-tah-tah]
    hu-　　　　　masculine singular patient – he

---

159. Toupin 1996:842.

160. Toupin 1996:878 as hotatiri.

161. Toupin 1996:842, 847, 849, and 854 and Connelley 1900:112: "Married into the tribe and given a Little Turtle name Quehnʔ-deh-sah-k-teh. Means vibrating voice or a voice which goes up and down. The voice intended to be described is the voice of the Little Turtle heard on summer nights." There is a similar looking word for a Large Turtle name recorded by Connelley 1900:113.

162. Toupin 1996:235 and 261. See chapter seven.

163. Toupin 1996:973.

	-k-	semi-reflexive voice
	-wist-	noun root – metal
	-ontat-	verb root – shake
	-a	habitual aspect

Hukyuhkwa?[164]
[hoo-kyooh-kwah-ah]

His group, his crowd, herd (male Deer)

	hu-	masculine singular patient – his
	-kyu-	verb root – be a lineage, clan
	-kw-	nominalizer instrumental root suffix
	-a?	noun suffix

Hukyukwanduro?[165]
[hoo-kyoo-wan-doo-ron-on]

He is of a valuable lineage, group. (male Striped Turtle)

	hu-	masculine singular patient – he
	-kyu-	verb root – be a lineage, clan
	-kw-	nominalizer instrumental root
	-a-	joiner vowel
	-nduro-	verb root – be valuable, difficult
	-?	stative aspect

Humęndanyęto[166]
[hoo-men-dah-nyeh-ton]

She or he is following what he has said. (male Large Turtle)

	hu-	feminine-zoic or masculine singular agent + masculine singular patient – she or he – him
	-męnd-	noun root – word, voice
	-a-	joiner vowel
	-nyęt-	verb root – follow
	-ǫ	stative aspect

Humęndayete[167]
[hoo-wen-dah-yeh-teh]

He bears a word, a voice. (male)

	hu-	masculine singular patient – he
	-męnd-	noun root – word, voice

164. Barbeau 1911:12.

165. Barbeau 1911:30. Toupin 1996:205, 209, 931 and 944 as otiok8endoron, 229 as otiok8andoron, 244 as tiok8oindoron, 260 as hokoinron, 824 as Tiok8oindoron, 825 and 833, as Otiok8andoron, 830 as Entiok8oindoron, 861, 876, 893, 950, 955, 961, 966, 973–5 and 971 as otiok8oindoron, and 963 as otiok8oineron See chapter nine for more references and discussion.

166. Toupin 1996:880 as ha8endanienton, 909 as ha8oindanienton, 910 as ho8oindanienton, 888 as h8andenienton, and 904 and 959 as ondanienton. A different version of the name, beginning with the repetitive -s- 'again' appears once (Toupin 1996:995). It doesn't change the meaning of the name significantly.

167. Toupin 1996:902 and 910.

-a-	joiner vowel
-yete	verb root – bear on a strap over the shoulder or neck + stative aspect

Humęndęnyandi[168]
[hoo-men-den-nyan-dee]   He is surpassing him in voice, word. (male)

hu-	masculine singular agent + masculine singular patient – he – him
-męnd-	noun root – voice, word
-ęnya-	verb root – surpass
-d-	dative root suffix
-i	stative aspect

Hundahšateyę?[169]
[hoon-dah-shah-teh-yen-en]   His tongue is burning. (male Snake)

hu-	masculine singular patient – he
-ndahš-	noun root - tongue
-atey-	verb root – burn
-ę?	stative aspect

[Hu]ndayuraten[170]
[hoon-dah-yoo-rah-ten]   The top of his head is dry (male Large Turtle)

hu-[171]	masculine singular patient – he
-ndayur-	noun root – top of the skull, head
-a-	joiner vowel
-ten	verb root – be dry + stative aspect

Hu'ndažuh[172]
[hoo-oon-dah-zhooh]   An arrow or quill kills him. (male Porcupine)

hu-	feminine-zoic agent and masculine patient – it – him
-'nd-	noun root – arrow
-a-	joiner vowel
-žu-	verb root – kill
-h	stative aspect

168. Toupin 1996:962 as h8endenngiandi.

169. As "ondachiateen" in Potier 1920:148, and Toupin 1996:173, 178, 185, 200, 206, 226, 238, 242 and 260.

170. Toupin 1996:222 as ndaaraton and 832, 892 and 972 as ndaoraten. As the name is Large Turtle clan I felt that 'top of the skull' as represented in the second example is more appropriate than 'antlers' as represented in the first example. Likewise, I thought that -ten- 'be dry' was more appropriate than 'stop' for -ten-.

171. In neither of the two references is there a pronominal prefix, so I added what I believe to be the appropriate one.

172. Barbeau 1915:xi. is This is informant John Kayrahoo's Wyandot name.

Hundešaręmąn[173]	He is floating (in) sand. (male Large Turtle).
[hoon-deh-shah-ren-man]	
hu-	masculine singular patient – he
-ndeš-	noun root – sand
-a-	joiner vowel
-rę-	verb root – be stable
-mą-	undoer root suffix
-n	stative aspect

Hundęngyandi[174]	He, she or it is beating him in battle. (male)
[hoon-den-gyan-dee]	
hu-	masculine/feminine-zoic singular agent
	+ masculine singular patient – (s)he – him
nengy-	verb root – surmount
-and-	dative root suffix
-i	stative aspect

Hunęharahwih[175]	He is turning corn upwards. (male)
[hoo-nen-hah-rah-weeh]	
hu-	masculine singular patient – he
-nęh-	noun root – corn
-ara-	verb root – turn upwards
-hw-	transitional root suffix
-ih	stative aspect

Hungwąnduhrǫʔ[176]	He has difficult rapids. (male Beaver)
[hoon-gwan-dooh-ron-on]	
hu-	masculine singular patient – he
-ngw-	noun root – rapids
-ą-	joiner vowel
-nduhrǫ-	verb root – be difficult or valuable
-ʔ	stative aspect

173. Toupin 1996:193 ("ndechiarenh8i"), 218, 228 ("hondechiaren8an") and 935 ("sarem-moin").

174. Toupin 1996:967 as h8endenngiandi. The first -e- is grammatically unlikely.

175. Toupin 1996:827, 833 and 840.

176. Barbeau 1915:65 fn4. Barbeau gave the meaning of the name as 'he makes a dam'. Maybe a dam was made because of the difficult rapids, and Barbeau did not catch the connection. This word could also have a nasal -ǫ- rather than a -u- as the second letter. A Frenchman with the name of Janis shared this name.

Hunǫmarure?¹⁷⁷	He is covering his head with it. (male Wolf)
[hoo-non-mah-roo-reh-eh]	
hu-	masculine singular patient – he
-nǫmar-	noun root – head, brains
-ure-	verb root – cover
-'	stative aspect
Huręndut¹⁷⁸	He is a standing stone, rock. (male)
[hoo-ren-doot]	
hu-	masculine singular patient – he
-ręnd-	noun root – rock, stone
-ut	verb root – stand + stative aspect
Huriwaętǫk¹⁷⁹	He is dealing with many matters. (male)
[hoo-ree-wah-en-tonk]	
hu-	masculine singular patient – he
-riw-	noun root – matter, affair
-a-	joiner vowel
-ę-	verb root – put
-tǫ-	distributive root suffix
-k	habitual aspect
Huriwahętǫh¹⁸⁰	He is leading in a matter, affair. (male)
[hoo-ree-wah-hen-tonh]	
hu-	masculine singular patient – he
-riw-	noun root – matter, affair
-a-	joiner vowel
-hęt-	verb root – lead, come first
-ǫh	stative aspect
Huriyehte?¹⁸¹	He bears a matter, a position of importance.
[hoo-ree-yeh-teh-eh]	(male Striped Turtle)
hu-	masculine singular patient – he
-ri-	noun root – matter
-yehte-	verb root – bear
-?	stative aspect

177. Barbeau 1911:8.

178. Toupin 1996:223 as oreend8t and 843 as horend8t.

179. Toupin 1996:870 as harih8aenton in 1755 as the father of a baptized girl and 875 as horih8aentonk in 1758.

180. Barbeau 1915:4, as Oriwahento (also Schoolcraft 1875:297–300).

181. Barbeau 1911:40.

The Names of the Wyandot

Huṛǫyaerita?[182]
[hoo-ron-nyah-eh-ree-tah-ah]

The sky used to furnish him with all that was necessary. (male)

    hu-   feminine-zoic singular agent
                     + masculine singular patient – it – him
    -rǫy-   noun root – sky
    -a-   joiner vowel
    -eri-   verb root – complete
    -t-   causative root suffix
    -a-   habitual aspect
    -?   past aspect suffix

Huṛǫyate[183]
[hoo-ron-yah-teh]

The sky is present in him, (male Striped Turtle)

    hu-   masculine singular patient – he
    -rǫy-   noun root – sky
    -a-   joiner vowel
    -te   verb root – exist + stative aspect

Huṛǫyahteywę[184]
[hoo-ron-yah-teh-ywen]

It is a great sky for him, an agreeable sky. (male)

    hu-   masculine singular patient – he
    -rǫy-   noun root – sky
    -ahte-   verb root – exist + stative aspect
    -ywę   augmentative clitic

Huṛǫyayehte[185]
[hoo-ron-yah-yeh-teh]

He bears the sky. (male Wolf)

    hu-   masculine singular patient – he
    -rǫy-   noun root – sky
    -yehte-   verb root – bear on a strap around the neck or shoulder
                     + stative aspect

---

182. Toupin 1996:866 and 872 as horonhiaeritak and 860 as horonhiaerito. The habitual as illustrated for this verb in Potier's dictionary is -s- with the past aspect suffix taking -kwa (Potier 1920:230), otherwise this is the best fit. There is also a form of what appears to be the same verb with horonhiaeri (Toupin 1996:889). It could be a separate name translated as "the sky is furnishing him with everything he needs".

183. Toupin 1996:208, 204, 864, 869–70, 876, 880, 883, 944 and 956 as horonhiate and 829 as aronhiate

184. Toupin 1996:966 as horonhia‘tei8oin. This could be linked with Hutrǫywę.

185. Toupin 1996:843. This was the Wyandot name given to Potier when he was adopted into the Wolf clan (Toupin 1996:261). See chapter seven.

Hurǫyǫkye[186]
[hoo-ron-yon-kyeh]
    hu-   masculine singular patient – he
    -rony-   noun root – sky
    -ǫky-   verb root – abandon, quit
    -e   purposive aspect

Hurǫyušrǫh[187]
[hoo-ron-yoo-ronh]
    hu-   masculine singular patient – he
    -rǫy-   noun root – sky
    -ušrǫ-   verb root – cover
    -h   stative aspect

Huskwehšandet[188]
[hoos-kweh-shan-det]
    hu-   masculine singular patient – he
    -skwehš-   noun root – axe blade
    -a-   joiner vowel
    -ndet   verb root – envelope, hold close + stative aspect

Hušęraę[189]
[hoo-shen-rah-en]
    hu-   masculine singular patient – he
    -šęr-   noun root – frost
    -ę   verb root – lie + stative aspect

Hušrandetak[190]
(hoo-shrahn-deh-tak)
    hu-   masculine singular patient – he
    -šhr-   noun root – axe
    -a-   joiner vowel
    -ndet-   verb root – hold close

He is going to abandon the sky. (no gender specified)

He is covered by the sky. (male)

He holds the axe blade close. (male).

He has frost on the ground. (male)

He used to hold an axe close. (male)

186. Toupin 1996:950. It is ironic that the verb root 'continue' takes the same form. It usually takes the cislocative.

187. Toupin 1996:883. There might be a transitional root suffix after this, as that is what is given in Potier 1920:404. There may have been a remnant of it dropped in the recording.

188. Toupin 1996:225 "kochiandet", 825 and "k8echiandet". There was an 18th-century Wendat named "hoskwechiandet" (Steckley 1998:10).

189. Toupin 1996:828 and 393 as ochienraen, and 841 as hochienraen. See chapter nine for discussion.

190. Toupin 1996: 871 "ochrahendetak", 877 "ochrandetak", 884-5 and 892 "ochrondetak" and 942 "ochrandetak".

| -a- | habitual aspect |
| -k | past aspect suffix |

Huhšaę?[191]
[hooh-shah-en-en]
    hu-   masculine singular patient – he
    -hšaę-   verb root – be slow
    -ʔ   stative aspect

He is a slow walker, is slow moving. (male Large Turtle)

Huhšruyuti[192]
[hooh-shroo-yoo-tee]
    hu-   masculine singular patient – he
    -hšr-   noun root – axe
    -uyu-   verb root – penetrate
    -t-   causative root suffix
    -i   stative aspect

He is causing an axe to penetrate it. (male Large Turtle)

Huhšęndayehte[193]
[hooh-shen-dah-yeh-teh]
    hu-   masculine singular patient – he
    -hšęnd-   noun root – name
    -a-   joiner vowel
    -yehte-   verb root – bear around neck or shoulder + stative aspect

He bears a name. (male Bear)

Huskwindehti[194]
    hu-   masculine singular patient – he
    -skwinde- verb root – go running (e.g., with a pack or crowd)
    -ht-   causative root suffix
    -i-   stative aspect

He is running with a group (e.g., a pack) (male Wolf)

Hustayehtak[195]
[hoo-stah-yeh-tahk]
    hu-   masculine singular patient – he
    -st-   noun root – bark
    -a-   joiner vowel
    -yeht-   verb root – bear around neck or shoulder
    -ak   habitual aspect – often

He often carries bark. (male Porcupine)

---

191. Barbeau 1911:2.

192. Barbeau 1915:xi as Striped Turtle Henry Stand, written as Cruˇyu'ˈtiʔ. Toupin 1996:908–9.

193. Toupin 1996:195, 221, 228, 256, 524, 846, 849-50, 852 and 859. In 1788 shendete was the principal chief of the Detroit River band (Buser 1989). Barbeau has what appears to be this name as belonging to the Large Turtle clan (Barbeau 1915:x).

194. See discussion in chapter nine.

195. See discussion in clan chapter.

Huhšraęwahs[196]
[hooh-shrah-en-wahs]
He often loses his axe. (male Deer)

    hu-   masculine singular patient – he
    -hšr-   noun root – axe
    -a-   joiner vowel
    -ę-   verb root – have
    -wa-   undoer root suffix
    -hs   habitual aspect

Huhtaraš[197]
[hah-ah-tah-rash]
He often eats mud or earth. Mudeater (male Striped Turtle)

    ha-   masculine singular agent – he
    -ʔtar-   noun root – mud, clay, wet earth
    -a-   verb root – eat
    -s   habitual aspect

Hutaseti[198]
[hoo-tah-seh-tee]
He is hiding himself (male)

    hu-   masculine singular patient – he
    -t-   semi-reflexive voice
    -aset-   verb root – hide
    -i   stative aspect

Hutaʔwiʔah[199]
[hoo-tah-ah-wee-ee-ah]
He sleeps frequently, often. (mythic uncle)

    hu-   masculine singular patient – he
    -taʔ-   verb root – sleep
    -wi-   transitional root suffix
    -ʔah   habitual aspect

Hutęrǫkyǫh[200]
[hoo-ten-ron-kyonh]
He is abandoning a palisade. (male)

    hu-   masculine singular patient – he
    -tęr-   noun root – palisade
    -ǫky-   verb root – abandon
    -ǫh   stative aspect

196. Barbeau 1915:xi.and 61, and Connelley 1900:113.

197. Barbeau 1915:xi John Whitewing. See discussion of the name Mudeater in the nicknames chapter.

198. See discussion of Adam Brown in the introductory chapter.

199. It is presented in Wyandot in Barbeau 1960:207 #52, and 208 #25, 31, 59, each one with no translation, just "Ts. n[ame]". In English texts it is found in Barbeau 1960:35 and 1915:214.

200. Toupin 1996:186, 208, 846 and 851.

Hutrǫywę[201]
[hoo-tron-ywen]
- hu- — masculine singular patient – he
- -t- — semi-reflexive voice
- -rǫ- — noun root – sky
- =ywę — augmentative clitic

He is a great, sky. (male Prairie Turtle)

Hutsihtsamęh[202]
[hoo-tseeh-tsah-menh]
- hu- — masculine singular patient – he
- -tsihts- — noun root – flower, blossom
- -a- — joiner vowel
- -mę- — verb root – have
- -h — stative aspect

He is holding a flower. (male Snake)

Hutsiʔtsuʔyaʔta?[203]
[hoo-tsee-ee-tsoo-oo-yah-ah-tah-ah]
- hu- — masculine singular patient – he
- -tsiʔts- — noun root – flower
- -uʔya- — verb root – penetrate
- -ʔt- — causative root suffix
- -aʔ — habitual aspect

He often penetrates flowers. (spirit uncle in myth)

Huʔtušrura?[204]
[hoo-oo-too-shroo-rah-ah]
- hu- — masculine singular patient – he
- -ʔtušr- — noun root – chest
- -ura — verb root – affix
- -ʔ — stative aspect

His Chest is Affixed. (male spirit in myth)

Huyęhwi[205]
[hoo-yen-hwee]
- hu- — masculine singular patient – he
- -yę- — verb root – clean

He is cleaning it off. (male)

---

201. Toupin 1996:216, 218, 229, 865, 885, 946 and 949 as otrenhi8oin, 218 as otreni8re, 943 as hotronhi8oin and 945 as otronhi8oin. The person had the first name Jean-Baptiste, and was a member of the elders council in 1747 (229).

202. Connelley 1900:109.

203. It is presented in Wyandot in Barbeau 1960:208 #25, 31, 59, each one with no translation, just "Ts. n". In English texts it is found in Barbeau 1960:35 and 1915:214. See discussion of names in narratives.

204. Barbeau 1960:199 #46, 204 #1, and 210 #29. See discussion of names in narratives.

205. Toupin 1996:871

	-hw-	transitional root suffix
	-i	stative aspect

Huyǫngyetsi[206]
[hoo-yon-gyeh-tsee]

		He has a long nose. (nickname for a particular Frenchman)
	hu-	masculine singular patient – he
	-yǫngy-	noun root – nose
	-ets-	verb root – be long
	-i	stative aspect

Imakǫšerǫ?[207]
[ee-ma-kon-sheh-ron-on]

		Its face is damaged. (male Large Turtle)
	im-	partitive – such
	-ak-	feminine-zoic singular agent – she, it + semi-reflexive voice
	-ǫš-	noun root – face
	-erǫ-	verb root – damage, injure
	-?	stative aspect

Iwanderes[208]
[ee-wan-deh-res]

		My waist is often long (female Bear)
	iw-	partitive
	-a-	1st-person singular patient – my
	-nder-	noun root – waist, torso
	-es	verb root – be long + habitual aspect

Iyatǫk[209]
[ee-ya-tonk]h]

		She often talks, says. (female)
	iy-	partitive
	-atǫ-	feminine-zoic singular agent – she + verb root – talk
	-k	habitual aspect

206. Toupin 1996:235 and 262.

207. Barbeau 1911:36.

208. Toupin 1996:850, 855, 861 and 877 as 8anderes, and 859, 863 and 870 as 8enderes. The former is more likely.

209. Toupin 1996:844.

Iža?ris[210] She cooks. (female Large Turtle)
[ee-zhah-ah-rees]
    iža- partitive + feminine-zoic singular agent – she
    -?ri- verb root – cook
    -s habitual aspect

Kandažawaka[211] Where there is a short knife, short knives (probably male[212])
[kan-dah-zhah-wah-kah]
    k- cislocative – where
    -a- feminine-zoic singular agent – she, it
    -ndaž-[213] noun root – knife
    -awak- verb root – be short + stative aspect
    -a diminutive aspect suffix

Kanęraę[214] Where there is a group. (male)
[kah-nen-rah-en]
    k-[215] cislocative – where
    -a- feminine-zoic singular agent – it
    -nęr- noun root – group
    -a- joiner vowel
    -ę verb root – lie + stative aspect

Karętuyęh[216] A calf, leg, her calf, leg is divided in two. (no gender specified)
[kah-ren-too-yenh]
    k- dualic
    -a- feminine-zoic singular agent – it, her
    -ręt- noun root – calf
    -uyę- verb root – divide, be divided
    -h stative aspect

210. Barbeau 1911:1 and 33, and Toupin 1996:223 as a,aris, 888 as ,aaris and 890 as a,aris. One problem with this connection is that Toupin has the name as belonging to the Bear clan. In addition, there are other verbs that could be expressed with this name: weave a web, spill, or chew (Potier 1920:345–6). It is shared with the Wendat.

211. Toupin 1996:954.

212. This name is presented in the midst of male names as people giving gifts at a mortuary ceremony.

213. There is an -e- in the middle, rather than an -a-, but there are no nouns in the language that have -e- there.

214. Toupin 1996:841.

215. The -t- of the cislocative combines with the -y- of the pronominal prefix to create -k-.

216. Toupin 1996:954 as karento,en.

Karǫtuʔ[217]	Log lying in the water, poles in water.[218] (male Large Turtle)
[kah-ron-too-oo]	
k-	cislocative
-a-	feminine-zoic singular agent – it
-rǫt-	noun root – tree, log, pole
-u-	verb root – be in water
-ʔ	stative aspect
Kawišruyęh[219]	It is the middle, the divide of a belt or sash. (gender not known)
[kah-wee-shroo-yenh]	
k-	dualic
-a-	feminine-zoic singular agent – it
-wi-	verb root – gird
-šr-	nominalizer
-uyę-	verb root – be at the merging, dividing point
-h	stative aspect
Kwęndindeʔs[220]	She often ties knots (female Bear)
[kwen-deen-deh-ehs]	
kw-	dualic
-ęndind-	feminine-zoic singular agent – she + verb root – tie knot(s)
-eʔs	habitual aspect
Kwiyǫteh[221]	It lives two ways. (male Large Turtle)
[kwee-yon-teh]	
kwiy-	dualic
-ǫnte	feminine-zoic singular agent – it + verb root - live
-h	stative aspect

217. Barbeau 1911:3 and 36. The name ‚aronto was held by a Frenchman named Godefroit (Toupin 1996:235).

218. This is cognate with the Mohawk word that became the city name 'Toronto.'

219. Toupin 1996:945 and 954 o8echro,en, 949 a8echro,en and 974 8echro,en. I have added the -k- as this verb requires the dualic.

220. Barbeau 1911:14 and 35, Toupin 1996:214 and 826 as ka8indes, 898 as k8endindes, 926 as k8indindes, and 978 as guannnedides.

221. Connelley 1900:113 " Quin'-děh "Two lives," or "he lives in the water and in the air," or "in living he goes up and down." This name is written and pronounced a little differently in the Little Turtle Clan, and has a different meaning." This has a cognate in a Mohawk sachem name.

Kyawęnyǫ⁷²²² It is where she walks, comes to many times. (female Deer)
[kyah-en-nyon-on]
    ky- cislocative
    -aw- feminine-zoic singular patient – she
    -ę- verb root – come, go, walk
    -nyǫ- distributive root suffix
    -ʔ stative aspect

Kayumęndata²²³ When, where one's voice, word ends. (male Snake)
[kah-yoo-men-dah-tah]
    k- cislocative – when, where
    -ayu- indefinite patient – one
    -męnd- noun root – voice, word
    -a- joiner vowel
    -ta- verb root – end + stative aspect

Kyǫndatǫyuti⁷²²⁴ When or where she penetrates a village, community. (female)
[kyon-dah-ton-yoo-tee-ee]
    ky- cislocative – when, where
    -ǫ- feminine-zoic singular patient – she
    -ndat- noun root – village, community
    -ǫyu- verb root – penetrate
    -t- causative root suffix
    -iʔ stative aspect

Kyǫnǫturęh²²⁵ Her leg is divided, split in two. (female)
[kyon-non-too-renh]
    ky- dualic
    -ǫ- feminine-zoic singular patient – her
    -nǫt- noun root – leg
    -urę verb root – split in two
    -h stative aspect

---

222. Barbeau 1915:x "the [deer's] many footprints or traces." Turner "The Deer's many footprints in the sky." There is a very similar term in Barbeau's earlier writing, with a name attributed to a Snake clan woman (Barbeau 1911:15, 36 and 49).

223. Barbeau 1911:14 and 35, and Connelley 1899b:87–8 and 1900:117–8 (see Barbeau 1915:341–2). See discussion in the clan chapter.

224. Toupin 1996:842.

225. Toupin 1996:956 and 968 tkionnontoren, 846, 849 and 871 tionnontoren and 852 tionnotoren.

Kyuherasa[226]	Where there are small stalks of corn. (male)
[kyoo-heh-rah-sa]	
-ky-	cislocative – where
-u-	feminine-zoic singular patient – it
-her-	noun root – stalks of corn
-a-	verb root – be a size + stative aspect
-s-	plural aspect suffix
-a	diminutive aspect suffix

Kyamęrǫyu[227]	Eel (it penetrates moss) (male)
[kyah-men-ron-yoo]	
ky-	dualic
-am-	feminine-zoic singular patient – it
-ę̈r-	noun root – moss
-ǫyu	verb root – penetrate + stative aspect

Kyumętarǫh[228]	It is a stick that goes across something. (male)
[kyoo-men-tah-ronh]	
ky-	dualic
-um-	feminine-zoic singular patient – it
-ęt-	noun root – stick
-a-	joiner vowel
-rǫ-	verb root – cross
-h	stative aspect

Kyurahkusę⁷[229]	Sun rays are pressing, shining against her. (female Bear)
[kyoo-rah-koo-sen-en]	
ky-	dualic
-u-	feminine-zoic singular patient – it
-ra-	verb root – for sun to rise
-ku-	instrumental root suffix nominalizer
-(i)se-	verb root – press against
-ʔ	stative aspect

226. Toupin 1996:874 "tioharase", 883 "tioïerasa", 887 "tkioherasa" and 889 "ndgioherasa". In Barbeau 1911:14 and 33 we have a Snake clan man named Ižuheraʔsah 'small stalks of corn'. I believe this is the same name. The -ʔ- marks the stative aspect.

227. Barbeau 1911:1 and 47. Toupin 1996:861 as tia8enrono and 867 ata8oinroiok. In Wendat it is tio8enron,o (Steckley 2010:44).

228. Barbeau 1911:1 and 36.

229. Barbeau 1911:16.

Kyuyaręnyǫˀ[230]	When spots have arrived on her. (female Snake)
[kyoo-yah-ren-nyon-on]	
ky-	cislocative – where
-u-	feminine-zoic singular patient – she, it
-yaręn-	noun root – spot(s)
-yǫ-	verb root – arrive
-ˀ	stative aspect
Ndikaratase[231]	They two (f) have twisted loins, flanks. (male Snake)
[ndee-kah-rah-tah-she]	
nd-	feminine-zoic dual agent – they two (f)
-ikar-	noun root – flank, loins
-a-	joiner vowel
-tase	verb root – twist, turn + stative aspect
Ngyawiš[232]	Turtle (nickname for Mary McKee, Bear)
[ngyah-weesh]	
N'ǫdaeˀ haǫ[233]	From them, those who (female, possible Wolf)
n'	definite article – those
ǫdaeˀ	third person particle pronoun – they, he, or she
haǫ	particle – from
Ǫmakǫšarǫk[234]	It often paints our faces many times. (male)
[on-mah-kon-sha-ronk]	
ǫm-	feminine-zoic singular agent + 1st-person plural patient – it – our
-ak-	semi-reflexive voice
-ǫs-	noun root – face
-a-	joiner vowel

230. Barbeau 1911:1,15, and 36. There is a similar name, also female Snake clan, tsŭtĕyārenď̌ˀŏ̆, which can be translated as 'she is again spotted'. It could be another version of the same name, or a name unto itself.

231. Potier 1920:148 has as "niskaratase" (see also Toupin 1996:243). Steckley 2014:158, 161, 186, 190–1, 207 and 221, and Toupin 1996:185–7, 207, 208, 228, 854 and 868.

232. Barbeau 1915:xi. Barbeau 1915:xi. As in a number of animal names (e.g., bear and dog), the initial syllable carrying the pronominal prefix has been dropped

233. Toupin 1996:839 and 846 as ondaiehaon, 850 as ondaihaon, 854 as nondaiehaon and 856 as nonaiaon. The possibility that the person was Wolf clan came from the involvement of Wolf clan members in two baptisms that she was part of (854 and 856).

234. Toupin 1996:872 as on8akonchiaronk, 878 and 888 as makonchiaron, 883 as makonchiaronk and 945 as Magonchiaron.

-r-	verb root – paint, represent[235]
-ǫ-	distributive root suffix – many
-k	habitual aspect

Ǫmandayǫ[236]
[on-man-dah-yon]
    Our oil, grease is pure. (female)

ǫma-	1st-person plural patient – our
-nd-	noun root – oil, grease
-ayǫ	verb – be pure + stative aspect

Ǫmandurǫ⁷
[on-man-doo-ronk]
    It is often difficult for us.[237] (male Wolf clan)

ǫma-	feminine-zoic singular + 1st-person plural patient – she/it – us
-nduron-	verb root – be difficult or valuable
-⁷	habitual aspect

Ǫmanduyarha[238]   Our poplar (no gender specified).
[on-man-doo-yar-hah]

ǫma-	1st-person plural patient – us, our
-nduyar-	noun root – poplar
-ha	noun suffix

Ǫmaskantha[239]
[on-mah-skan-t-hah]
    She or it often desires us. (male)

ǫm-	feminine-zoic singular agent + 1st-person plural patient – she/it – us
-askant-	verb root – desire
-ha	habitual aspect

---

235. I am not completely sure about the verb root plus root suffix combination, but it was better than the other choices available.

236. Toupin 1996:878. It could also mean 'in our arrow'.

237. Toupin 1996: 837, 854, 865 and 887. The name appears at the council held at Detroit, on April 26, 1781, as "Mandoron" (Curnoe 1996:205). In the Treaty of 1789 it is Maudoronk. For Treaty #2, 1790, we get Mondoro (Lajeunesse 1960:173). Hale 1883:479 gives a translation of "Unwilling" as the meaning for the name he writes as "Mandarong," the Anderdon Chief Joseph White, suggesting that the translation of 'hard, difficult' took precedence.

238. Toupin 1996:879. This contradicts what Potier wrote in two ways. He has it as appearing only with incorporated noun roots, and he has the habitual as -s- following -on- (Potier 1920:297).

239. Toupin 1996:872 as on,8askannha, 879 as on,8akata and 880 as on,8askanntnha.

Ǫmašrutǫywę[240] Our large number of (standing) great axes (male)
[on-mah-shroo-ton-ywen]

    ǫm- 1st-person plural patient – our
    -ašr- noun root – axe
    -ut- verb root – stand
    -ǫ- root suffix – distributive + stative aspect
    =ywę augmentative clitic

Ǫmaʔtaest[a][241] She or it often hits us with something. (male)
[ah-ah-on-mah-ah-tah-est]

    -ǫm- feminine-zoic singular agent + 1st-person plural patient – she/it – us
    -aʔt- noun root – body
    -ae- verb root – hit, strike
    -st- causative-instrumental root suffix
    -a habitual aspect

Ǫmatešatǫ[242] She or it is menacing us. (no gender referenced)
[on-mah-teh-shah-ton]

    ǫma- feminine-zoic singular agent + 1st-person plural patient – she/it – us
    -atešatǫ verb root – menace + stative aspect

Ǫmaʔtisati[243] She or it corners us. (male)
[on-mah-ah-tee-sah-tee]

    ǫm- feminine-zoic singular agent + 1st-person plural patient – she/it – us
    -aʔt- noun root – body
    -sa- verb root – press against
    -t- causative root suffix
    -i stative aspect

---

240. Toupin 1996:894 as on8achronton8a 899 as on8achr8ton8oin, 924 and 926 as on,8achr-8ton8a.

241. Toupin 1996:884 as On,8aataest. Something is missing in this word, possibly a factual at the beginning, which would then make the word mean 'She or it just struck us'. I chose a missing habitual. Both occur in Potier's recording of Wyandot names.

242. Toupin 1996:927. This verb root was used in the story of the Origin of the Sun Shower (Barbeau 1915, 53–6; 1960, 63–75), in which the son of a Wyandot woman and a thunderer was menacing ordinary boys.

243. Toupin 1996:888, 889 and 892 as on8atisati.

Ǫmaʔtukawih[244]
[on-mah-ah-too-kah-weeh]   It paints, colours us. (male)

    ǫm-   feminine-zoic singular agent + 1st-person plural patient – it – us
    -aʔt-   semi-reflexive voice (or noun root – body)
    -uka-   verb root – paint, colour
    -wi-   transitional root suffix
    -h   stative aspect

Ǫmayetahak[245]
[on-mah-yeh-ta-hak]   She or it used to bear or carry us. (male Deer)

    ǫma-   feminine-zoic singular agent + 1st- person plural patient – she/it – us
    -yet-   verb root – bear
    -a-   habitual aspect
    -hak   past aspect suffix

Ǫmętsašę[246]
[on-men-tsah-shen]   It is bad earth, land. (female)

    ǫmęts-   feminine-zoic singular agent – it + noun root – earth, land
    -a-   joiner vowel
    -šę   verb root – be bad + stative aspect

Ǫmętsinǫh[247]
[on-men-tsee-nonh]   She drags, takes the earth, land along. (female Porcupine)

    ǫmęts-   feminine-zoic singular agent – she + noun root – earth, land
    -in-   verb root – drag, take along
    -ǫh   stative aspect

Ǫndaižu[248]
[on-ah-ee-zhoo]   It is a great arrow. (male Wolf)

    ǫ-   feminine-zoic singular patient – it
    -nd-   noun root – arrow

---

244. Toupin 1996:214 on,8atoka8i, 836 honatoka8i, 854 honatoka8i, 857 on8atoka8i, 859 onatoka8i, 864 onatoka8i, 870 on,8atoka8i, 874 a on8aatoka8i, and 878 on,8âtoka8i.

245. Toupin 1996: 214 as Ma,eta, 887 Maie ̍tak and Mayetahak, and 891 as Maïe ̍tak for one way of writing the name and 879 and 884 as on,8a,etak, and 884, 886 and 892 as on8e,eta-ak.

246. Toupin 1996:852.

247. Connelley 1900:111.

248. Toupin 1996:220.

	-a-	joiner vowel[249]
	-ižu	verb root − be great + stative aspect

Qndašǫtakwih[250] She has a tongue of such a nature. (female)
[on-dah-shon-tah-kweeh]

	ǫ-	feminine-zoic singular patient − it
	-ndaš-	noun root − tongue
	-ǫt-	verb root − be attached
	-akw-	instrumental root suffix
	-ih	stative aspect

Qndatariǫ[251] (Her) cornbread is arriving. (female)
[on-dah-tah-ree-on]

	ǫ-	feminine-zoic singular patient − her, it
	-ndatar-	noun root − cornbread
	-iǫ	verb root − arrive + stative aspect

Qndatayętarak[252] She, it used to lie down in a bed. (probably female)
[on-ndah-tah-yen-tah-rak]

	ǫ-	feminine-zoic singular patient − she, it
	-ndat-	noun root − bed, personal space of a longhouse
	-a-	joiner vowel
	-yętara-	verb root − lie down + habitual aspect
	-k	past aspect suffix

Qndesǫk[253] (It is a) hawk. (male Hawk)

Qndešinyętǫk[254] She regularly follows the sand. (female Deer)
[on-deh-shee-nyen-tonk]

	ǫ-	feminine-zoic singular patient − she
	-ndeši-	noun root − sand
	-nyętǫ-	verb root − follow
	-k	habitual aspect

249. It is unusual for the joiner vowel to occur before this verb root.

250. Toupin 1996:850.

251. Toupin 1996:904.

252. Toupin 1996:963 as ondata,etarak.

253. Toupin 1996:822.

254. Toupin 1996:211, 219, 255, 827, 831, 867, 901, 903, 923 and 926 as ondechientonk, 252 as andechientonk, 830 as ondechrenton, 835 and 845 as ondechenton 867 as ondechinientonk and 928 as ondechiniente.

Ǫndehšuręs[255] She often finds sand. (female Large Turtle)
[on-deh-shoo-rens]

    ǫ- feminine-zoic singular patient – she
    -ndehš- noun root – sand
    -urę- verb root – find
    -s habitual aspect

Ǫndešǫngyahak[256] She used to make sand. (female Large or Striped Turtle)
[on-deh-shon-gyah-ak]

    ǫ- feminine-zoic singular patient – she
    -ndeš- noun root – sand
    -ǫngy- verb root – make
    -aha- habitual aspect
    -k past aspect suffix

Ǫndehšuri[257] She is covered with sand (female Prairie Turtle)
    ǫ- feminine-zoic singular patient – she
    -ndehš- noun root – sand
    -uri verb root – cover, be covered + stative aspect

Ǫndišraʔ ires[258] He often walks on ice. (male)
Ǫndišraʔ ice
[on-dee-shrah-ah]

    ǫ- feminine-zoic singular patient – it
    -ndišr- noun root – ice
    -aʔ noun suffix

ires He often walks.
[ee-rehs]

    -i- partitive
    -r- masculine singular agent – he
    -e- verb root – go, come, walk
    -s habitual aspect

255. Barbeau 1911:1, 2 and 7, as yaʔndešuręʔns. Powell 1881:60 as "Ya-däc-u-räs *(Finding Sand Beach)*." He has her belonging to the "Mud Turtle" clan. Toupin 1996:896 has andechi8rens and ondechi8rens.

256. Toupin 1996:217, as ondechionngiak with the -g- being a Wyandot feature written as a superscript, 863 and 873 as ondechionniak, 875 as hondechionniahak, 886, 962 and 963 as dechonngiahak, 878, 929 and 945 as ondechionniahak, 889, 892 and 975 as ondechionngiahak, 894 as ondechinngiahak, 897 as ondechronniahak, 900 as d'echionniahak, 904 as hondechronniahac, 905 and 909 as dechronngiahak, 962 and 963 as dechonngiahak and 839 as nndechonniahak. This noun root with the feminine-zoic singular patient and the noun stem ondechra 'country' are almost identical, but the fact that a clear majority of these from have the -i- tells me that the word for 'sand' is correct here.

257. Toupin 1996:194, 210, 220, 254, 847 and 850, and in Barbeau 1911:48.

258. Toupin 1996:895 and 905.

Ǫngwaęžat[259]
[on-gwah-en-zhat]

    ǫ-   feminine-zoic singular patient – it
    -ngw-   noun root – rapids
    -a-   joiner vowel
    -ęžat   verb root – be at the top of + stative aspect

It is the top of the rapids. (male)

Ǫndayarut[260]
[on-dah-rah-root]

    ǫ-   feminine-zoic singular patient - it
    -ndayar-   noun root – horn, antler
    -ut   verb root – stand + stative aspect

It is a standing horn, antler. (no gender specified)

Ǫndetu haǫ[261]
[on-deh-tu ha-on]

    ǫ-   feminine-zoic singular patient – she
    -ndet-   noun root – pine
    -u   verb root – be in water + stative aspect
    haǫ   from

She is from pines in water. (female)

Ǫneatęnyǫ[262]
[on-eh-ah-ten-nyon]

    ǫ-   feminine-zoic singular patient – it
    -ne-   noun root – bone
    -a-   joiner vowel
    -tęny-   verb root – change shape, form
    -ǫ   stative aspect

Bones are, a bone is changing form. (female Large Turtle)

Ǫnęharawi[263]
[on-nen-hah-rah-wee]

    ǫ-   feminine-zoic singular patient – it
    -nęh-   noun root – corn
    -a-   joiner vowel
    -ra-   verb root – roll up, set up
    -w-   transitional root suffix
    -i   stative aspect

Corn has been put up, set up. (male)

259. Toupin 1996:848, 897–8 and 956.

261. Toupin 1996:928 and 942.

261. Toupin 1996:822 and 828 as ndetohaon, 824 as ndahohaon and 833 as ondetohaon.

262. Toupin 1996:205 "annentenion" and Toupin 1996:851 "onneatennion." The first cannot be translated as stated.

263. Toupin 1996:827 and 840 as onnenhara8i.

Ǫneyaręndi[264] A bone is making noise. (male)
[on-neh-yah-ren-dee]

 Ǫ-   feminine-zoic singular patient – it
 -ne-   noun root – bone
 -yarę- verb root – make noise
 -nd-   inchoative root suffix
 -i   stative aspect

Ǫnǫdu[265] She has a cave. (female Bear)
[on-non-doo]

 Ǫ-   feminine-zoic singular patient – she, it
 -nǫd- noun root – depth
 -u   verb root – 'be in water' + stative aspect

Ǫnǫdu haǫ[266] It or she is from a cave. (female Bear)
[on-non-doo]

 Ǫ-   feminine-zoic singular patient – she or it
 -nǫd- noun root – depth
 -u   verb root – 'be in water' + stative aspect
[hah-on]   from (particle)

Ǫnǫkyęntawi?[267] She is or has a sleeping hill or mountain. (female)
[on-non-kyen-tah-wee-ee]

 -Ǫ-   feminine-zoic singular patient – she
 -nǫk- noun root – hill or mountain[268]
 -yęta- verb root – sleep
 -wi-   transitional root suffix
 -?   stative aspect

---

264. Toupin 1996:897 as onnearendi.

265. Toupin 1996: 188, 874, 901, 926, 928, 943, 944, 946, 948–52, 954, 959-60, 963, and 965.

266. Toupin 1996: Onnond8(-)haon 840, (as nnondohaon – bear elder as godfather of her child), 850, 952 – same ceremony as 951, 954, – same ceremony as onnon8, 957, 959. Without the pronominal prefix we have nondohaon 833, nnonohaon 840, and 850, and then nnondohan 850.

267. Toupin 1996:899.

268. The following -y- turns the -t- at the end of the noun root into a -k-. There is the possibility that the noun root -nǫt- 'leg' is used here

Ǫnǫrutęh²⁶⁹ [on-non-roo-tenh]		It is a scalp of such a nature. (male Bear)
	ǫ-	feminine-zoic singular patient – it
	-nǫr-	noun root – scalp
	-utę-	verb root – be of such a nature
	-h	stative aspect
Ǫnǫste²⁷⁰ [on-non-steh]		She is cheap, stingy. (nickname for female Striped Turtle)
	-ǫ-	feminine-zoic singular patient – she
	-nǫste-	verb root – be cheap, stingy + stative aspect
Ǫtareywę²⁷¹ [on-tah-reh-ee-wenh]		It is a very big lake. (male Deer)
	ǫtar-	feminine-zoic singular agent – it + noun root – lake
	-e-	verb root – be water + stative aspect
	=ywę-	augmentative clitic
Ǫtaręmaǫh²⁷² [on-tah-ren-mah-onh]		She is carrying a lake. (female Bear)
	ǫtar-	feminine-zoic singular agent – she + noun root - lake
	-ęmaǫ-	verb root – carry, bring
	-h	stative aspect
Ǫtarayǫrat²⁷³ [on-tah-rah-yon-rat]		It is a white lake (mythic figure). (male Large Turtle)
	ǫtar-	feminine-zoic singular agent – 'it' + noun root - lake
	-a-	joiner vowel
	-yǫrat	verb root – be white + stative aspect

269. Toupin 1996:215 (nickname "Port neuf"), 249, 869, 897, 899, 903 and 905. It is possible that the name is actually tsonnonr8ten, with the addition of the initial -ts- adding the meaning 'again' (Toupin 1996:895). The name exists in the form without the initial -ts- in Wendat (Steckley 1998:12 and JR20:23 and 25).

270. Toupin 1996:213 and 247. The individual had the clan name of te8arachiande. A form of this word, using the masculine singular agent, as "honnonste" was used to refer to one of the French officials, Deruisseau (Toupin 1996:262)

271. Toupin 1996:217 and 852.

272. Barbeau 1915:xi. He wrote the name without the initial ǫ- and presented two alternative translations. The one matching the one presented here is "carrying a pond." The alternative was "holding mud", hypothesizing that the noun root -tar- 'clay, mud' was in her name. I have chosen the first interpretation as in Toupin 1996:835, the mother of a baptized child in 1734 named "Ontaren8a," the translation given here (see Steckley 2011:203).

273. Toupin 1996:829 and 839. JR10:177

Shandatsuwaht[274]
[s-han-dah-tsah-what]   He is a very large pot, kettle. (male)

    s-   repetitive – very
    -ha-   masculine singular agent – he
    -ndats-   noun root – pot, kettle
    -uwaht   verb root – be large + stative aspect

Shandetsi[275]
[s-han-deh-tsee]   He has a very long arrow. (male)

    s-   repetitive – very
    -ha-   masculine singular agent – he
    -ets-   verb root – be long
    -i   stative aspect

Sharǫtat[276]
[s-ha-ron-tat]   He is one tree, log, pole (female)

    s-   repetitive
    -ha-   masculine singular agent – he
    -rǫt-   noun root – tree, log, pole
    -a-   joiner vowel
    -t   verb root – be one + stative aspect

Sharǫtayęraht[277]
[s-ha-ron-tah-yen-raht]   He is a very white tree, pole, log. (male)

    s-   repetitive – very
    -ha-   masculine singular agent – he
    -rǫt-   noun root – tree, pole, log

274. Barbeau 1911:44 and 45, Potier 1920:149 and Toupin 1996:173, 186, 201, 207, 238, and 243. He has the nickname of "le Bijou." It is written with an -o- instead of an -a- in Toupin 1996:909. The name in Wendat is presented in Vincent as Tsadatso8an Une large bouilloire [a large kettle]" (Vincent 1984:461). The form of the verb is slightly different, but the meaning is the same.

275. The Wyandot name associated with the father of François Marie Picote, Sieur de Belestre, commandant at Fort Pontchartrain in 1727–8 and again in 1758–60. His name was presented as Shandesti h8ena 'Shandesti has him as his child' (Toupin 1996:234), as well as simply as Sandetsi (Toupin 1996:262).

276. Barbeau 1915:4, referring to an "old woman" from the past among the Oklahoma Wyandotte. Ideally, to reflect the feminine-zoic singular agent, the word should have begun with -sk-. On page 82, fn 2, he presents a translation of "again she blows out the fire," which does not make fit with the roots in the word.

277. Toupin 1996:212 as saronta,enrat. This may refer to the white pine which is known to the Haudenosaunee as the Tree of Peace. White is a spiritual colour. There is a story in which a woman has a succession of visions of white animals (partridge, bear, beaver, deer, and turkey; Barbeau 1915:97–8 and 1960:77–91), as well as a story about a spiritual white otter (Barbeau 1915:65–72 and 1960:106–7).

-a-	joiner vowel
-yęraht	verb root – be white + stative aspect

Sharǫtǫkye[278]
[s-ha-ron-ton-kyeh]

s-	repetitive – again
-ha-	masculine singular agent - he
-rǫt-	noun root – tree, log, pole
-ǫkye	verb root – abandon + purposive aspect

He again is going to abandon[279] a tree. (male Deer)

Sharǫwas[280]
[shah-ron-was]

He cleans it off. (male)

s-	repetitive
-ha-	masculine singular agent – he
-r-	verb root – be with
-ǫ-	distributive root suffix
-wa-	undoer root suffix
-s	habitual aspect

Shastahǫretsi'?s[281]
[s-hah-stah-hon-reh-tsee-ees]

He has very long bone marrows. (male Deer)

s-	repetitive – very
-ha-	masculine singular agent – he
-stahǫr-	noun root – bone marrow
-ets-	verb root – be long
-i?	stative aspect
-s	plural aspect suffix

Shastaretsi[282]
[s-ha-star-eh-tsee]

He has very long antler spurs. (male Deer)

s-	repetitive – very
-ha-	masculine singular agent – he
-star-	noun root – antler spurs
-ets-	verb root – be long or tall
-i	stative aspect

278. Toupin 1996:217

279. It could also have a "continue to" before "abandon."

280. Barbeau 1911:45 –" scăro'owas = sweeping the earth or the flour (sp?)" "…sweeping…" It is possible that the name in Toupin 1996:855 "haron8a" refers to the same name.

281. Barbeau 1911: 12 and 45.

282. Toupin 1996:211, 226, 227, 239, 245, 259, 260, 825, 829–30, 833, 835, 931, 943–5, 947, 953, and 955. JR46:143.

Shašęnduwat[283] He has a very great, large name. (male)
[s-hah-shen-doo-wat]

    s-   repetitive – very
    -ha-   masculine singular agent – he
    -šęnd-   noun root – name
    -uhwat   verb root – be large + stative

Shaʔtsiʔtsuwaʔ[284] He very often picks flowers. (male Deer)
[s-hah-ah-tsee-ee-tsoo-wah-ah]

    s-   repetitive – very
    -ha-   masculine singular agent – he
    -ʔtsiʔts-   noun root – flower, flowers, blossoms
    -u-   verb root – be in water
    -aʔ   habitual aspect

Shayęʔtsuwat[285] He has a very big forehead. (male Large Turtle)
[s-hah-yen-en-tsoo-wah-aht]

    s-   repetitive prefix – very
    -ha-   masculine singular agent – he
    -yęʔts-   noun root – forehead
    -uwaʔt-   verb root – be large + stative aspect

Shękyukwes[286] He has a very long lineage. (male)
[s-hen-kyoo-kwehs]

    s-   repetitive – very
    -h-   masculine singular agent – he
    -ękyu-   verb root – be a lineage
    -kw-   instrumental root suffix/nominalizer
    -es   verb root – be long + habitual aspect[287]

283. He was an adopted "Iroquois". Toupin 1996:173, 183, 190, 196, 201, 214-5, 23, 249, 257, 837 sachiend8at, 842 sachiend8a, 844 sachiend8ann, 847 sachenn8at, 848 "sachiend8t, 851 sachiend8at, 855 and 849 sachiend8ann.

284. Barbeau 1915:x, 11,12, 45, and 47.

285. Barbeau 1915:272–4, 282–3, Toupin 1996:830, 832, 836-7, 942-4, 953, 955 and 965. Powell 1881:60 "Man of Mud Turtle … 'Sha-yän-tsu-wat' *(Hard Skull).*" Clarke 1870:22–4 in Barbeau 1915:367–8 as Soo-daw-soo-wat.

286. Toupin 1996:826

287. While the form appears to be for the habitual, the meanings seems to reflect the stative. This seems often to happen with this verb root.

Sayǫnǫhwažakǫh[288]
[sah-yon-non-hwah-zhah-konh]

    sayǫ-   masculine singular agent + indefinite patient – he - their
    -nǫhw-   noun root – head, brains
    -a-   joiner vowel
    -ža-   verb root – break
    -kǫ   distributive root suffix
    -h   stative aspect

He is breaking many of their heads. (male)

Sayuerakǫ[289]
[sah-yoo-eh-rah-kon]

He has done many things for them, for people. (male)

    sayu-   masculine singular agent + indefinite patient – he – them (ind)
    -era-   verb root – do
    -kǫ   distributive root suffix + stative aspect

Sayurewatha[290]
[sah-yoo-reh-wat-ha]

He criticizes, opposes them. (indefinite) (male)

    sayu-   masculine singular agent + indefinite patient – he – them (ind)
    -rewat-   verb root – oppose
    -ha   habitual aspect

Sayuhša'ih[291]
[sah-yooh-shah-ah-eeh]

He is finishing, killing them. (male)

    sayu-   masculine singular agent + indefinite patient – he – them
    -hša'-   verb root – finish
    -ih   stative aspect

Shahęteskǫ[292]
[s-hah-hen-teh-skon]

He very frequently leads. (male Porcupine)

    s-   repetitive – very
    -ha-   masculine singular agent – he
    -hęte-   verb root – go first, lead
    -skǫ   frequentative root suffix + stative aspect

---

288. Toupin 1996:853 and 855.

289. Toupin 1996:853.

290. Toupin 1996:869 as sa,ore8a't and 950 as sayo8e8aθa. It is possible that sa,or8tas, 893 also refers to this name.

291. Toupin 1996:217 tsa,ochiai", 833 "sa,ochia,i." and Wendat – Steckley 1998:13 Sa,ochiai.

292. Toupin 1996:825 as haenteskon, 830, 843, and 848 as saenteskon, 852 and 854 saonteskon. It is distinctly possible that -hu- masculine singular patient – 'he' was also used sometimes, see 213 as s8enteskon and 249 as s8en'teskon. In his signing the Huron Church reserve surrender on January 3, 1801, it was written as Sahenteskon (Lajeunesse 1960:208).

Shandetes[293]
[s-han-deh-tehs]

    s-   repetitive – very
    -ha-   masculine singular agent – he
    -ndet-   noun root – pine
    -es   verb root – be tall, long - habitual aspect

He is a very tall pine. (male)

Sharęhes[294]

He is very tall treetops, or long branch. (male Striped Turtle and Prairie Turtle)

[s-hah-ren-hehs]

    s-   repetitive – very
    -ha-   masculine singular agent – he
    -ręh-   noun root – treetops, branches
    -es   verb root – be tall. long + habitual aspect

Sharǫkye[295]
[s-hah-ron-kyeh]

Wind is going to continue again for him. (male)

    s-   repetitive – again
    -ha-   masculine singular agent – he, him
    -r-   noun root – wing, air
    -ǫky-   verb root – continue
    -e   purposive aspect

Shawęnǫtakwi[296]
[shah-wen-non-tah-kwee]

He is relearning a voice, a language. (male)

    s-   repetitive – again
    -ha-   masculine singular agent – he
    -węn-   noun root – voice, word
    -ǫt-   verb root – attach
    -akw-   instrumental root suffix
    -i   stative aspect

---

293. Toupin 1996:202, 225, 240, 259, 830 and 922. He was an adopted member of the Fox tribe.

294. Toupin 1996:175, 182, 206, 208–9, 244, 860 and 924.

295. This appears as Shaawrunthe in the Treaty of 1795 and as Shawrunthie in the Treaty of 1805.

296. Toupin 1996:845 and 847.

Skahwęndes[297]　　　　　　It is a very long island. (female Bear)
[skah-hwen-des]
    s-　　　　　　　　　repetitive – very
    -ka-　　　　　　　　feminine-zoic singular agent – it
    -hwęd-　　　　　　　noun root – island
    -es　　　　　　　　 verb root – be long + habitual aspect

Ši Huwaʔtenhwa[298]　　　　He comes carrying or being carried from afar. (male Large Turtle)
[shee] [hoo-wah-ah-ten-hwah]
Ši　　　　　　　　　　　far
    huw-　　　　　　　　masculine singular patient – he
    -aʔt-　　　　　　　　noun root – body
    -enhw-　　　　　　　verb root – carry, bring
    -ah　　　　　　　　 habitual aspect

Šiw ahate[299]　　　　　　　She exists far from the path. (female)
[sheew-ah-hah-teh]
Šiw　　　　　　　　　　　far
    ahate　　　　　　　　A path exists for her.
    ah-　　　　　　　　 feminine-zoic singular agent - she + noun root – path
    -a-　　　　　　　　 joiner vowel
    -te　　　　　　　　 verb root – exist + stative aspect

Ši yariwate[300]　　　　　　A matter exists far away. (female)
[shee-yah-ree-wah-teh]
Ši　　　　　　　　　　　far

    ya-　　　　　　　　 feminine-zoic singular agent – it
    -riw-　　　　　　　　noun root – matter, affair
    -a-　　　　　　　　 joiner vowel
    -te　　　　　　　　 verb root – exist + stative aspect

297. Toupin 1996: 214 as ka8indes, and 851 as ska8endes. The -h- that differentiates 'island' from 'word, voice' rarely shows up in the writing of any period of the recording of Wyandot.

298. I am not completely sure of the exact translation here. Steckley 2014:10 and 272, as Chi-hoatenhwa and Toupin 1996:871 and 882. There is a chance that the name written on Treaty #2 as She-hou-wa-te-mon is a representation of this name (Curnoe 1996:220). This name was last given to Darren English of the Kansas Wyandot late in the 20th century.

299. Toupin 1996:865 as chi-8âhate and 909 as chi-8ate.

300. Toupin 1996:823, 825, 836, 870, 874. One point of confusion with this name is that it is written in different ways in Toupin. It three of the examples (823, 825 and 836), we have just the -chi- (ši), in two (870 and 874) there is just ",arih8ate". Thirdly, in one example (860), there is "chiate ,arih8ate" which would be something like "all matters exist." I decided to take the first option.

Šiy awe[301]	She or it goes far (male)
[shee-yah-weh]	
Šiy	far

Awe	She or it goes
[ah-weh]	
aw-	translocative – go away
-e	feminine-zoic singular agent – she or it + verb root – go + purposive aspect

Shutrižuskǫ?[302]	He very frequently fights, kills. (male)
[s-hoo-tree-zhoo-skon-on]	
s-	repetitive – very
-hu-	masculine singular patient – he
-t-	semi-reflexive voice
-rižu-	verb root – fight, kill
-skǫ-	frequentative root suffix
-?	stative aspect

Skahęte[303]	She is going to lead, come first again. (female Deer)
[skah-hen-teh]	
s-	repetitive – again
-ka-	feminine-zoic singular agent – she
-hęte-	verb root – lead, go first + purposive aspect

Skahǫat[304]	It is one canoe. (male Deer)
[skah-hon-aht]	
s-	repetitive
-ka-	feminine-zoic singular agent – it
-hǫ-	noun root – canoe
-a-	joiner vowel
-t-	verb root – be one + stative aspect

301. This name appears in the Treaty of 1789 as Cheyawe, and as Shi-a-wa as the Wyandot name for John Solomon in the Treaty of 1832.

302. Toupin 1996:223, 256, 873, 900, 928, 962, and 974 (otrioskon). This is shared with a Wendat of the 17th century.

303. Toupin 1996:206, 857, and 870.

304. Toupin 1996:188, 212, 869, 872, 930. In the treaties and surrenders signed by One Canoe there is an -m- in the name: 1789 – Skahomat, 1801 – Ruhumatt, 1803, 1790 Skahoumat, and 1808 Skahomet. In the Treaty of 1807, the nickname of Black Chief was added, which would have had its origin in English.

Skamęndat³⁰⁵   She, it is or has one voice. (female Porcupine)
[skah-men-daht]

- s- — repetitive
- -ka- — feminine-zoic singular agent – it, she
- -męnd- — noun root – voice, word
- -a- — joiner vowel
- -t — verb root – be one + stative aspect

Skamęndižu³⁰⁶   She is a very great voice, is great in authority. (female)
[skah-men-dee-zhoo]

- s- — repetitive – very
- -ka- — feminine-zoic singular agent – she
- -męnd- — noun root – voice, word
- -ižu — verb root – be large, great + stative aspect

Skandaʔeʔ³⁰⁷   She again hits an arrow. (female)
[skan-dah-ah-eh-eh]

- s- — repetitive
- -ka- — feminine-zoic singular agent – she
- -nd- — noun root – arrow
- -aʔe- — verb root – hit, strike
- -ʔ — stative aspect

Skanǫhtawak³⁰⁸   She has very short legs. (female – probable nickname)
[skan-onh-tah-wahk]

- s- — repetitive – very
- -ka- — feminine-zoic singular agent – she
- -nǫht- — noun root – leg, legs
- -awak — verb root – be short + stative aspect

Skarǫyatih³⁰⁹   It is on the other side of the sky. (male)
[skah-ron-yah-tee]

- s- — repetitive – other
- -ka- — feminine-zoic singular agent – she or it
- -rǫy- — noun root – sky
- -a- — joiner vowel

---

305. Connelley 1900:110.

306. Toupin 1996:894 and 896.

307. Barbeau 1915:246 fn5. In one example, it was written as skanda,e, which I believe to be incorrect (Toupin 1996:84).

308. Barbeau 1911:35.

309. Toupin 1996:880, 886, 889, 891, 893, 895, 898 and 910.

-ti-	verb root – be on a side
-h	stative aspect

Skahšęnduwat[310]
[skah-shen-doo-wat]

s-	repetitive – very
-ka-	feminine-zoic singular agent – she
-hšęnd-	noun root – name
-uwat	verb root – be large, great + stative aspect

She has a very great name (female)

Skangywes[311]
[skan-gy-wehs]

It is very long moosehide. (female)

s-	repetitive – very
-ka-	feminine-zoic singular agent – it
-ngyw-	noun root – moosehide
-es	verb root – be long + habitual aspect

Skękyuhkwes[312]
[sken-kyooh-kwehs]

She has a very long family, lineage. (female Bear)

s-	repetitive – very
-k-	feminine-zoic singular agent – she
-ękyu-	verb root – be a lineage, group
-kw-	instrumental nominalizer
-es	verb root – be long + habitual aspect

Skwętuwat[313]
[skwen-too-wat]

It is a very large, great day. (male)

skw-	repetitive – very
-ęt-	feminine-zoic singular agent – it + noun root – day
-uwat	verb root – be large, great + stative aspect

---

310. Toupin 1996:855

311. Toupin 1996:885 as skandgi8es.

312. Barbeau 1911:17.

313. Toupin 1996:848.

Sundakwa?[314]	Eagle. (male, [315]Sturgeon and Yaa?tayętsi?[316])
[soon-dah-kwah-ah]	
s-	repetitive[317]
-u-	feminine-zoic singular patient – she, it
-ndakw-	noun root – eagle
-a?	noun suffix

Šamętaha[318]	At the same time she concluded, finished it. (female)
[shah-men-tah-hah]	
š-	coincident – at the same time
-am-	factual
-ęta-	feminine-zoic singular agent – she, it -verb root – conclude, finish
-ha	inchoative root suffix + punctual aspect

Šarehti?[319]	At the same time he walks and goes at that place. (male Deer)
[shah-reh-tee-ee]	
ša-	coincident
-r-	masculine singular agent – he
-e-	verb root – go, come, walk
-ht-	causative root suffix
-i?	stative aspect

Šatehaǫmętsati[320]	He is in the middle of the land. (male)
[shah-teh-ha-on-men-tsah-tee]	
ša-	coincident
-te-	dualic
-ha-	masculine singular patient – he
-ǫmęts-	noun root – land
-a-	joiner vowel
-ti	verb root – be on a side + stative aspect

314. Toupin 1996:173–4, 178, 182, 184, 185, 196–7, 200, 202, 205, 224–5, 238, 243, 257–8 and 260.

315. This combined clan, Hotira,on and Ti,ata,entsi (Toupin 1996:260), belonged to the Wolf phratry during the 18th century, but would disappear by the 19th century.

316. This is the name of the first woman in the Origin Story, as well as a few other traditional tales. She fell from the sky world and became the first woman on earth.

317. It may be that this is not the repetitive, but what linguists call a "prosthetic," adding sound but no concrete meaning. Many animal names begin with a -(t)s- that has no clear connection with the repetitive (see Steckley 2021: 166).

318. Toupin 1996:889 and 909.

319. Barbeau 1911:12.

320. Toupin 1996:903 as chiate haon8aesati and haonh8ensati.

Šatehuroyati[321]
[shah-teh-hoo-ron-yah-tee]   He is in the middle of the sky, half the sky. (male Bear)

    ša-   coincident
    -te-   dualic
    -hu-   masculine singular patient – he
    -roy-   noun root – sky
    -a-   joiner vowel
    -ti   verb root – be on a side + stative aspect

Šateyarihwate[322]
[shah-teh-yah-ree-hwah-teh]   Two equal matters or statements. (male)

    ša-   coincident
    -te-   dualic
    -ya-   feminine-zoic singular agent – it
    -rihw-   noun root – matter, affair
    -ate   verb root – exist + stative aspect

Šateyaroyah[323]
[shah-teh-yah-ron-yah]   It is as big as the sky, half the sky. (male Porcupine)

    ša-   coincident
    -te-   dualic
    -ya-   feminine-zoic singular agent – it
    -roy-   noun root – sky
    -ah   verb root – be a size + stative aspect

Šateyaroyati[324]
[shah-teh-yah-ron-yah-tee]   She or it is in the middle of the sky. (probably female)

    ša-   coincident
    -te-   dualic
    -ya-   feminine-zoic singular agent – it, she
    -roy-   noun root – sky
    -a-   joiner vowel
    -ti   verb root – be on a side + stative aspect

---

321. Toupin 1996:958. This name is also reported by Hancks as Shah-tah-hooh-rohn-teh Half the Sky, and belonging to Ebenezer Zane, son of Isaac Zane Jr., a white man adopted by the Wyandot.

322. Toupin 1996:823 as chiarih8ata, 825 as chiarih8ate, 860 as chiate ,arih8ate and possibly the entry on 887 which is the sole source for the next name. This name relates to one of the Mohawk sachem names.

323. Buser 1989. He had the nickname of Leatherlips.

324. Toupin 1996:887.

Šateyaroyes[325]	It is often as tall, as long as the sky. Half the height of the sky. (male Large Turtle)
[shah-teh-yah-ron-yehs]	
ša-	coincident
-te-	dualic
-ya-	feminine-zoic singular agent – it
-roy-	noun root – sky
-es	verb root – be tall, long + habitual aspect

Shumęnduwat[326]	He is very large, in word, voice, authority (male Striped Turtle)
[s-hoo-men-doo-wat]	
s-	repetitive – very
-hu-	masculine singular patient – he
-męnd-	noun root – word, voice
-uwat	verb root – be large + stative aspect

Skamęndanduro[327]	She has a very valuable voice, word. (female)
[skah-men-dan-doo-ron]	
s-	repetitive – very
-ka-	feminine-zoic singular agent – she
-męnd-	noun root – voice, word
-a-	joiner vowel
-nduro	verb root – be valuable + stative aspect

Skahmęndati[328]	She is on the other side of the island. (female Porcupine)
[skah-mend-ah-tee]	
s-	repetitive
-ka-	feminine-zoic singular agent – she
-hmęnd-	noun root – island
-a-	joiner vowel
-ti	verb root – be on a side + stative aspect

---

325. Toupin 1996:217.

326. Toupin 1996: 187, 209, 229, 244, 828, and 945. C.A. Buser "Our Great Chiefs" https://www.wyandotte-nation.org/culture/history/general-history/our-great-chiefs/, and S.C. Andrews https://www.wyandotte-nation.org/culture/history/timeline/1534-1842/ and Finley 1840:285 as sum-mun-de-wat.

327. Toupin 1996:829, 831, 840 and 844.

328. Connelley 1900:110 "Skah'-mëhn-dah-teh." Toupin 1996:880, 883, 896, 929, 945, 947 and 953. She was the daughter of Monocue.

Skandare[329]	It exists again. (female and male)
[skan-dah-reh]	
s-	repetitive – again
-ka-	feminine-zoic singular agent – it
-ndare	verb root – exist + stative aspect

Skandatatih[330]	It is on the other side of the village. (male)
[skan-dah-tah-teeh]	
s-	repetitive – other
-ka-	feminine-zoic singular agent – it
-ndat-	noun root – village
-a-	joiner vowel
-ti-	verb root – be on a side
-h	stative aspect

Skandawati[331]	It is on the other side of the river (mythic male).
[skan-dah-wah-tee]	
s-	repetitive – other
-ka-	feminine-zoic singular agent – it
-ndaw-	noun root – river
-a-	joiner vowel
-ti	verb root – be on a side + stative aspect

Skanderęhaǫh[332]	Her waist is carrying again. (female)
[skan-deh-reh-ha-onh]	
s-	repetitive – again
-ka-	feminine-zoic singular agent – she
-nder-	noun root – waist, torso
-ęhaǫ-	verb root – carry
-h	stative aspect

Skandešrisǫh[333]	She is again up against a lot of sand. (female)
[skan-deh-shree-sonh]	
s-	repetitive
-ka-	feminine-zoic singular agent – she
-ndešr-	noun root – sand
-is-	verb root – be up against

329. Toupin 1996:832, 837, 841 and 843 female and 839, 840, 846, 849, 852 and 856 male.

330. Toupin 1996:205 and 242. It is possible that the Skawduutoutee in the Treaty of 1817 is a bad attempt at writing this name.

331. Barbeau 1915:61.

332. Toupin 1996:874, 879-80, 899, 929, and 952. The translation may not be completely accurate.

333. Toupin 1996:892, 894, 897, 902 and 967.

-ǫ-	distributive – a lot
-h	stative aspect

Skangyeretsih[334] It is a very long bird's tail, pipestone, canoe point (male).
[skan-gyeh-reh-tseeh]

s-	repetitive – very
-ka-	feminine-zoic singular agent – it
-ngyer-	noun root – bird's tail
-ets-	verb root – be long
-ih	stative aspect

Skaʔngyuwat[335] She has a very big finger, big fingers. (female Large Turtle)
[skah-an-gyoo-wat]

s-	repetitive – very
-ka-	feminine-zoic singular agent – she or it
-ʔngy-	noun root – finger
-uwat	verb root – be large + stative aspect

Skanętarǫʔ[336] Evergreens are often again distant from each other. (female)
[skah-nen-tah-ron-on]

s-	repetitive – again
-ka-	feminine-zoic singular agent – it
-nęt-	noun root – evergreen, evergreens
-a-	joiner vowel
-rǫ-	verb root – be distant
-ʔ	habitual aspect

Skanętatih[337] She is on the other side of the evergreen(s). (female)
[skah-nen-tah-teeh]

s-	repetitive – other
-ka-	feminine-zoic singular agent – she, it
-nęt-	noun root – evergreen
-a-	joiner vowel
-ti-	verb root – be on a side
-h	stative aspect

---

334. Potier 1920:148. Toupin 1996:182–3, 200, 204, 224, 238, 241, 845–6, 859, 864, 871, 879, and 957–8.

335. Barbeau 1911:1. Barbeau also spelled this as Skaʔengyuwat with the possible addition of the semi-reflexive voice -e- (Barbeau 1911:45).

336. Toupin 1996:826 gannentarhon, 831 skannentaronk, 833 skannentar8t, 834, skannentaront, 836 skannentaronk, 837 kannenkaron, 845 skanneentaron, 846, skannentaron, 871 skannentaronk, 888 skannentaron, 899 skannentaron and 903 skannentaronk.

337. Toupin 1996:892

Skanetato³³⁸   It is becoming evergreen again (perhaps a forest). (female)
[skah-nen-tah-ton]

    s-   repetitive – again
    -ka-   feminine-zoic singular agent – it
    -net-   noun root – evergreen
    -ato   verb root – become + stative aspect

Skanodes³³⁹   It is a very long mark. (female)
[skah-non-dehs]

    s-   repetitive – very
    -ka-   feminine-zoic singular agent – it
    -nod-   noun root – mark
    -es   verb root – be long + habitual aspect

Skanotaro³⁴⁰   She is crossing a hill, mountain again. (female)
[skah-non-tah-ron]

    s-   repetitive – again
    -ka-   feminine-zoic singular agent – she
    -not-   noun root – hill, mountain
    -a-   joiner vowel
    -ro   verb root – cross + stative aspect

Skwahskyaro³⁴¹   She is moving very fast. (female Snake)
[skwahs-kyah-ron]

    skw-   repetitive – very
    -ahskyaro   feminine-zoic singular agent – she + verb root – move fast + stative aspect

Skwatandi³⁴²   She is very afraid (female Striped Turtle)
[skwah-tan-dee]

    skw-   repetitive – very
    -ata-   verb root – fear, be afraid
    -nd-   inchoative root suffix
    -i   stative aspect

---

338. Toupin 1996:822, 829 and 888. An alternative translation would be "Evergreens are disappearing again" with the verb -ato- be lost, disappear.

339. Toupin 1996:850 as Skannondes.

340. Toupin 1996:826. This verb usually takes the dualic, but perhaps that is cancelled out by the repetitive.

341. Barbeau 1911:15 and 44, and Connelley 1900:111: "Snake Clan. Squäh:-skah-rōh. She moves quickly; or she moves suddenly; or she turns unexpectedly."

342. Toupin 1996:208, 234, 826, 832–3, 837, 851, 904, 910 and 921.

Skwaterę[343]	She is missed, missing again. (female Deer)	
[skwah-ten-reh]		
	skw-	repetitive – again
	-at-	feminine-zoic singular agent – she + semi-reflexive voice
	-ęre	verb root – for something to be missing + stative aspect
Skwętuwat[344]	It is a very large, great day. (male)	
[skwen-too-wat]		
	skw-	repetitive – very
	-ęt-	feminine-zoic singular agent – it + noun root – day
	-uwat	verb root – be large, great + stative aspect
Skweyatęsti[345]	She again thickens the water, liquid (female)	
[skweh-yah-ten-stee]		
	sk-	repetitive – again
	-w-	feminine-zoic singular patient - she
	-ey-	noun root – water, liquid
	-atęs-[346]	verb root – be thick
	-t-	causative root suffix
	-i	stative aspect
Sǫmanduyareskwa[347]	Our poplar(s) used to be very tall. (male)	
[son-man-doo-yah-reh-skwah]		
	s-	repetitive - very
	ǫma-	masculine singular agent + 1st-person plural patient – he – us
	-nduyar-	noun root – poplar
	-es-	verb root – be tall, long + habitual aspect
	-kwa	past aspect suffix

---

343. Toupin 1996:829 and 830 as sk8ateenre, 830–3, 840, 842, 844 and 968 as sk8atenre. It is also found in Wendat.

344. Toupin 1996:848.

345. Toupin 1996:855 as sk8a,atensti. I changed the first -a- to an -e- as it does not seem grammatical any other way.

346. The actual verb root is -tęts- but it is affected by the -t- of the causative-instrumental root suffix that follows.

347. Toupin 1996:835

Shǫnǫkyakǫ⁷³⁴⁸ He is breaking a mountain or hill into very many pieces. (male Bear)
[s-hon-on-kyah-kon-on]

    s-   repetitive – very
    -hǫ-   masculine singular patient – he
    -nǫk-   noun root – hill or mountain
    -ya-   verb root – break
    -kǫ-   distributive root suffix
    -ʔ   stative aspect

Suhkaratsiwayę³⁴⁹ Wood chips are smelling very strong (just gnawed by a beaver). (male)
[s-ooh-kah-rah-tsee-wah-yen]

    s-   repetitive – very
    -u-   feminine-zoic singular patient – it
    -hkar-   noun root – wood chips
    -a-   joiner vowel
    -tsiway-   verb root – smell strong
    -ę   stative aspect

Sundeyęh³⁵⁰ She is joining again. (female Bear)
[soon-deh-yenh]

    s-   repetitive – again
    -u-   feminine-zoic singular patient - she
    -ndeyę-   verb root – join, be joined
    -h   stative aspect

Shuriwaętǫ⁷³⁵¹ He is putting, dealing with very many matters. (male)
[s-hoo-ree-wah-en-ton-on]

    s-   repetitive – very
    -hu-   masculine singular patient – he
    -riw-   noun root – matter, affair
    -a-   joiner vowel
    -ę-   verb root – put
    -tǫ-   distributive root suffix
    -ʔ   stative aspect

---

348. Toupin 1996:865 as Sonnontkiakonk, 926 as Sonnontkiaxon and 974 as Ts8nnontkiakonk. It is probable that the name presented as Sonnentiaxon in 225 and 258 represents the same name. This name is shared with the Wendat.

349. Toupin 1996:838.

350. Toupin 1996:183, 188, 195, 202, 221, 222, 228, 256 and 257.

351. Toupin 1996:830. The name appears without the initial -s- in 870, 875 and with the 1758 death anniversary ceremony of orih8aenton in 942.

Shutetsęnskǫh[352]
[s-hoo-teh-tsen-skonh]

	He is quite frequently a healer, curer. (male Wolf)
s-	repetitive – very
-hu-	masculine singular patient – he
-te-	semi-reflexive voice
-tsęn-	verb root – cure, heal, doctor
-skǫ-	frequentative root suffix
-h	stative aspect

Shutra'tes[353]
[s-hoo-trah-ah-tehs]

	His quills are very long. (male Porcupine)
s-	repetitive – very
-hu-	masculine singular patient – his
-tra't-	noun root – quills
-es	verb root – be long + habitual aspect

Tahakye[354]
[tah-hah-kyeh]

	He is not going to abandon it. (male Prairie Turtle)
t-	negative
-a-	factual
-h-	masculine singular agent – he
-aky-	verb root – abandon, quit, throw
-e	purposive aspect

Taharihǫkye[355]
[tah-hah-ree-hon-kyeh]

	His affair, news is not going to continue. (male)
t-	negative
-a-	factual
-ha-	masculine singular agent – he
-rih-	noun root – matter, affair, news
-ǫky-	verb root – continue
-e	purposive aspect

352. Toupin 1996:221. Barbeau 1911:7 and 44.

353. Barbeau 1911:10 and 45. This name was also given to a Frenchmen called Courtmanche in the 18th century (Toupin 1996:235).

354. Toupin 1996:229, 631, 834, 837, 878–9 and 956 as tahatie, 250 and 494 as rakiet, and 539 as takiet,; Lajeunesse 1960:94 as "Takay."

355. Toupin 1996:203, 571, 831 (te,ariontie), 881, 945–6, 947–8, 954, and 953 (t'aharihontie) and 954.

Taharǫyutęh[356]	He stuck out in the sky. (male Deer)
[tah-hah-ron-yoo-tenh]	
t-	dualic
-a-	factual
-ha-	masculine singular agent – he
-rǫy-	noun root – sky
-ut-	verb root – stand
-ęh	punctual aspect

Tanduyares[357]	Where the poplars are often tall. (female Prairie Turtle)
[tan-doo-yah-rehs]	
t-	cislocative
-a-	feminine-zoic singular agent – it, she
-nduyar-	noun root – poplar
-es	verb root – be tall + habitual aspect

T[h]atęriʔa[358]	He is (the little/younger one) left behind. (male mythic figure)
[t-hah-ten-ree-ee-ah]	
t-	dualic
-h-	masculine singular agent – he
-at-	semi-reflexive voice
-ęri-	verb root – omit or leave behind
-ʔ-	stative aspect
-a	diminutive aspect suffix

Tehašitawanęs[359]	He has two big feet. (male Porcupine)
[teh-hah-shee-tah-wah-nens]	
te-	dualic
-h-	masculine singular agent – he
-ašit-	noun root – foot
-a-	joiner vowel
-wanę-	verb root – be large + stative aspect
-s	plural aspect suffix

356. Barbeau 1911:11, 46 "when daylight is breaking … appearing" and Barbeau 1915:x. In his biographical panel of Hiram Star Young, Jeremy Turner has John Solomon, Young's uncle as bearing the name "Taharoʔuteʔ he sticks out of the sky."

357. This appears as tandoares in Toupin 1996:208, 216, 876, 882, 888, and 957–8. The problem with this form is that it appears to be taking the masculine singular agent form. The feminine-zoic agent form with the stative aspect, kando[,]aretsi 'where poplars are tall, where a poplar is tall,' which is more accurate, only appears once (Toupin 1996:962).

358. Barbeau 1960: 169, 170, 172-5, 177, 179, 180, 181, !82, and 183.

359. Divine 2019:141–4.

Tehunyę'nhažu'kye?[360]   He has fringes alongside his leggings (uncle in myth[361])
[teh-hoo-nyen-en-hah-zhoo-oo-kyeh-eh]

te-	dualic
-hu-	masculine singular patient – he
-nyę'nhaž-	noun root – fringe, fringes on leggings
-u'kye-	verb root – be alongside, continue
-?	stative aspect

Teyanǫęs[362]   She does not often fall into deep water. (female)
[teh-yah-non-ens]

te-	negative
-ya-	feminine-zoic singular agent – she
-nǫ-	noun root – deep water[363]
-ę-	verb root – fall
-s	inchoative root suffix + habitual aspect

Thahmęndarǫs[364]   His voice is often heard twice, echos. (male Bear)
[t-hah-men-dah-rons]

t-	dualic
-ha-	masculine singular agent – he
-męnd-	noun root – voice, word
-arǫ-	verb root – hear
-s	habitual aspect[365]

Thandawias[366]   He often cuts the river in two. (male)
[t-han-dah-wee-yas]

t-	dualic
-ha-	masculine singular agent – he
-ndaw-	noun root – river
-ia-	verb root – cut in two
-s	habitual aspect

360. Barbeau 1960:208 #50–1, 209 #13, 24 and 51–2, and 210 #2.

361. The Old Bear and the Nephew (Barbeau 1960:197–210).

362. Toupin 1996:254 and 842 as te ,annonens, 843 as te annonnens and 223, 847, 852 and 922 as te ,annonnens.

363. There is an identically sounding noun root that means 'chasm' or 'precipice'. It might be the same noun root.

364. Barbeau 1911:16.

365. This is not the form the habitual takes in Potier 1920:173.

366. Toupin 1996:833 as toanda8ias, 845 as taonda8ias and 848 as tanda8ias. He was an adopted Abenaki.

Thanęhušreh[367]	Water is not going to flow in his corn. (male Snake)
[t-hah-nen-hoo-shreh]	
t-	negative
-ha-	masculine singular agent – his
-nęh-	noun root – corn
-u-	verb root – be in water
-šr-	dislocative root suffix
-eh	purposive aspect

Tharatuwaht[368]	He has two large heels. (male)
[t-hah-rah-too-waht]	
t-	dualic – two
-ha-	masculine singular agent – he
-rat-	noun root – heel
-uwaht	verb root – be large + stative aspect

Thayǫšǫtakwi[369]	He has a face of two forms, natures. (male Bear)
[t-hah-yon-shon-tah-kwee]	
t-	dualic
-ha-	masculine singular agent – he
-yǫš-	noun root – face
-ǫt-	verb root – attach, be attached
-akw-	instrumental root suffix
-i	stative aspect

Thanǫwarurę[370]	He is splitting the head, brains in two. (male)
[t-hah-non-wah-roo-ren]	
t-	dualic
-ha-	masculine singular agent – he
-nǫwar-	noun root – head, brain
-urę	verb root – split in two + stative aspect

367. I am not sure that this is the exact translation. Steckley 2014:43, 158, 161, 207 and 233. Toupin 1006:198, 226, 228, 259, 833, 878, 881, 883, 885, 901–2, 904, 95, 947, 949 and 954. His nickname is "Coupe-jarret" which could mean 'cut on the back of the leg'.

368. Toupin 1996:886 as tara8at, 888 as tarr8at, 893-4 and 896 as tara8a't.

369. Toupin 1996:215 as tonchiontonk8i, 248 as ïonchiontak8i, 845 as taonchientonk8i (2 times), and 852, 854 and 855 as tonchiontonk8i. The various representations made this hard to translate. I believe that the extra -ǫ- in the verb came about as the product of the -a- coming after two nasal vowels.

370. Toupin 1996:958.

Thanyęduyęh³⁷¹ His skill, ability is divided. (male Prairie Turtle)
[t-ha-nyen-doo-yenh]
    t- dualic
    -ha- masculine singular agent – he, his
    -nyęd- noun root – skill, ability
    -uyę- verb root – be divided
    -h stative aspect

Thaǫndešrurę?³⁷² He is splitting the country in two. (male Large Turtle).
[t-ha-on-deh-shroo-ren-en]
    t- dualic
    -ha- masculine singular agent – he
    -ǫnde- verb root – have as country
    -šr- nominalizer
    -urę- verb root – split in two
    -? stative aspect

Thaǫtariayi³⁷³ He is cutting the lake in two. (male)
[t-ha-on-tah-ree-ah-yee]
    t- dualic
    -ha- masculine singular agent – he
    -ǫtar- noun root – lake
    -iay- verb root – cut in two
    -i stative aspect

Taǫtǫwętsatase³⁷⁴ Where one twisted, turned the land. (male)
[tah-on-ton-wen-tsah-tah-she]
    t- cislocative – where
    -a- factual
    -ǫ- indefinite agent – one, they
    -t- semi-reflexive voice
    -ǫwęts- noun root – land
    -a- joiner vowel
    -tase verb root – twist, turn + punctual aspect

371. Toupin 1996:216, 218, 229, 250, 252, 864, 867, 888–9, 907, 953 and 966.

372. Toupin 1996:217 and 223. Taondechoren.

373. Toupin 1996: 826, 832, 843, 874–6, 879, 881, 887, 890, 895, 909, 961, 874 and 895. This may be a reference to the name for Quebec, a statement of where the first by that name came from. It was passed down to several people. Potier wrote the place name as Te,atontari,e – referring to how Isle D'Orleans divides the St. Lawrence River in two.

374. Toupin 1996:828 as taonton8entsatas and 833 as taoton8entsatas. Adding the -e- at the end of this word follows the example of Tehatǫtaratase where the word appears both with and without the final -e.

Taǫtrạndeyẹh[375]
[tah-on-ten-deh-yenh]

t-	dualic
-a-	factual
-ǫ-	indefinite agent – they (ind)
-tẹ-	semi-reflexive voice
-ndeyẹ-	verb root – be joined
-h	punctual aspect

Taretande[376]
[tah-reh-tan-deh]

t-	cislocative
-a-	factual
-r-	masculine singular agent – he
-e-	verb root – go
-t-	causative root suffix
-and-	dislocative root suffix
-e	purposive aspect

He is at the point of going. (male Bear)

Tarhe[377]
[tar-heh]

(male Porcupine)

Thatǫhwẹtsurẹh[378]
[t-hah-ton-hwen-tsoo-renh]

He splits the land in two. (male)

t-	dualic
-h-	masculine singular agent
-at-	semi-reflexive voice
-ǫhẹts-	noun root – land, earth
-urẹ-	verb root – split, divide in two
-h	stative aspect

Taurhẹdihakye[379]
[teh-oo-rhen-dee-hah-kyeh]

When, or where day(light) is continuing to come. (male)

t-	cislocative[380]
-a-	factual

---

375. Toupin 1996:822 "tao8arande,en" and 839 "taonrande,en."

376. Steckley 2014:117, 158, 162–3, 186, 191, 198, 207 and 231. Toupin 1996:182, 195, 221, 228, 238, 244 and 256.

377. See "Tarhe: A Man with Two Nicknames" in chapter five.

378. Toupin 1996:902 taton8ensoren and 903 toton8ensoren.

379. Toupin 1996:895, 929 and 956.

380. This could also be the dualic, with no significant change to the meaning, or the negative.

-u-	feminine-zoic singular patient - it
-rhę-	verb root – for day to come
-d-	inchoative root suffix
-i-	stative aspect
-haky-	progressive root suffix
-e	purposive aspect

Taurhęšre?[381]
[tah-oo-rhen-shreh-eh]

When day is dawning, going to dawn. (male Striped Turtle)

-t-	cislocative
-a-	factual
-u-	feminine-zoic singular patient - it
-rhę-	verb root – dawn
-šr-	inchoative + dislocative root suffix
-e?	purposive aspect

Tawašruwanęh[382]
[tah-wah-shroo-wan-enh]

Where there is a large axe. (male)

taw-	cislocative - where[383]
-ašr-	feminine-zoic singular agent + noun root – axe
-uwanę-	verb root – be large
-h	stative aspect

Thawęntaestih[384]
[t-hah-wen-tah-eh-steeh]

He is striking it with a stick. (male Bear)

t-	dualic
-haw-	masculine singular patient – he
-ęt-	noun root – stick
-ae-	verb root – hit, strike
-st-	causative-instrumental root suffix
-ih	stative aspect

381. Barbeau 1915:x and 1911:44: Isiah Walker named. Connelley 1900:111 claims it is a Large Turtle clan name, possibly a mistake and that the implications of the name include "The Turtle sees the light," i.e., "when he floats up to the surface of the water." He mentions that Isiah Walker married a woman of the Large Turtle clan, Ayanyęmiha, which would have been against the rules of clan exogamy among the Wyandot. This furthers the possibility that he got Isiah Walker's clan wrong. This name also exists in Wendat (Vincent 1984:72, 83, 87, 179, 324, 433 and 461, and JR17:145).

382. Toupin 1996:234 and 261. This name was recorded for a Frenchman, not a Wyandot (see Naming the Incomers).

383. It is also possible that it is the negative.

384. Toupin 1996:203, 840 and 842.

Tawinde[385]	Otter (female and male name)
[tah-win-deh]	

Taya'nǫkye?[386]	An arrow is continuing on its way (this way) (male Deer)
[tah-yah-an-non-kyeh-eh]	
t-	dualic
-a-	factual
-ya-	feminine-zoic agent – it
-n-	noun root – arrow
-ǫky-	verb root – continue
-e	purposive aspect

Tayeąndrak[387]	Look at me! (male Prairie Turtle)
[tah-yeh-an-drak]	
t-	imperative
-aye-	1st-person singular patient – me
-yąndra-	verb root – look at
-k-	imperative aspect

Tayehšatę[388]	Carry me on your back! (male Wolf)
[tah-yeh-shah-ten]	
t-	imperative
-aye-	1st-person singular patient – me
-hšatę	verb root – carry on the back + imperative aspect

Tehaa'tat[389]	He, his body is standing. (male Striped Turtle)
[teh-hah-ah-tat]	
te-	dualic
-ha-	masculine singular agent – he
-a't-	noun root – body
-a-	joiner vowel
-t	verb root – stand + stative aspect

385. Toupin 1996:826 (female), 831 and 834 (male). It was also used to refer to a French officer at Detroit named Demuisseau (Toupin 1996:234 and 261).

386. Barbeau 1911:11.

387. Steckley 2014:145, 158, 166–7, 186, 199, 208, 284 and Toupin 1996:186, 187, 208, 210, 229, 238 and 245.

388. Potier 1920:148, Toupin 1996: 173, 176, 184, 189, 194, 196, 200, 206, 213, 220, 224, 227, 238, 242, 247, 254, 257 and 260, and JR69:249 and 263.

389. Toupin 1996:208. This name belonged to a nine-year-old boy.

Tehaa’tureş[390]
[teh-hah-ah-too-rens]
- te- — dualic
- -ha- — masculine singular agent + feminine-zoic singular patient – he – it
- -a’t- — noun root – body
- -ureę- — verb root – split in two
- -s — habitual aspect

Tehandakwayeh[391]
[teh-han-dah-kwah-yeh]
- te- — dualic
- -ha- — masculine singular agent – he
- -ndakw- — noun root – drum, barrel
- -a- — joiner vowel
- -ye- — verb root – number
- -h — stative aspect

Tehangyasaroǫ[392]
[teh-ha-ngyah-sah-ron]
- te- — dualic
- -ha- — masculine singular agent – he
- -ngyas- — noun root – neck
- -a- — joiner vowel
- -roǫ — verb root – cross + stative aspect

Teharǫyureş[393]
[teh-hah-ron-yoo-reh-eh]
- te- — dualic
- -ha- — masculine singular agent – he
- -rǫy- — noun root – sky
- -ureę- — verb root – split in two
- -s — habitual aspect

---

390. Signed Treaty 2 with a wolf's head (1790) and the name te-ha-to-rence (Curnoe 1996:135). Signed the Greenville Treaty of 1795 as te-haaw-to-rens. https://www.wyandotte-nation.org/culture/treaties/treaty-of-1795/.

391. Toupin 1996:864 handak8a,e, 929 te hendak8a,e, 948 te handak8a,e and 960 te ,andak8a.

392. Toupin 1996:832 as tanniatsaron and 839 as te hondiasaron.

393. Steckley 2014:117, 152–3, 158, 168, 177–8, 196, 207, 225 and 286. Toupin 1996:213, 220, 239, 246 and 260. Connelley 1900:111, 38: Big Turtle Clan ….Têh'-häh-rōhn'-yooh-rĕh. Means "Splitting the sky," i.e., the Big Turtle is rushing across the sky, dividing it with his course." It is written as "taronhi8rens," which shows the habitual aspect and not the stative as in the text here.

Tehahšęndayeh[394] He has two names. (male name)
[teh-hah-sen-day-yeh]

    te-　　　　　　　　dualic
    -ha-　　　　　　　masculine singular agent – he
    -hšęnd-　　　　　　noun root – name
    -a-　　　　　　　　joiner vowel
    -ye-　　　　　　　verb root – number
    -h　　　　　　　　stative aspect

Teharęhǫt[395] He is not putting the branch into the fire. (male)
[teh-hah-reh-hont]

    te-　　　　　　　　negative
    ha-　　　　　　　　masculine singular agent – he
    -ręh-　　　　　　　noun root – branch, branches, treetops
    -ǫt　　　　　　　　verb root – be, put in a fire + stative aspect

Teharhatase?[396] He is going around the forest. (male Large Turtle)
[teh-har-hah-tah-seh-eh]

    te-　　　　　　　　dualic
    -ha-　　　　　　　masculine singular agent – he
    -rh-　　　　　　　noun root – forest
    -a-　　　　　　　　joiner vowel
    -tase-　　　　　　verb root – turn, twist
    -?　　　　　　　　stative aspect

Tehašituwanęh[397] He has two big feet. (male Porcupine clan)
[teh-hah-shee-too-wah-nenh]

    te-　　　　　　　　dualic
    -h-　　　　　　　　masculine singular agent – he
    -ašit-　　　　　　noun root – foot
    -uwanę-　　　　　　verb root – be large
    -h　　　　　　　　stative aspect

---

394. Toupin 1996:883. The Wendat version of this name was recorded in Vincent 1984:161.

395. Toupin 1996:872.

396. Connelley 1900:111 46. Big Turtle Clan. Brother of Governor William Walker. Name Räh'-hahn-tah'-sĕh. Means "Twisting the forest," i.e., as the wind moves, waves, and twists the willows along the banks of the stream in which the turtle lives.

397. Big Foot was a big man who was killed in 1782 (Divine 2019:141–4 and 148-9). I have not seen his name in Wyandot, but I believe that the translation from English that I have made is a likely one. It was probably a nickname. He had an older brother by the name of Haskutaše.

Tehatas[398] He often stands up. (male)
[tch-hah-tas]
    te- dualic
    -ha- masculine singular agent – he
    -t- verb root – stand
    -as inchoative root suffix + habitual aspect

Tehatatatǫh[399] He is surrounding it (i.e., with arms wrapped around a tree). (male Bear)
[teh-hah-tah-tah-tonh]
    te- dualic
    -h- masculine singular agent – he
    -atat- reflexive voice
    -atǫ- verb root – surround
    -h stative aspect

Tehatǫtaratase[400] He is going around a lake. (male Striped Turtle)
[teh-hah-ton-tah-rah-tah-seh-eh]
    te- dualic
    -h- masculine singular agent – he
    -at- semi-reflexive voice
    -ǫtar- noun root – lake
    -a- joiner vowel
    -tase- verb root – turn, twist + stative aspect

Tehatrǫuyuhta?[401] He often penetrates the sky at a particular place. (male Snipe)
[te-hah-tron-oo-yooh-tah-ah]
    te- dualic
    -h- masculine singular agent – he
    -at- semi-reflexive voice
    -rǫ- noun root – sky
    -uyu- verb root – penetrate
    -ht- causative root suffix
    -a? habitual aspect

---

398. Toupin 1996:884.

399. Barbeau 1911:16.

400. Toupin 1996:186, 201, 209, 238, 244 and 836 as taotontaratase. Powell 1881:60 "Ta-há-so[n]-ta-ra-ta-se *(Going Around the Lake)*." One thing that I find curious about this name as Striped Turtle, is that in the Snake clan's story of origin are songs entitled "He twists himself in the lake" and "I go around the lake." (Barbeau 1915:91, fn2).

401. Barbeau 1911:18.

Tehatrǫyatase'[402]	His sky is twisted; he is twisting the sky. (male Bear)
[teh-hah-tron-yah-tah-seh-eh]	
te-	dualic
-h-	masculine singular agent – he
-at-	semi-reflexive voice
-rǫy-	noun root – sky
-a-	joiner vowel
-tase-	verb root – turn, twist
-ʔ	stative aspect

Tehaukęh	He has two things opposite each other; his teeth are tartared.[403] (male)
[teh-hah-oo-kenh]	
te-	dualic
-ha-	masculine singular patient – he
-ukę-	verb root – be opposite each other
-h	stative aspect

Tehažahšuwanęʔs[404]	He has two large arms. (male)
[teh-hah-zhah-shoo-wah-nens]	
te-	dualic
-ha-	masculine singular agent – he
-žahš-	noun root – arm
-uwanę-	verb root – be large
-ʔ-	stative aspect
-s	plural aspect suffix

Tehǫmandušrakwa[405]	They (f) often grab his robe. (male)
[teh-hon-man-doo-shrah-kwah]	
te-	dualic
-hǫma-	feminine-zoic plural agent + masculine singular patient – they (f) – him
-ndušr-	noun root – robe
-a-	joiner vowel
-kwa	verb root – seize, grab + habitual aspect

402. Toupin 1996:223 (with initial -t-), 239, 256 (with initial -t-), 872 and 882.

403. Barbeau 1911:46 has it translated as "your teeth are tartared", although there is no 2nd-person pronominal prefix. I suspect that this is a nickname.

404. Barbeau 1911:46, and Toupin 1996:894 and 896. There is a name in the Treaty of 1814 which is presented as Zashuona – Big Arm – which is probably the same. There is a possibility that this name is a nickname.

405. Toupin 1996: 834 as ta8ond8chak8a and taond8chak8a and 928 as tehonand8chrak8a.

Tehǫmatsarandih[406] — They are pushing him over. (male Porcupine)
[ton-mah-tsah-ran-deeh]

- t- — dualic
- -hǫm- — masculine plural agent + masculine singular patient – they – him
- -atsar- — verb root – push over
- -and- — inchoative root suffix
- -ih — stative aspect

Tehǫmayandra[407] — They (m) are looking at him. (male)
[teh-hon-mah-yan-drah]

- te- — dualic
- -hǫma- — masculine plural agent + masculine singular patient – they – him
- -ayandra- — verb root – look at + stative aspect

Tehuhǫrandeyęh[408] — He has feathers joined. (male)
[teh- hoo-ran-deh-yenh]

- te- — dualic
- -hu- — masculine singular patient – he
- -hǫr- — noun root – feather
- -a- — joiner vowel
- -ndeyę- — verb root – join
- -h — stative aspect

Tehukakašra[409] — He has double eyes. (male Bear - nickname)
[te-hoo-kah-kah-shrah]

- te- — dualic
- hu- — masculine singular patient – he
- -k- — semi-reflexive voice
- -(y)ak- — noun root – white of the eye, eye
- -ašra — verb root – be double + stative aspect

---

406. Toupin 1996:859, 863, 865, 870, 877, 929, 944 and 947. Barbeau 1915:103 fn1 has the name given to an old man called Littlechief who told the Wolf clan story. It appears that the first reference to this name occurred concerning the talks in July and August preceding the Great Peace of Montreal in 1701. The name Houatsarant is included with that of Kondiaronk, and the Bear leader Quarante Sols, representing the Deer phratry (La Potherie 4:222).

407. Toupin 1996:832 and 851.

408. Toupin 1996:902.

409. This was a name given to Robert Robitaille, adopted into the Bear clan. Connelley presented it as: "Teh-hooh'-kah-quah'-shrooh," which he interpreted as meaning: "'Bear with four eyes,' so named because he wore spectacles when he was adopted'" (Connelley 1899b:36 and 110).

Tehumayęs[410]   They (indefinite), people, one cannot see him. (male Snake)
[teh-hoo-mah-yens]

     te-   negative
     -huma-   indefinite agent + masculine singular patient – they or one – him
     -yę-   verb root – see
     -s   habitual aspect

Tehuratati[411]   He is running. (male Wolf)
[teh-hoo-rah-tah-tee]

     te-   dualic
     -hu-   masculine singular patient – he
     -ratat-   verb root – run
     -i   stative aspect.

Tehurǫtatiri[412]   A tree is not supporting him. (male)
[teh-hoo-ron-tah-tee-ree]

     te-   negative
     -hu-   feminine-zoic singular agent + masculine singular patient – it – him
     -rǫt-   noun root – tree
     -atiri   verb root – support + stative aspect

Tehurǫyateh[413]   He exists as two skies or he is not the sky. (male)
[teh-hoo-ron-yah-teh]

     te-   dualic or negative
     -hu-   masculine singular patient – he
     -rǫy-   noun root – sky
     -ate-   verb root – exist
     -h   stative aspect

---

410. "This was given to Charles L of the Snake clan and was said to mean 'You cannot see him,' or 'He is invisible'" (Connelley 1900:36). 111:26. Snake Clan. Těh-hŏŏh-mah-yěhs. Means "you cannot see him; or invisible."

411. Potier 1920:149, and Toupin 1996:192, 217, 221, 246, 251, and 255. The name seems also to be found as "Tha-ra-tou-hat" at the Council held at Detroit April 26, 1781 (Lajeunesse 1960:126).

412. Toupin 1996:249 as te orontatirhon, 836 as ,arentatiri, 841 as te ,arontatiron,843 as te yarontatire, 847 as orontatiri, 843 te ,arontatiri, 850 as te horontatiri, and 854 as te horontatiri.

413. Toupin 1996:909. There was a temptation to conflate this name with Hurǫyate, but they were married to two different women.

Tehuroyateka[414]	He does not burn the sky.[415] (male Large Turtle)
[teh-hoo-ron-yoo-teh-kah]	
te-	negative
-hu-	masculine singular patient – he
-roy-	noun root – sky
-atek-	verb root – burn
-a	habitual aspect

Tehonęhawehtih[416]	He does not have all of the corn. (male Deer)
[teh-hon-nen-hah-weh-teeh]	
te-	negative
-ho-	masculine singular agent – he
-nęh-	noun root – corn
-a-	joiner vowel
-we-	verb root – be together
-ht-	causative root suffix
-ih	stative aspect

Tehuroyureta[417]	He often examines, considers the sky. (female)
[teh-hoo-ron-yoo-reh-tah]	
te-	dualic
-hu-	masculine singular patient – he
-roy-	noun root – sky
-uret-	verb root – examine, consider
-a	habitual aspect

Tehušititako[418]	He has two feet seized by the cold. (male Miami chief)
[teh-hoo-shee-tee-tah-kon]	
te-	dualic
-hu-	masculine singular patient – he
-šit-	noun root – foot
-itako	verb root – be seized by the cold + stative aspect

414. Barbeau 1915:xi Jacob Whitewing as Striped Turtle. Steckley as Large Turtle, 2014:117, 158, 164, 186-7, 207 and 227. Perhaps there was some confusion with the male Striped Turtle name that precedes this one. Potier has it as Large Turtle, but also has a -o- or -u- where the -a- would normally be: Toupin 1996:206 as te horonhiotexa, 217 and 228 as tehoronhi8texa, 250 as taronnioteka.

415. This could also mean 'He is not a burning sky', but it seems a lot less likely.

416. See discussion of Adam Brown in introductory chapter.

417. Toupin 1996:849 and 851. In both these cases the person presented is the mother of a baptized child. In these examples there is no dualic, but this verb, like others that involve two eyes, takes the dualic.

418. Toupin 1996:237 and 261 as te hochitaxon. The name as presented there would refer to 'mouth' rather than 'foot'. The Miami chief was known to the French as Pied-Froid 'Cold Foot', which presumably was a translation, as is the Wyandot word, from the original Miami name.

Tehutrǫturę?⁴¹⁹ He is splitting a log in two. (male)
[teh-hoo-tron-too-ren-en]
    te- dualic
    -hu- masculine singular patient – he
    -t- semi-reflexive voice
    -rǫt- noun root – tree, log, pole
    -urę- verb root – split in two
    -ʔ stative aspect

Tehuwehturę⁴²⁰ He is splitting nails, talons in two. (male)
[teh-hooh-too-ren]
    te- dualic
    -huw- masculine singular patient – he
    -eht- noun root – nails or talons
    -urę verb root – split in two + stative aspect

Temękyaʔs⁴²¹ She breaks sticks in two. (female Striped Turtle)
[teh-men-kyah-ahs]
    tem- dualic
    -ęk- feminine-zoic singular agent – she + noun root – stick
    -yaʔ- verb root – break, split in two
    -s habitual aspect

Teǫnęditakon⁴²² Cold is seizing the front of her two legs. (female Wolf)
[teh-on-nen-dee-tah-kon]
    te- dualic
    -ǫ- feminine-zoic singular patient – her
    -nęd- noun root – front of the leg
    -itakǫ verb root – for cold to seize a part of the body + stative aspect

419. Splitlog is a common last name in Barbeau 1911. I don't have it written out in Wyandot in any of the sources.

420. Toupin 1996:840 as 8ectoren and 884 as te hectoren.

421. Barbeau 1911: 4, 44 and 48.

422. This name appears with seven different spellings: nenditaxon (Toupin 1996:221, 229, 862 and 873), nnienditakonk (844), nnenditakon (846 and 849), nnenditaxon (851 and 854), nnditaxon (851). nenditak (859), and nienditaxon (861), all of them incomplete. The only way -itaxon- can appear in a word is with the verb root itaxon 'for cold to seize a part of the body' (Potier 1920:239–40). That much is easy, although it requires the dualic at the beginning. Finding the noun root that precedes it is difficult. There is no -nnend- as a noun root in Potier's dictionary. The noun root -nnient- 'front of the leg' (Potier 1920:451) seems to be the best choice.

Tesayumẹndakwa[423]   He picks up, grabs their words, voices. (male)
[teh-sah-yoo-men-dah-kwah]
    te-   dualic
    -sayu-   masculine singular agent + indefinite patient – he – their (ind)
    -mẹnd-   noun root – word, voice
    -a-   joiner vowel
    -kwa-   verb root – grab, pick up + habitual aspect

Teukyukwaratẹh[424]   It is climbing up the group. (male)
[teh-oo-kyoo-kwah-rah-tenh]
    te-   dualic[425]
    -u-   feminine-zoic[426] singular patient – it
    -kyu-   verb root – be clan or group
    -kw-   instrumental root suffix nominalizer
    -a-   joiner vowel
    -ratẹ-   verb root – climb, mount
    -h   stative aspect

Te'undisewas[427]   She does not often delay. (female Snake)
[teh-eh-oon-dee-se-wahs]
    te'-   negative
    -u-   feminine-zoic singular patient – she
    -ndisewa-   verb root – delay
    -s   habitual aspect.

Teutrǫyuta[428]   She or it does not often stand up in the sky (female)
[teh-oo-tron-yoo-tah]
    te-   negative
    -u-   feminine-zoic singular patient – she or it
    -t-   semi-reflexive voice
    -rǫy-   noun root – sky
    -ut-   verb root – stand
    -a   habitual aspect

423. Barbeau 1911:15.

424. Toupin 1996:886 otkiok8araten (-k- is superscript to indicate Wyandot form), 887 otiok-k8araten, 889 otiak8araten, 894, otkiak8araten, 897 tokiok8araten, 900 tkiok8araten, 904 otkiok8araten and 905 te-otkiak8araten.

425. It seems that the dualic has a special use for names that involve change.

426. This could be the masculine patient, with the -h- nor heard or written by the recorder.

427. Steckley 2014: 35, 120, 157, 161, 166, 186, 190–1, 198, 209 and 231. Toupin 1996:208, 228 and 244. It is written as "te ondise8a" and "tiaondese8a", in which case it is referred to as being of the Striped Turtle clan (see discussion in Steckley 2014:35). An alternative translation could be "It does not often delay her," with the pronominal prefix indicating feminine-zoic singular agent 'it' and the feminine-zoic singular patient 'she'.

428. Toupin 1996:896.

Tewasęhaǫh[429]
[teh-wah-sen-hah-on]

	She is not carrying a spoon, dish, or bowl. (female)
tew-	negative
-a-[430]	feminine-zoic singular agent – she
-s-	noun root – spoon, dish, or bowl
-ęhaǫ-	verb root – carry
-h	stative aspect

Tewašrayeh[431]
[teh-wash-rah-yeh]

	Two axes (male)
tew-	dualic
-ašr-	feminine-zoic singular agent – she or it + noun root – axe
-a-	joiner vowel
-ye-	verb root – number
-h	stative aspect

Tewatǫmętsinde'[432]
[teh-wah-ton-men-tseen-deh-eh]

	Land is not going to be dragged or drawn. (female Bear)
tew-	negative[433]
-at-	feminine-zoic singular agent + semi-reflexive voice
-ǫmęts-	noun root – land, country
-ind-	verb root – to drag or draw
-e'	purposive aspect

Tewatrǫyahkwa[434]
[teh-wah-tron-nyah-kwah-ah]

	She often picks up, takes hold of, lifts the sky.[435] (female Deer)
tew-	dualic
-at-	feminine-zoic singular agent – she + semi-reflexive voice
-rǫy-	noun root – sky
-a-	joiner vowel
-hkwa-	verb root – grab, take hold + habitual aspect

429. Toupin 1996:899.

430. There is a problem here with the conjugation of the noun root. It is a consonant stem, so the feminine-zoic singular agent should be -ya-, but no other noun root even comes close to being suitable here.

431. Toupin 1996:876.

432. Toupin 1996:214 and 248 without the negative.

433. This could include the future or even be the dualic, although there is no apparent reason for the latter.

434. Barbeau 1915:xii Catherine Armstrong. In "Leonard Nicholas Cotter." Sallie Cotter Andrews refers to Lizzie Arms Cotter of the Deer clan having the name Tewatronyahkwa 'Lifting the Sky." https://www.wyandotte-nation.org/culture/history/biographies/leonard-nicholas-cotter-sr/ nation.org/culture/history/biographies/leonard-nicholas-cotter-sr/

435. Barbeau 1911:35 translates it as "sky moving or raising."

Tewesǫh[436] (When) she is walking in, coming to many places. (female Deer)
[teh-weh-sonh]
    tew- cislocative
    -e- feminine-zoic singular agent + verb root – go, walk
    -sǫ- distributive root suffix
    -h stative aspect

Temęndehwatiri[437] They are or one is not being supported by pelts. (male)
[te-men-ndeh-hwah-tee-ree]
    tem- negative
    -ę- indefinite agent – they, one
    -ndehw- noun root – pelt, pelts
    -atiri verb root – support + stative aspect

Tewętut[438] A stick is not standing in the ground. (male)
[teh-wen-toot]
    te- negative
    -w- feminine-zoic singular patient – it
    -ęt- noun root – stick
    -ut verb root – stand + stative aspect

Teyamęnęs[439] Her voice often falls. She often lowers her voice. (female Large Turtle)
[teh-yah-men-nens]
    te- dualic
    -ya- feminine-zoic singular agent – her, she
    -męn- noun root – voice, word
    -ę- verb root – fall
    -s inchoative root suffix + habitual aspect

436. Barbeau 1915:xi – Mary Whitewing Kelley. This name looks like Jane Zane Gordon's sister's name of Ta-we-so, which is translated as 'where the Deer slept last night' but translates like her name of "as the deer runs" (SCA).

437. Toupin 1996:870. There is also in this list the near opposite of this, with the masculine singular instead of the indefinite agent: Handehwatiri 'He is supported by pelts.'

438. Toupin 1996:222 and 226 "te 8ent8t", 856, 860, 865, 883, 885, 925 and 926 "te8entet".

439. Barbeau 1911:2 and 43

Teyąndakwahsęh[440] It is twenty barrels or drums. (male Deer)
[teh-yan-dah-kwah-senh]

    te- dualic
    -ya- feminine-zoic singular agent – it
    -ndakw- noun root – drum, barrel
    -asę- verb root – be ten
    -h stative aspect

Teyandatakwa[441] She or it often seizes a village. (female)
[teh-yan-dah-tah-kwah]

    te- dualic
    -ya- feminine-zoic singular agent – she or it
    -ndat- noun root – village, camp
    -a- joiner vowel
    -kwa verb root – seize, grab + habitual aspect

Teyandatamę[442] She does not have a village. (female)
[te-yahn-dah-tah-wan]

    te- negative
    -ya- feminine-zoic singular agent – she
    -ndat- noun root – village
    -a- joiner vowel
    -mę verb root – have + stative aspect

Teyangyasteyęh[443] Fingers are joined. (male)
[te-yan-gyah-steh-yenh]

    te- dualic
    -ya- feminine-zoic singular agent - it
    -ngy- noun root – finger, fingers
    -a- joiner vowel
    -steyę-[444] verb root – join
    -h stative aspect

440. Barbeau 1915:203 fn 3. It refers to Catherine Johnson's mother's uncle, who was probably her mother's maternal uncle, and therefore of the same clan.

441. Toupin 1996:904.

442. Toupin 1996:885 'te andata8oin'. The noun root could also refer to 'space, room'.

443. Toupin 1996:833.

444. The general rule is that a -š- changes the -nd- beginning of this verb root into an -st-. The noun root for finger does not have that ending, but neither does any noun root or noun stem that I know of.

Teyarihuyęh[445] A matter is divided, at a dividing point. (male Striped Turtle)
[teh-yah-ree-hoo-yenh]

    te-   dualic
    -ya-   feminine-zoic singular agent – it
    -rih-   noun root – matter
    -uyę-   verb root – divided
    -h   stative aspect

Teyarǫtandeyęh[446] Two trees, logs are joined, close together. (male)
[teh-yah-ron-tan-deh-yenh]

    te-   dualic
    -ya-   feminine-zoic singular agent - it
    -rǫt-   noun root – tree
    -a-   joiner vowel
    -ndeyę-   verb root – be joined, be close
    -h   stative aspect

Teyarǫtayeh Two trees[447] (male Bear)
[teh-yah-ron-tah-yeh-eh]

    te-   dualic – two
    -ya-   feminine-zoic singular agent – it
    -rǫt-   noun root – tree
    -a-   joiner vowel
    -ye-   verb root – number
    -h   stative aspect

Teyarǫtuyęh[448] It is between two logs. Between the Logs. (male Bear)
[teh-yah-ron-too-yenh]

    te-   dualic – two
    ya-   feminine-zoic singular agent – it
    -rǫt-   noun root – tree, log, pole
    -uyę-   verb root – be at the meeting, merging point, the divide
    -h   stative aspect

445. Barbeau 1911:5, Toupin 1996:858 and 881. This is also the name of the primary Mohawk sachem, usually written as tekarihogen (see discussion in Shared Names).

446. Toupin 1996:204 (as t'aontondeen) and 864 (as te ,arontande,en).

447. This name is presented in the Bear list so probably is a Bear name. Finley 1840:31 gives a Bear clan name as being "Three Logs." The Wyandot for that would be ahsęhk harǫtaye 'three. It is such a numbers of logs, trees'.

448. Connelley 1900:113 refers to this as a "famous" name. James B. Finley stated that "Between-the-logs, Three-logs [two logs], &c., refers to the Bear tribe, denoting the manner in which the bear crouches, or sleeps' (Finley 1840;31). See chapter nine.

Teyawęndayeh[449]
[teh-yah-wen-dah-ye]

te-	dualic
-ya-	feminine-zoic singular agent – it
-węnd-	noun root – island
-a-	joiner vowel
-ye-	verb root – number
-h	stative aspect

It is two islands. (male Snake)

Teyatak[450]
[teh-yah-tahk]

te-	dualic
-ya-	feminine-zoic singular agent – it
-t-	verb root – stand
-a-	habitual aspect
-k	past aspect suffix

It used to stand. (male Large Turtle)

Tharihit[451]
[t-hah-ree-heet]

t-	cislocative – where
-ha-	masculine singular agent – he
-rihit	verb root – be a tree + stative aspect

Where he is a tree. (male Porcupine – nickname)

Tihǫnǫšarak[452]
[tee-hon-non-shah-rahk]

ti	cislocative – when, where
-hǫ-	masculine singular agent + masculine singular patient – he – his
-nǫš-	noun root – house
-a-	joiner vowel
-r-	verb root – be inside
-a-	habitual aspect
-k	past aspect suffix

When, where he used to be inside his house. (male)

449. Barbeau 1911:15 and 48, and Toupin 1996:859, 875, 899, 925 and 926. They have an -h- rather than a -y-.

450. Toupin 1996:837, 840, 846, 850–1, 853, 859, 870, 876, 882, 884–5, 894, 905, 907, 909, 932, 937 (1788 – wife of theata), 940, and 941. Written as Tyachta at the Detroit Council concerning the Schieffelin Deed, October 22, 1783 (Curnoe 1996:218). In Treaty #2 of 1790 we have Te-dy-a-ta (Lajeunesse 1960:173).

451. See discussion in the nicknames chapter. Buser, Charles Aubrey, https://www.wyandotte-nation.org/culture/history/biographies/tarhe-grand-sachem/.

452. Toupin 1996:825 as tionnonchiara and 886 as tsinnonchiarak.

Tihšǫ[453]	Morning star (nickname for male Wolf)
Tihšǫt[454]	Strawberry or the turtle's eye (male Large Turtle)
Tihšǫywę [teeh-shon-wah-nenh]	Large star (female Striped Turtle)[455]
tihšǫ	star (particle)
=ywę	augmentative clitic
Tiǫndešara[456] [tyon-deh-shah-rah]	Where she or it is on top of the sand. (probably female)
ti-	cislocative – where
-ǫndeš-	feminine-zoic singular agent – she or it + noun root – sand
-a-	joiner vowel
-ra	verb root – be on top + stative aspect
Tǫmatares[457] [ton-mah-tah-rehs]	When our clay (possibly clan) is often long. (no gender given)
t-	cislocative – when
-ǫma-	feminine-zoic singular agent + 1st-person plural patient – it – us
-tar-	noun root – clay (symbolically also clan)
-es	habitual aspect
Tǫmętsakahkwiʔ[458] [toh-meh-tsah-kah-kwee-ee]	She is looking at the land. (female Striped Turtle)
t-	dualic
-ǫmęts-	feminine-zoic singular patient – she + noun root – land
-akakw-	verb root – look
-iʔ	stative aspect

453. Barbeau 1911:7 and 11, and 1915:x. He was given this nickname as he was born early in the morning.

454. Connelley 1900:111 35. "Big Turtle Clan. Teh-shōnt' Strawberry, or the turtle's eye. The Big Turtle has a strawberry-colored eye."

455. This name was recorded in the 18th century by Jesuit Father Pierre Potier as tichion8oin, tichi8oin and tichion8an. Toupin 1996:186, 203 (without the clitic), 210, 219, 252, 869, 873, 875, 879, 881, 883, 886–7, 889, 896, 926, 946–7, 949-50, 957, 959–60, 965, 971–2, and 975. It seems to be a Wendat term as well, with the miswritten Tichion8amie and Tichionwamie JR35:58–59.

456. Toupin 1996:212.

457. Toupin 1996:879 as ton8atiris and 884 ton8,atarès.

458. Barbeau 1911:4 and 48.

Tǫndešrisǫ?⁴⁵⁹	Where she comes up against the sand in many places. (female Porcupine)
[ton-deh-shree-son-on]	
t-	cislocative
-ǫ-	feminine-zoic singular patient – she
-ndešr-	noun root – sand
-is-	verb root – be against
-ǫ-	distributive root suffix
-ʔ	habitual aspect

Tǫngyatǫyuti⁴⁶⁰	She is penetrating it with a pestle. (female)
[ton-ngyah-ton-yoo-tee]	
t-	dualic
-ǫ-	feminine-zoic singular agent – she feminine-zoic singular patient – it
-ngyat-	noun root – pestle⁴⁶¹
-ǫyu-	verb root – penetrate
-t-	causative root suffix
-i	stative aspect

Thǫtaritakye⁴⁶²	He going to embark, pack (to cross) a lake. (male)
[t-hon-tah-ree-tah-kyeh]	
t-	dualic
-h-	masculine singular agent – he
-ǫtar-	noun root – lake
-it-	verb root – embark, load, pack + stative aspect
-aky-	progressive root suffix
-e	purposive aspect

Tǫti⁴⁶³	Named after a French commandant at Fort Pontchartrain (male)
[ton-tee]	

459. Toupin 1996:202, 860, 896-7, 900-1 as taondechris 875, 959 and 971. There are a few small problems with this name, including what is usually a dualic form being translated as a cislocative, and the dropping of -ǫʔ with a few cases.

460. Toupin 1996:834.

461. The noun roots for 'bridge' and 'throat' also take this form, but seem semantically less likely for this word.

462. Toupin 1996:822, 824, 825 and 826.

463. Pierre Alphones de Tonty was the commandant of nearby Fort Pontchartrain from 1717 to 1729. One of the "Considerés" or candidates for at least phratry chief had this name (as Tonti, which would be easily pronounced by a Wyandot speaker, as a nickname (Toupin 1996:219, 253. He was Honda8annhont 'he has a river in his mouth" a prominent figure in the Deer clan. It is possible, then that the Deer clan had adopted him. Interestingly, it was a demand from the Wyandot that was a major contributor to his being removed from the commandant position (Steckley 2014:75).

Tsahǫndinǫ[464]
[tsah-hon-dee-non-dee-non]

    ts-   repetitive – again
    -a-   factual
    -hǫ-   masculine singular patient – he
    -ndinǫ   verb root – desire, dream wish + punctual aspect

He again has a powerful desire, dream, wish. (male Bear)

Tsamęhinǫh[465]
[tsah-men-hee-nonh]

    ts-   repetitive – again
    -a-   feminine-zoic singular patient[466] – it
    -męh-   noun root – bud, buds
    -innǫ-   verb root – lead, drag
    -h   stative aspect

Buds are coming again. (female Porcupine)

Tsamęhuhi?[467]
[tsah-men-hoo-hee-ee]

Osprey, eagle (female Large Turtle)

Tsamahskuwat[468]
[tsah-mah-skoo-wat]

    ts-   repetitive – very
    -am-   feminine-zoic singular patient – it
    -hsk-[469]   noun root – beaver dam
    -uwat   verb root – be large + stative aspect

It is a very big beaver dam. (female)

Tsamęndakaę[470]
[tsah-men-dah-kah-enh]

    ts-   repetitive – very
    -a-   feminine-zoic singular patient – she[471]
    -męnd-   noun root – voice, word
    -akaę   verb root – be slow + stative aspect

She is speaking very slowly. (female Bear)

464. Toupin 1996:212, 228, and 255 sohondinnon and 222 sohoninnonn.

465. Toupin 1996:898, 900, 928, 943, 950, 952, 957-60, 962, 964, 967, 971–5,

466. This is the weak spot of this translation, as this is an unusual form. It appears that when consonant stem feminine-zoic singular patient pronominal prefixes come before noun roots that begin with an -m- in Wyandot, they are shortened to just being represented with an -a-.

467. Barbeau 1911:47 female Large Turtle. Toupin 1996: 839 (male and possibly Porcupine) 950 (female).

468. Barbeau 1911:44.

469. The -hš- of the word for beaver dam and the -y- of the verb root combine to form -hsk-.

470. Powell 1881:60 has this name as "Tsá-ma-da-ka-é *(Grunting for her Young)*."

471. This is the one problematic element in this word, as instead of -tsa- there should be -ska- for the first two parts of this name. This is another case of a shortened feminine-zoic simgular patient coming before a noun root.

Tsamęse[472] She is greatly esteemed. (female)
[tsah-men-seh]

    ts-   repetitive – greatly
    -am-   feminine-zoic singular patient – she
    -ęse   verb root – esteem + stative aspect

Tsamętǫdi[473] She is again growing. (female Prairie Turtle)
[tsah-men-ton-dee]

    ts-   repetitive – again
    -am-   feminine-zoic singular patient – she
    -ętǫ-   verb root – grow
    -d-   inchoative root suffix
    -i   stative aspect

Tsaǫndešres[474] Her country is very long. (female)
[tsah-on-deh-shres]

    ts-   repetitive – very
    -a-   feminine-zoic singular patient – her
    -ǫnde-   verb root – be country to
    -šr-   nominalizer
    -es   verb root – be long + habitual aspect

Tsaurahsti?[475] She again is taking it out of the fire. (female Deer or Snake)
[tsah-oo-rah-stee-ee]

    ts-   repetitive – again
    -a-   feminine-zoic singular patient – she
    -urahst-   verb root – take out of the fire
    -i?   stative aspect

Tsawę ahęhaǫ[476] He said again. (female)
Tsawę It is said again.
[tsah-wen]

    ts-   repetitive – again
    -aw-   feminine-zoic singular patient – she or it
    -ę   verb root – say + stative aspect

---

472. Toupin 1996:836, 841, 847, 850. 938 as tamoinsée, and 957 as tsa8oinhes.

473. Toupin 1996:229, 893, 968 and 970 as tsa8ointondi – Prairie Turtle elder.

474. Toupin 1996:217, 869, 888 and 948 as tsaondechres, 964 and 969 as tsaondechris and 881 as Sa,ondechres.

475. Barbeau 1911:12 and 43 as Snake clan, 47 as Deer clan.

476. Toupin 1996:959 as Tsa8oinïahenhaon. This representation of the name is a little confusing as it ungrammatically links two separate words.

Ahęhaǫ	He said.
[ah-hen-hah-on]	
-a-	factual
-h-	masculine singular agent – he
-ęhaǫ	verb root – say + punctual aspect

Tsawę Hinǫ	Thunder[477] speaks again (female Porcupine)
Tsawę	She or it speaks again.
[tsah-wen]	
ts-	repetitive – again
-aw-	feminine-zoic singular patient – she or it
-ę	verb root – say, speak + stative aspect
Hinnon	thunderer

Tsihunǫšuręs[478]	He very often finds houses, his house. (male)
[tsee-hoo-non-shoo-rens]	
tsi-	repetitive – very
-hu-	masculine singular patient – he
-nǫš-	noun root – house
-urę-	verb root – find
-s	(inchoative root suffix) + habitual aspect

Tsǫndehšratih[479]	It is the other side of the country. (male)
[tson-deh-shah-teeh]	
ts-	repetitive – other
-ǫnde-	feminine-zoic singular agent – it + verb root – have as country
-hšr-	nominalizer
-a-	joiner vowel
-ti-	verb root – be on a side
-h	stative aspect

477. I am taking a big chance with this one. Several points lead to it. One is that I can find no other semantic or grammatical interpretation. Second is that in most recording of this name, there is a dash between the two parts of the name like what exists with the augmentative clitic: Toupin 1996:182, 186, 847, 852, 857, 898, 900, 928, 950, 964, 969, 972–3 and 974. Most of the others join the two parts in one way or another: Toupin 1996:240, 840, 943, 959, 962, 968 and 975. What suggests to me that the second part is hinnon comes regrettably from only three recordings: 202 tsa8oin-hinnon, 840 tsa8enhinnon, and 968 tsa8ohinnon. Thirdly, there is another name that definitely joins two words in similar fashion: Toupin 1996:959: Tsa8oinïahenhaon Again he said. Ahenhaon means 'he said'. There is another example of a name with an -innon separated from the rest of the word "otena-innon" (Toupin 1996:971), but I cannot as yet make sense of it.

478. Toupin 1996:821 as tsinnonchioren, 829 as tsonnonchioren and 837 as tsinnonchiorens.

479. Toupin 1996:841, 846 and 851.

Tsǫndehšratęh[480]
[tson-deh-shrah-tenh]
- ts-   repetitive
- -ǫ-   feminine-zoic singular patient – it
- -ndehšr-   noun root – sand
- -a-   joiner vowel
- -tę-   verb root – dry
- -h   stative aspect

It is very dry sand. (female Large Turtle)

Tsǫnęrižuh
[tson-nen-ree-zhooh]
- ts-   repetitive – very
- -ǫ-   feminine-zoic singular patient – it
- -nęr-   noun root – group
- -ižu-   verb root – be large
- -h   stative aspect

It is a very large group. (female)

Tsuahayehte[481]
[tsoo-ha-yeh-teh]
- ts-   repetitive
- -u-   feminine-zoic singular patient – she, it, one
- -ah-   noun root – sack
- -a-   joiner vowel
- -yehte   verb root – bear + stative aspect

One bears a sack again. (male Bear)

Tsukarayuwanęh[482]
[tsoo-ksh-rah-yoo-wah-nenh]
- ts-   repetitive – very
- -u-   feminine-zoic singular patient – it
- -kar-   noun root – wood chip
- -a-   joiner vowel
- -yuwanę-   verb root – be large
- -h   stative aspect

It is a very large wood chip. (male)

---

480. Connelley 1900:111 gives the clan and the name, the latter without a translation, claiming that the meaning was "lost."

481. Toupin 1996:857, 860, 871, 879, 883, 885–6, 888–9, 892, 895–6, 942–3, 961–2, 966, 968–9, 972–3, 975. Although every example ends with -en- and not -e-, there appears to be no grammatical way in which that can be the imperative or punctual, both of which take that ending.

482. Toupin 1996:898 – two times as ts8karaï8aen.

Tsukares[483] Very long wood chips. (male)
[tsoo-kah-res]

    ts- repetitive – very
    -u- feminine-zoic singular patient – it
    -(a)kar- noun root – wood chips
    -es verb root – be long + habitual aspect

Tsukętaranǫ[484] It stretches itself out very many times. (male Large Turtle)
[tsoo-ken-tan-ran-non]

    ts- repetitive – very
    -u- feminine-zoic singular patient – it
    -k- semi-reflexive voice
    -ętara- verb root – stretch out
    -nǫ distributive root suffix + stative aspect

Tsukwęnderǫʔ[485] She again plays tricks with her words. (female)
[tsoo-kwen-deh-ron-on]

    ts- repetitive – again
    -u- feminine-zoic singular patient – she
    -k- semi-reflexive voice
    -węnd- noun root – word, voice
    -erǫ- verb root – play tricks
    -ʔ habitual aspect

Tsundakwanęh[486] It is a very large barrel, drum (female)
[tsoon-dah-kwah-nenh]

    ts- repetitive – very
    -u- feminine-zoic singular patient
    -ndakw- noun root – barrel, drum
    -(w)anę- verb root – be large
    -h stative aspect

483. Toupin 1996:210, 858 and 861 (as ts8karis), 209, 863, 869, 875, 882, 889, 895, 900, 902, 909, 949, 961–2, 966, 972 and 975 as tsk8ares. This likely also includes Tihockeres, recorded at a meeting of 1781 (Lajeunesse 1960:126).

484. Connelley 1900:110. Normally this verb root refers to lying down, but it appears to work here.

485. Toupin 1996:210, 881, 884 as ts8k8oindoronk, 884 ts8k8oinderon, 869 tsk8enderon, 874 tsok8enderonk and 882 tsk8oinderonk. Normally this verb does not incorporate a noun root, and usually with the semi-reflexive voice the agent form is used.

486. Toupin 1996:848 as sondak8ennen, 851 as tsondak8annen and 964 as ts8ndak8annen.

Tsundara'ti[487] She again is causing her, it to exist. (female)
[tsoon-dah-rah-tee]

    ts-   repetitive – again
    -u-   feminine-zoic singular patient – she
    -ndar-   verb root – exist
    -a't-   causative root suffix
    -i   stative aspect

Tsundaskwayah[488] It is a very small domestic animal, pet. (male)
[tsoon-dah-skwah-yah]

    ts-   repetitive – very
    -u-   feminine-zoic singular patient – it
    -ndaskw-   noun root – domestic animal, pet
    -a-   verb root – be a size
    -y-   stative aspect
    -ah   diminutive aspect suffix

Tsundawinǫn[489] It again drags, leads a river. (male Large Turtle)
[tsoon-dah-win-non]

    ts-   repetitive – again
    -u-   feminine-zoic singular patient – it
    -ndaw-   noun root – river
    -inǫn   verb root – drag + stative aspect

Tsundayati[490] She is planting again in a particular place. (female)
[tsoon-dah-yat-ee]

    ts-   repetitive – again
    -u-   feminine-zoic singular patient – she
    -nday-   verb root – plant
    -at-   causative root suffix
    -i   stative aspect

---

487. Toupin 1996;956 as ts8ndare'ti.

488. Toupin 1996:872, 898, and 966 as ts8ndask8aia, 879 as ts8ndask8aea, 885 as ts8ndask8aëa, 888, 904, 969 and 974, 891 as ts8ndak8aïa, 962 as tsondak8aïa, 962 as tsondak8aïa, 964 as tsondask8aia.

489. Toupin 1996:217, 844, 845, 964–5 and 971.

490. Toupin 1996:212. This is a name for a three-year-old.

Tsunduwanẹh⁴⁹¹ It is a very large arrow. (male)
[tsoon-doo-wah-nenh]
    ts-   repetitive – very
    -u-   feminine-zoic singular patient – it
    -nd-   noun root – arrow
    -uwanẹ-   verb root – be large
    -h   stative aspect

Tsihundeǫskǫ⁴⁹² He holds very many sweat lodges. (male Striped Turtle).
[tsee-hoon-deh-on-skon]
    tsi-   repetitive – very
    -hu-   masculine singular patient – he
    -ndeǫ-   verb root – hold a sweat lodge
    -skǫ   frequentative root suffix + stative aspect

Ts(ih)ǫndešraseha⁴⁹³ It is or he has a very new little country. (male)
[tsee-hon-deh-shrah-seh-ha]
    ts(i)-   repetitive – very
    -(h)-   feminine-zoic singular patient or masculine singular patient – it or he
    -ǫnde-   verb root – have as country
    -šr-   nominalizer
    -ase-   verb root – be new
    -h-   stative aspect
    -a   diminutive aspect suffix

Tsundihšrẹhaǫh⁴⁹⁴ She is carrying ice again. (female)
[tsoon-deeh-shren-hah-on-on]
    ts-   repetitive – again
    -u-   feminine-zoic singular patient – she
    -ndihšr-   noun root – ice
    -ẹhaǫ-   verb root – carry
    -h   stative aspect

491. This is the Wyandot name of a man with the surname of Greyeyes. ("Mary Greyeyes" by Ashley Simmons and Sallie Cotter Andrews https://www.wyandotte-nation.org/traditions/biographical-panels/mary-greyeyes/).

492. Toupin 1996:186 and 210. This name is shared with the Wendat (JR37:95 and 46:109). I am not sure about having the masculine as the pronominal prefix here as it generally only appears with a repetitive prefix taking the -s- rather than the -ts- form.

493. Toupin 1996:206 hondechronseha, 868 ondechrasea, 877 hondechrasea and 895 ts8ndechrasea.

494. Toupin 1996:901.

Tsungwasteh[495]
[tsoon-gwah-steh]

	It is a very strong, violent current, rapids. (male)
ts-	repetitive – very
-u-	feminine-zoic singular patient – it
-ngw-	noun root – rapids
-aste	verb root – be hard, firm
-h	stative aspect

Tsunǫrašę[496]
[tsoo-non-rah-shen]

	She has, or it is a very bad scalp. (female Porcupine)
ts-	repetitive – very
-u-	feminine-zoic singular patient – she or it
-nǫr-	noun root – scalp
-ašę	verb root – be bad + stative aspect

Tsunǫšes[497]
[tsoo-non-sheh]

	It is a very long house (male)
ts-	repetitive – very
-u-	feminine-zoic singular patient – it
-nǫš-	noun root – house
-es	verb root – be long + habitual aspect

Tsunǫyašehte[498]
[tsoo-non-yah-sheh-teh]

	It again bears a beak. (male)
ts-	repetitive – again
-u-	feminine-zoic singular patient – it
-nǫyaš-	noun root – beak, muzzle, canoe tip
-ehte	verb root – bear + stative aspect

---

495. Toupin 1996:937.

496. Toupin 1996:203, 223, 255, 864, 866 Ts8nnonrachien, 881 tsonnonrachien, and 204 Onnonrachien and 241, 859 ,annonrachien.

497. Toupin 1996:896, 899, 903, 910 and 962–3. This looks to be the same name as is found held by a Mr de s pierre: "Sonnonchiès (Toupin 1996:234). The name seems to appear with a different pronunciation in the Treaty of 1815 as "Sanohskee or long house" https://www.wyandotte-nation.org/culture/treaties/treaty-of-1815/. This is one of those instances in which the habitual form of the verb -es- is used but the meaning is stative. This looks to be part of the way this verb appears in names.

498. Toupin 1996:863–4.

Tsurašu[499] She again has a shoe. (female Bear)
[tsoo-rah-shoo]

    ts-　　　　　repetitive – again
    -u-　　　　　feminine-zoic singular patient – she
    -rašu　　　　verb root – be a shoe + stative aspect

Tsurawayi?[500] It takes hold of the air, the wind again. (male)
[tsoo-rah-wah-yee-ee]

    ts-　　　　　repetitive – again
    -u-　　　　　feminine-zoic singular patient – it
    -r-　　　　　noun root – air, wind
    -a-　　　　　joiner vowel
    -way-　　　　verb root – take hold
    -i　　　　　 stative aspect

Tsuriwaht[501] He is one affair, matter (male).
[ts-hoo-ree-what]

    ts-　　　　　repetitive
    -(h)u-　　　　masculine singular patient – he
    -riw-　　　　 noun root – affair, matter
    -a-　　　　　joiner vowel
    -ht　　　　　verb root – be one + stative aspect

Tsurǫtaętandih[502] A tree falls, is falling again. (male)
[tsoo-ron-tah-en-tan-deeh]

    ts-　　　　　repetitive – again
    -u-　　　　　feminine-zoic singular patient - it
    -rǫt-　　　　 noun root – tree
    -a-　　　　　joiner vowel
    -ę-　　　　　verb root – lie
    -t-　　　　　causative root suffix
    -and-　　　　inchoative root suffix
    -ih　　　　　stative aspect

499. Toupin 1996:214 and 248 as sorachi8t, 866 and 875 as tsorachi8 and 955 as s'orachi8. Although the last form uses a masculine pronominal prefix, I suspect that that is a mistake, as the possessor of the name is female.

500. Barbeau 1911:12

501. Toupin 1996:867 as tsoï8ha, 872 as s'ori8a, 879 as tsorihia a Seneca, 881 as horih8a, 882 as tsorih8a't, 889 as tsorih8at and 977 as tsorih8a. In the French/Wyandot meeting in 1781 regarding the death of Father Pierre Potier it is recorded as "joriha", the -j- signifying the -ts- sound (Lajeunesse 1960:126).

502. Toupin 1996:833. On Toupin 1996:859 there is oronta,entandi, which, with the -,en- would change the verb root to 'prefer, esteem highly', which to me seems rather unlikely.

Tsušaę⁵⁰³ She puts her mouth in place again. (female Porcupine)
[tsoo-shah-en]
    ts- repetitive – again
    -u- feminine-zoic singular patient – she
    -š- noun root – mouth
    -a- joiner vowel
    -ę verb root – put, place + stative aspect

Tsuhšraę?⁵⁰⁴ She is a very slow walker. (female Large Turtle)
[tsooh-shrah-en-en]
    ts- repetitive – very
    -u- feminine-zoic singular patient – she
    -hšr- dummy noun root
    -aę- verb root – be slow
    -ʔ stative aspect

Tsuteses⁵⁰⁵ It is very long ribbon work, lacework. (female)
[tsoo-teh-sehs]
    ts- repetitive – very
    -u- feminine-zoic singular patient – it
    -tes- noun root – ribbon work, lacework
    -es verb root – be long + habitual aspect

Tsuweyǫkyǫ⁵⁰⁶ She has abandoned or is abandoning the water. (female Striped Turtle)
[tsoo-weh-yon-kyon]
    ts- repetitive – again
    -uw- feminine-zoic singular patient – she
    -ey- noun root – water
    -ǫky- verb root – abandon
    -ǫ stative aspect

Tsuyęnrǫ⁵⁰⁷ Spring is coming, has come again. (female Wolf)
[tsoo-yen-ron]
    ts- repetitive – again
    -u- feminine-zoic singular patient – it
    -yęnrǫ verb root – for spring to come + stative aspect

---

503. Toupin 1996:204 and 212.

504. Barbeau 1911:2. Powell 1881:60 "woman of Smooth Large Turtle … Tsu-ca-e *(Slow Walker)*."

505. Toupin 1996:204 and 217. This individual, a child, could be either Striped Turtle or Large Turtle.

506. Powell 1881:60 "Tso-we-yuñ-kyu *(Gone from the Water)*."

507. Toupin 1996:221, 255, 825, and 856.

Tehutrǫnyure[508]	He is not covered by the sky. (male)
[teh-hoo-tron-yoo-reh]	
te-	negative
-hu-	masculine singular patient – he
-t-	semi-reflexive voice
-rǫy-	noun root – sky
-ure	verb root – cover + stative aspect
tuw atrǫnaȩs[509]	There the sky often falls. (female, Wolf clan)
tuw	there
[t-hoow]	
Atrǫnaȩs	The sky often falls.
[ah-tron-ah-ens]	
at-	feminine-zoic singular agent – it + semi-reflexive voice
-rǫn-	noun root – sky
-a-	joiner vowel[510]
-ȩ-	verb root – fall
-s	inchoative root suffix + habitual aspect
Tuh yandawias[511]	There the river often breaks. (male)
Yandawias	A river often breaks.
[yan-dah-wee-yas]	
ya-	feminine-zoic singular agent – it
-ndaw-	noun root – river
-ia-	verb root – break
-s	habitual aspect
tuh yaraskwan	(From) there I am departing, leaving. (male)
[tuh yah-rah-skwan]	
tuh	there
Yaraskwan[512]	I am departing, leaving.
y-	1st-person singular agent – I
-araskwa-	verb root – depart, leave
-n	stative aspect

508. Toupin 1996:219 and 854 as te hotronhiore and 219 and 859 as i8tronhiore (with the same wife as the one indicated by the other spelling). Possibly included as well is hotronhi8re, 896.

509. Barbeau 1915:xii. He added in square brackets an initial "[tuwa]". This was one of Catherine Armstrong's names. She also had a Large Turtle name.

510. This would not normally be present in an -e- conjugation verb such as -ȩ- 'fall'. Barbeau was probably inaccurate in putting this sound here.

511. Toupin 1996:833 as toanda8ias, 845 as taonda8ias, and 848 tanda8ias.

512. Toupin 1996:835 (three times) as θo,arask8a, and 869 as θo ,arask8a. I have added the nasal vowel at the end to make the stative aspect, as I do not think that there is a factual -a- between the two words, although it is possible.

Tuh yarihǫkye[513]	There a matter, affair is going to continue. (male)
[tooh yah-ree-hon-kyeh]	
Yarihǫkye	A matter is going to continue.
ya-	feminine-zoic singular agent – it
-rih-	noun root – matter, affair
-ǫky-	verb root – continue
-e	purposive aspect

Tukwęndahyutęh[514]	(When/where) her voice is, her words are soft. (female Deer)
[too-kwen-dah-hyoo-tenh]	
t-	cislocative – when, where
-u-	feminine-zoic singular patient – her
-k-	semi-reflexive mood
-węnd-	noun root – voice, word
-hyutę-	verb root – be soft, supple
-h	stative aspect

Tukwęnǫnyuti[515]	She or it is being penetrated by words, voice. (female Striped Turtle)
[too-kwen-non-nyoo-tee]	
t-	dualic
-u-	feminine-zoic singular patient
-k-	semi-reflexive voice
-węn-	noun root – word, voice
-ǫnyu-	verb root – penetrate
-t-	causative root suffix
-	stative aspect

Tureyęšuyęh[516]	Two river mouths are merging. (male Porcupine)
[too-reh-yen-shoo-yenh]	
t-	dualic
-u-	feminine-zoic singular patient – it
-reyę-	verb root – be a river mouth
-š-	nominalizer
-uyę-	verb root – merge or split
-h	stative aspect

513. Toupin 1996:847 as togarihontie, 831 as te ,ariontie and 933 as ariontie.

514. Connelley 1900:109. I am not sure why the initial -t- is in this word, written by Connelley as Tŏŏh-kwah'-nah-yŏŏh-teh. It would make more sense to me if it were -ts-, the repetitive, meaning 'very'.

515. Toupin 1996:204, 241, 845, 850, 853–4, 857, 888, 930, 957, 960–4, 966, 970–2 and 975.

516. Toupin 1996:182, 192, 203, 219, 240 (as torenchonien), 252 (as torenchoi,en), 861, 869, 873, 879, 883, 887, 948, and 953. The noun typically took the form -rench- or -ronch- (861) on the pages mentioned, but, as there are no nouns that fit either pattern, and as semantically this translation is a good fit, I have gone with it.

Tusatędi[517]	Smoke, fog, mist, steam is not falling. (female)
[too-sah-ten-dee]	
t-	negative
-u-	feminine-zoic singular patient – it
-sat-	noun root – smoke, fog, mist, steam
-ędi	verb root – fall + stative aspect

Umędaterih[518]	She recognizes her voice. (female)
[oo-men-dah-teh-reeh]	
u-	feminine-zoic singular agent + feminine-zoic singular patient – she – her
-męd-	noun root – voice, word
-ateri-	verb root – now
-h	stative aspect

Ukwędindes[519]	She often drags an island. (female)
[oo-kwen-deen-dehs]	
u-	feminine-zoic singular patient – she
-k-	semi-reflexive voice
-węd-	noun root – island
-inde-	verb root – drag
-s	habitual aspect

Ukwęnǫdih[520]	It is round, a circle, a wheel. (male Bear)
[oo-kwen-non-deeh]	
u-	feminine-zoic singular patient – it
-k-	semi-reflexive voice
-węnǫdi-	verb root – make round, encircle
-h	stative aspect

Ukwista'[521]	metal (female Large Turtle)
[oo-kwee-stah-ah]	
u-	feminine-zoic singular patient – it
-k-	semi-reflexive voice
-wist-	noun root – metal
-aʔ	noun suffix

517. Toupin 1996:887.

518. Toupin 1996:905.

519. Toupin 1996:847, 849, and 852

520. Barbeau 1911:18.

521. Barbeau 1911:35 kwíʔijaʔa = "old tin" (can etc) possibly a nickname.

Ukwišriwę[522]
[oo-kwee-shree-wen]   She is a great force (female)

    u-   feminine-zoic singular patient – she
    -k-   semi-reflexive voice
    -wišr-   noun root – force
    =iwę   augmentative clitic

Ukyatatęnyǫ[523]
[oo-kyah-tah-ten-nyon]   She is transfiguring, changing herself. (female)

    u-   feminine-zoic singular patient – she
    -ky-   semi-reflexive voice
    -at-   noun root – body
    -a-   joiner vowel
    -tęny-   verb root – change
    -ǫ   stative aspect

Umęndaes[524]
[oo-men-dah-ehs]   She often strikes an island. (female)

    u-   feminine-zoic singular patient – she
    -męnd-   noun root – island
    -ae-   verb root – strike, hit
    -s   habitual aspect

Umęhmąh[525]
[oo-menh-manh]   Putting[526] tobacco   (male Large Turtle)

    u-   feminine-zoic singular patient – it
    -męhm-   noun root – tobacco
    -ą-   verb root – put
    -h   stative aspect

---

522. Toupin 1996:958. This looks different for an augmentative clitic in that the preceding noun does not end with a noun suffix.

523. Toupin 1996:924 and 926 as Otkiatatïen (the Wyandot -k- replacing the Wendat -t-), 889 as otïtatïen, 964, 971 and 975 as tkiatatïen, 893 as Tkiata,en, 896 as tiata,en, and 974 as tkiatatihen.

524. Toupin 1996:926–7.

525. Toupin 1996:218 and 228.

526. The verb root -ę- (-en- in Potier) could be 'have, lie or put.' I chose 'put' as putting or placing tobacco is a sacred act.

Umęndateri[527]　　　　　　She recognizes or knows her voice. (female)
[oo-men-dah-teh-ree]

    u-　　　　　　feminine-zoic singular agent + feminine-zoic
　　　　　　　　　　singular patient –　she – her
    -męnd-　　　　noun root – voice
    -a-　　　　　　joiner vowel
    -teri　　　　　verb root – recognize, know + stative aspect

Undaętǫ[528]　　　　　　She putting, placing many arrows. (female Deer)
[oon-dah-en-ton]

    u-　　　　　　feminine-zoic singular patient – she
    -nd-　　　　　noun root – arrow
    -a-　　　　　　joiner vowel
    -ę-[529]　　　　verb root – put, place
    -tǫ　　　　　　distributive root suffix + stative aspect

Undatižu[530] haǫ　　　　She is from a large village. (female Striped Turtle)
[oon-dah-tee-zhoo]

    u-　　　　　　feminine-zoic singular patient – she[531]
    -ndat-　　　　noun root – village, community
    -ižu　　　　　verb root – be large, great + stative aspect

Unęta?[532]　　　　　　　Evergreen (female)
[oo-nen-tah-ah]

    u-　　　　　　feminine-zoic singular patient – it
    -nęt-　　　　　noun root – evergreen
    -a?　　　　　　noun suffix

---

527. Toupin 1996:905.

528. Christine 8ndaenton was regularly referred to as "la vielle reine" [the old queen] (Toupin 1996:219, 239, 253, 923 and 927). This suggests that she was a woman of some influence in the Deer clan, even though she was not listed as a member of the elders council. She died in 1751 (Toupin 1996:923).

529. There are a number of potential verbs for this name. The verb root -ę- 'have' is one, but Potier crossed out the form with the distributive root suffix (Potier 1920:221). On the same page is -ę- 'lie on the ground' is another, but Potier stated that it was used without any people involved as agents or patients. The verb root I chose is not eliminated by anything Potier wrote.

530. I thought at first that this might be a nickname, but it was passed down from a Francisca, and when she died a Marie-Magdalene, a woman adopted from the Fox tribe was given the name. Toupin 1996:209, 826, 833, 841, 846, 851, 865, 872, 884, 921, 928, 944 and 948

531. This part was added by me, as all examples begin with -n-: ndatïohaon

532. Toupin 1996:859.

Ungwiruhwi?
[oon-gwee-ron-hwee-ee]

Treetops in the water. (male Bear)

u-	feminine-zoic singular patient – it
-ngwir-	noun root – corn tassels, treetops
-u-	verb root – be in water
-hw-	transitional root suffix
-?	stative aspect

(H)unǫrandurǫh
[oo-non-ran-doo-ronh]

He is or has a difficult scalp. (male Large Turtle)[533]

u-	feminine-zoic singular patient – it
-nǫr-	noun root – scalp
-a-	joiner vowel
-ndurǫ-	verb root – be valuable or difficult
-h	stative aspect

Urayehte[534]
[oo-rah-yeh-teh]

It bears air, wind. (male)

u-	feminine-zoic singular patient – it
-r-	noun root – air, wind
-yehte	verb root – bear + stative aspect

Urǫtǫndih[535]
[oo-ron-ton-deeh]

A pole is (being) made; Warpole. (male Porcupine)

u-	feminine-zoic singular patient - it
-rǫt-	noun root – tree, log, pole
-ǫndi-	verb root – make
-h	stative aspect

533. Barbeau 1911:17 and 32, gives it as being a Large Turtle and a Bear clan name. The name was given to Robert Armstrong (1775–1825), a white man captured when a boy and adopted by the Large Turtle clan (Sallie Cotter Andrews, "Robert Armstrong", https://www.wyandotte-nation.org/culture/history/biographies/robert-armstrong/. She presents his name as being o-no-Ran-Do-Roh, and meaning 'hard scalp'.

534. Toupin 1996: 212, 880, 892, 895, 943–4.949–50, 952–4 and 962.

535. Potier 1920:148 and 153 (as Nicolas), Steckley 2014:12, 15, 18, 60–1, 80, 83-89, 97, 105, 117, 122, 133, 143, 152–3, 155-6, 158, 167–8, 197, 205–7, 212, 217, 220 and 232.Toupin 1996:171, 173, 176, 178, 182–3, 187, 191, 192, 195, 197, 200–2, 204, 215, 225–6, 229, 238–41, 249, 258 and 26, as "orontondi." https://www.wyandotte-nation.org/culture/treaties/treaty-of-1836/ Rontondee or Warpole, https://www.wyandotte-nation.org/culture/treaties/treaty-of-1842/ Warpole and Barbeau 1911:10 "rŏntonde".

Uskęnǫtǫha[536]	Little Deer (male Deer)
[oo-sken-non-ton-wah]	
-u-	feminine-zoic singular patient - it
-skę-	verb root – be the dead[537]
-ǫ-	dislocative root suffix
-tǫ-	distributive roof suffix + stative aspect
-wa	diminutive aspect suffix

Uskwirarǫˀ[538]	Bush is in many places, everywhere. (male Bear)
[oo-skwee-rah-ron-on]	
u-	feminine-zoic singular patient – it
-skwir-	noun root – bush, undergrowth
-a-	joiner vowel
-r-	verb root – be with
-ǫ-	distributive root suffix
-ˀ	stative aspect

Uskwiratayi[539]	It is dense undergrowth, bush. (nickname for a Frenchman)
[oo-skwee-rah-tah-yee]	
u-	feminine-zoic singular patient – it
-skwir-	noun root – branches, undergrowth
-atay-	verb root – be dense, thickly grown
-i	stative aspect

Uskwirǫtaˀta	It (often) shakes bushes, undergrowth. (male Bear)
[oo-skwee-ron-tah-ah]	
u-	feminine-zoic singular patient[540] – it
-skwir-	noun root – bushes, undergrowth2
-ǫtat-	verb root – shake
-a	habitual aspect

---

536. Toupin 1996:828 as oskennontona and 832 as oskennontonha.

537. It should be noted that this verb root does not show up elsewhere in the Wyandot material. This morphological analysis is largely conjecture, but the reference to deer is a fact.

538. Barbeau 1911:17.

539. Toupin 1996:234. From 1710 to 1712, Charles Regnault, Sieur Dubuisson was interim commandant of Fort Pontchartrain. The Wyandot translated 'buisson' which means 'bush' into their language.

540. This could be -hu- 'he' as the pronominal prefix was dropped.

Ustamęšrǫt[541]	It has a turtle shell rattle attached, rattlesnake. (male, probably Snake).
[oo-stah-men-shront]	
u-	feminine-zoic singular patient – it
-stamęšr-	noun root – turtle shell rattle
-ǫt	verb root – attach, be attached + stative aspect

Uhtahtawastih[542]	It is a beautiful, good piece of wood (male nickname).
[ooh-tah-tah-wah-steeh]	
u-	feminine-zoic singular patient – it
-htaht-	noun root – wood, piece of wood
-a-	joiner vowel
-wast-	verb root – be good, beautiful
-ih	stative aspect

Utęrut[543]	It is a standing palisade, a tower. (male nickname for a Frenchman)
[oo-ten-root]	
u-	feminine-zoic singular patient – it
-tęr-	noun root – palisade
-ut	verb root – stand + stative aspect

Utesędi[544]	She is grinding corn for her. (female)
[oo-teh-sen-dee]	
u-	feminine-zoic singular agent + feminine-zoic singular patient – she – her
-te-	verb root – grind corn
-sędi	dative root suffix + stative aspect

Utratękwi[545]	It is a quill that is being used for something. (male)
[oo-trah-ten-kwee]	
u-	feminine-zoic singular patient – it
-trat-	noun root – quill, quills

541. Toupin 1996:223, 851, 855 and 861. This name was held in 1733 by the French Commandant at Fort Pontchartrain Ives Pean (Toupin 1996:234). It is also the name of one of the Mohawk sachems.

542. Toupin 1996:234 and 262. This was the Wyandot nickname given to Louis Henry Deschamps Sieur de Boishebert, commandant at Fort Portchartrain from 1728–9. See chapter seven.

543. This was translated into French as "la tour" or 'the tower' (Toupin 1996:234). Jesuit Brother Frère Pierre Gournay received this name in the 18th century (Toupin 1996:234 and 261).

544. Toupin 1996:220 as 8tesendi, 829 and 861 as tesendi, 866, 876 and 926 as tensendi, and 903 as te-sândi.

545. JR60:51 as Otratenkoui, a man who lived at the Michilimackinac home of the Wyandot

-ękw-	verb root – use
-i	stative aspect

Utręhętǫʔ	A branch is hanging down[546] (female Striped Turtle)
[oo-tren-hen-ton-on]	
u-	feminine-zoic singular patient – it
-t-	semi-reflexive voice
-ręh-	noun root – branch
-ętǫ-	verb root – be suspended
-ʔ	stative aspect

Utrewatih[547]	She is opposing, resisting, criticizing it. (female)
[oo-treh-wah-teeh]	
u-	feminine-zoic singular patient – she
-trewat-	verb root – oppose, resist, criticize
-ih	stative aspect

Utriwąndet[548]	She holds an important matter, responsibility close to her. (female Striped Turtle)
[oo-tree-wan-det]	
u-	feminine-zoic singular patient – she
-t-	semi-reflexive voice
-riw-	noun root – matter, affair
-a-	joiner vowel
-ndet	verb root – envelope + stative aspect

Utrǫywę[549]	It is a great sky to her, a pleasant sky (female)
[oo-tron-ywen]	
u-	feminine-zoic singular patient – she
-t-	semi-reflexive voice
-rǫ-	noun root – sky
=ywę	augmentative clitic

---

546. Barbeau 1911:48, Connelley 1900:112 translates this as "Tree shaking," i.e., by the current, or flow of water against it."

547. There is some confusion in Toupin concerning this name and hatrewatih. There is one instance in which I can be fairly sure that a female is being referred to with otre8ati and that is in Toupin 1996:854.

548. Toupin 1996:833, 1733 and 880, 1760. There is also a mother of a baptized child given the male version of the name hatrih8andet 830; Barbeau 1911:1.

549. Toupin 1996:203 as otronnion8an, 929 and 947 as otronhi8oin and 959 and 974 as Otronhi8an. The idea that the concept of 'pleasant' is involved comes from Potier 1920:371 ",aronhiaï8en c. Etre agreable divertissant ... haronhiaï8en il est agreable ,aronhiaï8en elle est [agreable] [He is pleasant, nice, She is pleasant, nice]."

Utroyayęk[550]	She is often seen in the sky. (female Large Turtle)
[oo-tron-nyah-yenk]	
u-	feminine-zoic singular patient - she
-t-	semi-reflexive voice
-roy-	noun root – sky
-a-	joiner vowel
-yę-	verb root – see
-k	habitual aspect
Utroyowąh[551]	Sky is coming out of the water. (female)
[oo-tron-nyon-wanh]	
u-	feminine-zoic singular patient – it
-tr-	semi-reflexive voice
-roy-	noun root – sky
-o-	verb root – be in water[552]
-wą-	undoer root suffix
-h	stative aspect
Utsistateyęh[553]	It is a burning fire. (male)
[oo-tsee-stah-teh-yenh]	
u-	feminine-zoic singular patient – it
-tsist-	noun root – fire
-atey-	verb root – burn
-ęh	stative aspect
Uture[554]	It is cold (the weather). (male)
[oo-too-reh]	
u-	feminine-zoic singular patient – it
-ture	verb root – be cold + stative aspect

---

550. Toupin 1996:850, 854, 857, 860, 871, 877, 879, 883, 885–6, 888, 892, 946, 952, 956, 958–60, 962, 964–8, 970, and 972.

551. Toupin 1996:203

552. Normally this vowel would not be nasalized, but it may be that there being a nasal vowel both before and after it nasalized this vowel.

553. Toupin 1996:832.

554. Toupin 1996:832. This name was first recorded in 1650, as Outouré, as the name of a Petun who had been captured then released by one of the Haudenousaunee tribes. This verb root usually does not distinguish for gender. An exception appears in one of the Narratives, in which a masculine term is used to identify the north (Barbeau 1960:68).

Uyehtęhaǫh[555]	Throughout the summer. (female)
[oo-yeh-ten-hah-onh]	
u-	feminine-zoic singular patient – it
-yeht-	noun root – summer
-ęhaǫ-	verb root – carry
-h	stative aspect

Warǫ[556]	(Wyandot version of Baron (male)

Watrǫyanǫnę[557]	She took care of the sky (in the past). (female Striped Turtle)
[wah-tron-yan-non-neh]	
w-	ø
-at-	feminine-zoic singular agent – she + semi-reflexive voice
-rǫy-	noun root – sky
-a-	joiner vowel
-nǫ-	verb root – take care of + stative aspect
-nę	past aspect suffix

Węnenharižu?[558]	They (indefinite) have a large maypole. (male)
[wen-nen-hah-ree-zhoo-oo]	
wę-	indefinite agent – they (indefinite)
-nęnhar-	noun root – maypole
-ižu-	verb root – be large
-?	stative aspect

555. Toupin 1996:834, 836, 838, 840, 841, 844, 856, 942, and 950. Two of the citations combine the Wendat form with another -n- with what I believe is a superscript -t-—",e'tnnhenhaon" (838), and o,e'tnnhenhaon (856)—and one takes the Wendat form o,ennhenhaon (844).

556. The -b-, which does not exist in the Wyandot language was changed to -8- or -w-. The individual first known as 'the Baron', acted independently from other Wyandot leaders in the 1690s (see Steckley 2014:61–3), trying to negotiate some kind of Haudenosaunee-friendly deal. A person by that name had children from four different mothers baptized from 1729 to a newborn in 1736 (Toupin 1996:826, 829, 832 and 839). If he were an older man during his politically active days, then this person may well have been a descendant or young brother of the original. In a 2014 publication, I hypothesized that clan exogamy would have kept him from belonging to the Deer, Snake, Large Turtle and Striped Turtle, and the leadership opposing him was coming from the Deer and the Wolf clans, that he may have been Prairie Turtle clan (Steckley 2014:63).

557. Connelley 1900:112 "She takes care of the sky," or "Keeper of the heavens."

558. Potier 1920:450 translated the noun in this word as "espece de mai ou les algonquins mettoient les prix aux fetes des morts [a kind of maypole where the Algonquins put the prizes in the Feast of the Dead." Potier 1920:148 and Toupin 1996:182–3, 194, 198–201, 203, 220, 238–9, 241, 254, 259, 905–6 and 921.

Wętaywę[559]	It is a great, a large stick. (no gender stated)
[wen-tah-yweh]	
w-	feminine-zoic singular patient – it
-ęt-	noun root – stick
-a-	noun suffix
=ywę	augmentative clitic

Wehtęhaǫh[560]	She is carrying a field. (female)
[weh-ten-hah-on]	
w-	feminine-zoic singular patient – she[561]
-eht-	noun root – field
-ęhaǫ-	verb root – carry
-h	stative aspect

Yaaʔtamahkah[562]	It has a small body. (joking name for a bear)
[yah-ah-tah-mah-kah]	
ya-	feminine-zoic singular agent – it
-aʔt-	noun root – body
-mahka-	verb root – be small
-h	stative aspect

Yaaʔtandureh[563]	She, her body, is fast. (female)
[yah-ah-tan-doo-reh]	
ya-	feminine-zoic singular agent – she
-aʔt-	noun root – body
-o-	verb root – be fast
-h	stative aspect

Yaaʔtaseh[564]	Her body is new. (female Snake)
[yah-ah-tah-seh]	
ya-	feminine-zoic singular agent – her
-aʔt-	noun root – body
-ase-	verb root – be new
-h	stative aspect

559. Toupin 1996:924.

560. Toupin 1996:187 as 8etenhaon, 211 as 8ę˙tenhaon (the -ę- is used inconsistently by Toupin, so I cannot be sure it indicates a nasal -e-), and 245 as 8ętenhaon. There is a possibility that the noun root is -ent- 'day.'

561. Normally for a -w- to be there, a vowel would be in front of it.

562. Barbeau 1915:209 fn 2. See Names in Narratives for an explanation.

563. Toupin 1996:204 as "aatandore". Possibility of 941 "tandouray."

564. Connelley 1900:111. "Yah'-äh-täh-sĕh. Means, "A new body". Said of the snake when she slips off her old skin, as snakes do once a year." Toupin 1996:895.

Yaa'tayęhtsih[565]
[ya-ah-tah-yenh-tseeh]
    ya-   feminine-zoic singular agent – she
    -a'ᵗ-   noun root – body
    -a-   joiner vowel
    -yęhts-   verb root – be an old person
    -ih   stative aspect

She is an old person. (female – mythic)

- ya- : feminine-zoic singular agent – she
- -a'ᵗ- : noun root – body
- -a- : joiner vowel
- -yęhts- : verb root – be an old person
- -ih : stative aspect

Yaa'tetsis[566]
[yah-ah-teh-tsees]

Tall or long bodies (female)

- ya- : feminine-zoic singular agent – she or it
- -a'ᵗ- : noun root – body
- -ets- : verb root – be tall or long
- -i- : stative aspect
- -s : plural aspect suffix

Yaa'tiha[567]
[yah-ah-tee-hah]

She is frequently a unique person. (female)

- ya- : feminine-zoic singular agent – she
- -a'ᵗ- : noun root – body
- -i- : verb root – be the only, a unique person
- -ha : habitual aspect

Ya,ęnǫkyǫ[568]
[yah-en-non-kyon]

I am abandoning the bow. (female)

- Y- : 1st-person singular agent
- -aęn- : noun root – bow
- -ǫky- : verb root – abandon
- -ǫ : stative aspect.

---

565. There is a double -a- here where there is only one later on in this list for other words. This reflects the use in the original texts. Barbeau 1960:77 #37, 86 #53, 87 #16, 52, 88 #32, 49, 89 #21, 46, 90 #7, 91 ##9, 158 #34, 47, 160 #20, 161 #19, 163 #1, 14, 165 #50, 166 #35, 167 #12, 176 #28, 177 #2, 178 #3, 39, 179 #39, 50, 180 #23, 245 #60, 246 #2 and 254 #28.

566. Toupin 1996:887 and 959.

567. Toupin 1996:859.

568. Toupin 1996:845: ,aenontion, 849 ,aennontion, and 923 ,ennontkion. My translation goes against the presence of the initial subscript -,-. However, the noun root for 'bow' is somewhat unusual, looking like a consonant conjugation noun root, so it would be easy for the outside recorder to make an incorrect assumption. Further, there is no noun root of the consonant conjugation that fits.

Yaętandeyęh[569] Sticks are joined. (male)
[ya-en-tan-deh-yenh]
    ya- feminine-zoic singular agent – it
    -ęt- noun root – stick, sticks
    -ndeyę- verb root – be joined
    -h stative aspect

Yaherindeʔ She, it is going to drag a corn stalk. (possible female Porcupine)
[yah-heh-reen-deh-eh]
    ya- feminine-zoic singular agent – she, it
    -her- noun root – corn stalk
    -in- verb root – drag
    -de purposive aspect

Yatǫhǫk[570] She, it used to say, talk. (female)
[yah-ton-honk]
    y- feminine-zoic singular agent – she, it
    -atǫ- verb root – say
    -hǫ- habitual aspect
    -k past aspect suffix

Yahwęntaʔ Small fish (male)
[yah-hwen-tah-ah]
    ya- feminine-zoic singular agent – it
    -hwęnt- noun root – small fish
    -aʔ noun suffix

Yahwišayaste[571] Her force is firm, resistant. (female)
[yah-hwee-shah-yah-steh]
    ya- feminine-zoic singular agent – her
    -hwiš- noun root – force
    -a- joiner vowel
    -yaste verb root – be firm, resistant + stative aspect

Yamęndaweyiʔ[572] Her word, voice is closed. (female Striped Turtle)
[yah-men-dah-weh-yee-ee]
    ya- feminine-zoic singular agent – her
    -męnd- noun root – word, voice
    -a- joiner vowel
    -wey- verb root – close
    -iʔ stative aspect

569. Toupin 1996:828

570. Toupin 1996:830, and 880 as ,atonhonk and 833 ,atonhon.

571. Toupin 1966:826 as h8ichaste, and 827, and 834 8ichaste.

572. Toupin 1996:208 as a8endâ8e,i, 871 as ,a8enda8e,ik and 878 as,a8enda8e,i. There is also o8enda8e,i on 873. This is probably not another name, just a misspelling of this one.

Yamęndandureh⁵⁷³ She is speaking quickly, her words are fast. (female)
[yah-men-doo-reh]
    ya-   feminine-zoic singular agent – she
    -męnd-   noun root – word, voice
    -a-   joiner vowel
    -ndure-   verb root – be quick, fast
    -h   stative aspect

Yamęndatęs⁵⁷⁴ Her voice, her words often stop. (female)
[ya-men-dah-tens]
    ya-   feminine-zoic singular agent – her
    -męnd-   noun root – voice, word
    -a-   joiner vowel
    -tę-   verb root – stop
    -s   habitual aspect

Yamęndindetih⁵⁷⁵ She is causing her voice to come. (female Deer)
[yah-men-deen-deh-teeh]
    ya-   feminine-zoic singular agent – she
    -męnd-   noun root – voice, word
    -inde-   verb root – drag, lead
    -t-   causative root suffix
    -ih   stative aspect

Yąnaasa?⁵⁷⁶ Small bones (male)
[yan-nah-ah-sah-ah]
    yą-   feminine-zoic singular agent – it
    -na-   noun root – bone, bones
    -a-   verb root – be a size
    -sa   stative aspect + diminutive aspect suffix + plural aspect suffix

Yandarekwi⁵⁷⁷ She is living, has lived there long. (female Snake)
[yan-dah-reh-kwee]
    -ndare-   verb root – reside, dwell, exist
    -kw-   instrumental root suffix
    -i   stative aspect

573. Toupin 1996:209 and 210 as a8endaandore, 858 as 8andandore, 870 and 877 as a8endandore, and 870 as handandore.

574. Toupin 1996:844 8endatens and 858 a8endatens, and possibly 904 as 8endates.

575. "[T]he echo; the wonderful talker; what she says goes a long way and then comes back again. Refers to the deer's voice echoing in the night when calling his fellows" (Connelley 1900:35 and see 110). Barbeau 1911:11, "the call of the Deer goes far" and 37 "When the deer calls, it goes a long way" or "echo." Toupin 1996:875, 881 and 926.

576. Toupin 1996:838, 847, 850 and 853.

577. Toupin 1996:872, 874, 883, 887, 888, , 889, 894, 961 and possibly 975 ("te ,andarak8i").

Yandataę[578]
[yan-dah-tah-en]

	There is a village. (male)
ya-	feminine-zoic singular agent – it
-ndat-	noun root – village
-a-	joiner vowel
-ę	verb root – have, be in a place + stative aspect

Yandatase[579]
[yan-dah-tah-seh]

	It is a new village. (male)
ya-	feminine-zoic singular agent – it
-ndat-	noun root – village
-ase	verb root – be new + stative aspect

Yandatawanęh[580]
[yan-dah-tah-wah-nenh]

	It is a large camp, village. (no gender indicated).
ya-	feminine-zoic singular agent – it
-ndat-	noun root – camp, village, community
-a-	joiner vowel
-wanę-	verb root – be large
-h	stative aspect

Yandatasa[581]
[ya-ndat-ah-sah]

	Small villages (male)
ya-	feminine-zoic singular – it
-ndat-	noun root – village
-a-	verb root – be a size + stative aspect
-s-	plural aspect suffix
-a	diminutive aspect suffix

Yandatsarǫ?[582]
[yan-dah-tsah-ron-on]

	She often puts pots at a distance from each other. (female Porcupine)
ya-	feminine-zoic singular – she
-ndats-	noun root – pot
-a-	joiner vowel
-r-	verb root – be a distance[583]
-ǫ-	distributive root suffix
-?	habitual aspect

578. Toupin 1996:895.

579. "Datasay" in the Treaty of 1789. https://www.wyandotte-nation.org/culture/treaties/treaty-of-1789/.

580. Barbeau 1911:24.

581. Toupin 1996:204 as andatasa.

582. Toupin 1996:203 andatsaron, 863–4 ndatsaronk, and 877 handatsaronk.

583. I am not exactly sure of the construction of the verb before the habitual, or its ultimate meaning.

Yandatsuyęnęh[584]
[yan-dah-tsoo-yenh]
    ya-   feminine-zoic singular agent – she
    -ndats-   noun root – pot
    -uyęnę-   verb root – be under
    -h   stative aspect

Yandatuyęnę[585]
[yan-dah-too-yen-nen]
    ya-   feminine-zoic singular agent – she
    -ndat-   noun root – village, community
    -uyęnę   verb root – be under + stative aspect

Yandawayęs[586]
[yan-dah-wah-yens]
    ya-   feminine-zoic singular agent – she
    -ndaw-   noun root – river
    -a-   joiner vowel
    -yę-   verb root – go out
    -s   habitual aspect

Yandeša[587]
(yan-deh-šah-ah)
    ya-   feminine-zoic singular agent – it
    -ndeš-   noun root – sand
    -aʔ   noun suffix

Yandešarǫs[588]
[yan-deh-shah-rons]
    ya-   feminine-zoic singular agent – she
    -ndeš-   noun root – sand
    -a-   joiner vowel
    -rǫ-   verb root – pierce
    -s   habitual aspect

584. Toupin 1996:874, 881, 899 and 956.

585. Toupin 1996:898 as ndatoennen. I added the -ya- pronominal prefix as that regularly appears with nouns incorporated into this verb (Potier 1920:405).

586. Toupin 1996:909.

587. Toupin 1996:941. This name maybe only partially recorded. Father François-Xavier Dufaux was the priest who performed the baptism ceremonies and recorded the participants from 1787 to 1796 (Toupin 1996:936-41). He was a poor recorder of Wyandot names, his work being more with the French than the Wyandot. There are eight names with sand in them in this text. This word could be one of them.

588. Toupin 1996:879.

Yandetu haon[589]	She is from a pine in water. (female[590])
[yan-deh-too hah-on]	

Yandetu

ya-	feminine-zoic singular agent
-ndet-	noun root – pine
-u	verb root – be in water + stative aspect

haon	from

Yandihatętsih[591]	It has a thick hide. (joking name in story)
[yan-dee-hah-ten-tseeh]	

ya-	feminine-zoic singular agent - it
-ndih-	noun root – hide
-a-	joiner vowel
-tętsi-	verb root – be thick
-h	stative aspect

Yandinǫʔ[592]	She desires, wants something greatly. (female Wolf)
[yan-dee-non-on]	

ya-	feminine-zoic singular agent - she
-ndinǫ-	verb root – desire
-ʔ	stative aspect

Yandišraʔ ire[593]	He walks on ice. (male)
[yan-dee-shrah-ah ee-reh]	

ya-	feminine-zoic singular agent – it
-ndišr-	noun root – ice
-aʔ	noun suffix
i-	partitive
-r-	masculine singular agent – he
-e	verb root – walk + purposive aspect

Yandurǫkwa[594]	She is often considered valuable. (female)
[yan-doo-ron-kwah]	

ya-	feminine-zoic singular agent – she

589. Toupin 1996:927–8.

590. Even though both examples of the word begin with the -h- masculine singular agent marker, that the individual is female suggests that the recorder might have got it wrong.

591. Barbeau 1915:209 fn 4. This is what rabbit calls himself. See Names in Narratives.

592. Barbeau 1911:7 and Toupin 1996:902. Powell 1881:60 said that it meant "always hungry."

593. Toupin 1996:971

594. Toupin 1996:865.

-nduro̱-	verb root – be valuable or difficult
-kw-	instrumental root suffix
-a	habitual aspect

Yanduš rayet[595]
[yan-doo-shrah-yeht]   She is scraping her shell. (female Large Turtle).

ya-	feminine-zoic singular agent – she
-ndušr-	noun root – shell
-a-	joiner vowel
-yet	verb root – scrape + stative aspect

Yanduyarha[596]
[yan-doo-yah-rhah]   Poplar (male)

ya-	feminine-zoic singular agent – it
-nuyarh-	noun root – poplar
-a	noun suffix

Yane̱duk[597]
[ah-ya-nen-dook]   She is corn in water. (female)

-ya-	feminine-zoic singular – she
-ne̱d-	noun root – corn[598]
-u-	verb root – be in water
-k	stative aspect

Yane̱ho̱tak[599]
[yah-nen-hon-tak]   Corn used to be in the fire. (female)

ya-	feminine-zoic singular agent – it
-ne̱h-	noun root – corn
-o̱t-	verb root – be in fire
-a-	habitual aspect
-k	past aspect suffix

---

595. Barbeau 1911:3.

596. Toupin 1996:835 (interestingly as godfather to child of son8ando,aresk8a, which also uses the same verb root) and 974 following otrioskon 'she frequently fights' in a place where there should be only one name.

597. Toupin 1996:828 as yannendo and 831 as yannend8k.

598. This is the questionable part of the translation, as the noun root for corn is -ne̱h-, with no -d-. But 'corn' appears in a good number of words, and there is no noun root -ne̱d-. It is possible though not very likely that the -d- would emerge with the u- following.

599. Toupin 1996:842 ennontak, 843 ,annennontak, 862 annennontak and 937 enontak. The Wendat version is written by Vincent as annennontak (Vincent 1996:461)

Yanętaye	At the evergreen (female)
[ya-nen-tah-yeh]	
ya-	feminine-zoic singular agent – she, it
-nęt-	noun root – evergreen
-a-	noun suffix
=ye	external locative clitic

Yanęti[600]	It is an entire, intact evergreen (female)
[yah-nen-tee]	
ya-	feminine-zoic singular agent – it
-nęt-	noun root – evergreen
-i	verb root – be entire, full + stative aspect

Yangǫta⁷[601]	Horned snake, snake charm (female Snake)
[yan-gon-tah-ah]	
ya-	feminine-zoic singular agent – it
-ngǫt-	noun root – horned snake, snake charm
-a⁷	noun suffix

Yangwęta⁷[602]	Long pouch (female)
[yan-gwen-tah-ah]	
ya-	feminine-zoic singular agent – it
-ngwęt-	noun root – long pouch
-a⁷	noun suffix

Yangwirut	Standing corn tassels[603] (male Prairie Turtle)
[yan-gwee-root]	
ya-	feminine-zoic agent – it
-ngwir-	noun root – corn tassels, treetops
-ut	verb root – stand + stative aspect

600. She participated in baptisms from 1739 to 1769, as mother (Toupin 1996:842 and 854) or as godmother (870, 881, 884, and 950) and gave gifts at mortuary ceremonies from 1760 to 1770 (950–1, 953, 960, 963, 967 and 970).

601. Toupin 1996:198, 202, 226, 240 and 259. Her nickname is "la Caliere," which I believe to mean "the wedge."

602. This is the name given to a woman adopted from the Fox nation. Steckley 2014:99–101 and 285. She was possibly adopted by the Bear clan (see Steckley 2014:101). Toupin 1996:99–100, 285, 840 and 851.

603. This could also be a fishtail. Steckley 2014:81–4, 86, 92, 111, 134, 139, 142, 151, 156–7, 167–8, 185, 205–7, 212, 226, 279, and Toupin 1996:174, 176, 183, 190, 192, 201, 214, 217, 227, 239, 260, 849–50 and 923. See Curnoe 1996:5-6.

Yangwišaha[604]   It regularly finishes, completes rapids. (male)
[yan-gwee-shah-hah]

    ya-   feminine-zoic singular agent – she or it
    -ngw-   noun root – rapids
    -iša-   verb root – finish, complete
    -ha   habitual aspect

Yanǫduwanęh[605]   She has, or it is a large mark, line, or sign (female Deer)
[yan-on-doo-wan-nenh]

    ya-   feminine-zoic singular agent – she, it
    -nǫd-   noun root – mark, line, or sign
    -uwanę-   verb root – be large
    -h   stative aspect

(Ya)nyękyǫdi[606]   She has the front of her leg sticking out. (female)
[ya-nyen-kyon-dee]

    ya-   feminine-zoic singular agent – she or it
    -nyęk-   noun root – front of the leg
    -yǫdi   verb root – stick out + stative aspect

Yarakǫnęta[607]   She often comes down on a ray of sun. (female)
[yah-rah-kon-en-tah]

    ya-   feminine-zoic singular agent – she
    -ra-   verb root – sun to rise
    -k-   instrumental root suffix as nominalizer
    -ǫnęt-   verb root – come down, descend
    -a   habitual aspect

Yaręngyakǫh[608]   She is breaking rocks into many pieces. (female)
[yah-ren-gyah-konh]

    ya-   feminine-zoic singular agent – she or it
    -ręng-   noun root – rock
    -ya-   verb root – cut, break
    -kǫ-   distributive root suffix
    -h   stative aspect

---

604. Toupin 1996:877.

605. Toupin 1996:222, 227, 256 and 849.

606. Toupin 1996:946 as nientkiondi. As there is no pronominal prefix presented in the name, the -ya- is just a guess.

607. Toupin 1996:872, 878, 882, 886, 889, 890, 892, 929, 946, 950, and 959.

608. Potier 1920:148, Toupin 1996:205, 221, 241, 255 868 and 905. On 938 there is sarédiacon, which could add 'very' or 'again' to the name. It also depicts a female's name.

Yaręha'tsih[609]
[yah-ren-hah-ah-tseeh]

ya-	feminine-zoic singular agent – she
-ręh-	noun root - treetops, branches
-'ats-	verb root - name, be called
-ih	stative aspect

She is called treetops, branches. (female)

Yaręnyakǫ[610]
[yah-ren-nyah-kon]

Branch(es) or treetops are broken in many pieces. (female)

ya-	feminine-zoic singular agent – it
-ręn-	noun root – branch or treetops
-ya-	verb root – break
-kǫ	distributive root suffix + stative aspect

Yarhata'[611]
[yah-rhah-tah]

She is at the end of the forest. (female)

ya-	feminine-zoic singular agent – she
-rh-	noun root – woods, forest
-a-	joiner vowel
-ta-	verb root – be at the end + stative aspect
-'	stative aspect

Yarhǫnęs[612]
[yar-hon-nens]

She often makes the forest fall. (female Large Turtle)

ya-	feminine-zoic singular agent – she, it
-rh-	noun root – forest
-ǫnę-	verb root – make fall
-s	habitual aspect.

Yarihǫnęta'[613]
[yah-ree-hon-nen-tah-ah]

She often drops matters, affairs. (female Snake)

ya-	feminine-zoic singular agent – she
-rih-	noun root – matter, affair
-ǫnęt-	verb root – fall, drop
-a'	habitual aspect

---

609. Toupin 1996:870–1. 876–7, 901, 946 and 960.

610. Toupin 1996:846 as Arenniakon.

611. Toupin 1996:193, 828–9, 835, 839, 852, 861, 896, 904, and 925–6.

612. I am not completely sure about this translation. Toupin 1996:196.

613. Toupin 1996:198, 226, 834, 837, 845, 850, 876, 878, 885, 964, 968 and 970.

Yariuta⁷ tehat⁶¹⁴	A rock, he stands. (male)
[yah-ree-oo-tah teh-hat]	
ya-	feminine-zoic singular agent – it
-riut-	noun root – rock, stone
-a⁷	noun suffix
te-	dualic
-ha-	masculine singular agent – he
-t-	verb root – stand + stative aspect

Yariwase⁷⁶¹⁵
[yah-ree-wah-seh-eh]   It is new news, a new matter, law. (female Bear)
    ya-   feminine-zoic singular agent – it
    -riw-   noun root – matter, news, law
    -ase-   verb root – be new
    -⁷   stative aspect

Yarǫkyakǫ⁶¹⁶
[yah-ron-kyah-kon]   A tree is broken, breaking into many pieces. (female)
    ya-   feminine-zoic singular agent – it
    -rǫk-   noun root – tree, pole, log
    -ya-   verb root – break
    -kǫ   distributive root suffix + stative aspect

Yarǫyaye⁶¹⁷
[yah-ron-yah-yeh]   In the sky (male)
    ya-   feminine-zoic singular agent – it
    -rony-   noun root – sky
    -a-   noun suffix
    =ye   external locative clitic

Yarǫyayi⁶¹⁸
[ya-ron-yah-yee]   She is eating the sky. (female)
    ya-   feminine-zoic singular agent – she
    -rǫy-   noun root – sky

---

614. Toupin 1996:888 and 962.

615. Barbeau 1911:17 and 22.

616. Toupin 1996:853 as ,arentiaxon and 897 as ,arentkiaxon. There is a noun root -'rent- 'calf, lower leg' that appears in Wendat (Potier 1920:452), but there is no strong evidence that it exists in Wyandot.

617. This name was given to a commandant at Fort Pontchartrain, Pierre Joseph Céleron (Toupin 1996:234 and 262).

618. Toupin 1996:895 as aronhia,i. It is also possible that the verb root is -iay- 'break'.

-a-	joiner vowel
-yi-	verb root – to eat + stative aspect

Yarǫtayęrat[619]
[ya-ron-tah-yen-rat]

ya-	feminine-zoic singular agent – she, it
-rǫt-	noun root – tree, pole, log
-a-	joiner vowel
-yęrat	verb root – be white + stative aspect

She, it is a white tree, pole, log. (female)

Yarǫtęntawih[620]
[yah-ron-ten-tah-weeh]

It is a tree sleeping. (male)

ya-	feminine-zoic singular agent – it
-rǫt-	noun root – tree, pole, log
-ęnta-	verb root – sleep
-w-	transitional root suffix
-ih	stative aspect

Yarǫtuwanęh[621]
[yah-ron-too-wah-nenh]

It is a big, large tree. (female Bear)

ya-	feminine-zoic singular agent – it
-rǫnt-	noun root – tree, log, pole
-uwanę-	verb root – be large
-h	stative aspect

Yarǫyawayih[622]
[yah-ron-nyah-wah-yee]

She is holding, grasping the sky. (female Large Turtle)

ya-	feminine-zoic singular agent – she
-rǫy-	noun root – sky
-a-	joiner vowel
-way-	verb root – grasp, hold
-ih	stative aspect

Yarǫyatiri[623]
[yah-ron-yah-tee-ree]

She, it is supporting the sky. (male)

ya-	feminine-zoic singular agent – it

619. Toupin 1996:878–9, 945–6, 951, 963–4, 966 and 971 as ,aronta,onra, 851 as eronta,onra, 900 as taronta,onra, 900 and 902 as onta,onra.

620. Toupin 1996:855, 887, 889, 893, 896 (the only example that begins with a masculine pronominal prefix -h-, 902 as harentonta8i, 909, 966, 971, 974 and 975.

621. Barbeau 1911:17 and 23.

622. Barbeau 1911:3 and 22.

623. Toupin 1996:893 and 945. This might be the name that Hancks presents as Rohn-yau-tee-rah Leaning Sky, held by Isadore Chaine or Chesne.

	-rǫy-	noun root – sky
	-atiri	verb root – support + stative aspect

Yarǫyą'wi[624]
[yah-ron-nyan-an-wee-ee] — She is canoeing or floating in the sky (female Deer)

	ya-	feminine-zoic singular agent – she
	-rǫy-	noun root – sky
	-yąwi-	verb root – go by canoe
	-'	stative aspect

Yarǫyures[625]
[yah-ron-yoo-rehs] — The sky is often covered. (female)

	ya-	feminine-zoic singular agent – it
	-rǫy-	noun root – sky
	-ure-	verb root – cover
	-s	habitual aspect

Yarǫyurę'ˀs[626]
[ya-ron-yoo-ren-ens] — She (often) finds the sky. (female)

	ya-	feminine-zoic singular agent – she
	-rǫy-	noun root – sky
	-urę-	verb root – find
	-ˀs	habitual aspect

Yašęndaes[627]
[yah-shen-dah-ehs] — She often hits names. (female Snake)

	ya-	feminine-zoic singular agent – she
	-šęnd-	noun root – name
	-ae-	verb root – hit, strike
	-s	habitual aspect

Yašwanęh[628]
[yash-wah-nenh] — She or it has a large mouth (male)

	ya-	feminine-zoic singular agent – she, it
	-š-	noun root – mouth
	-wanę-	verb root – be large
	-h	stative aspect

624. Barbeau 1915:ix, and Connelley 1900:113: "Yah-rōhn'-yäh-ah-wih' The Deer goes in the sky and everywhere."

625. Toupin 1996:866, 934, 954 and 967 with an -e- before the final -s, and 929 as ,aronhi8ris. There is a chance that this and the next word are the same, but I do not believe that they are.

626. Barbeau 1911:9 and 21. Toupin 1996:928, 942, and 955.

627. Toupin 1996:185, 206–7, 836, 839, 845, 848–9, 850, 853, 921 and 925.

628. Toupin 1997:967 as yachi8annen.

Yatera[629]	Tree root (female Porcupine)
[yah-teh-rah]	
ya-	feminine-zoic singular agent – it
-ter-	noun root – tree root
-aʔ	noun suffix

Yateθa	She often grinds corn with it. (female)[630]
[yah-teh-t-ha]	
ya-	feminine-zoic singular agent – she
-te-	verb root – grind corn
-t-	causative root suffix
-ha	habitual aspect

Yatsistarǫʔ[631]	It is often a fire at diverse distances. (male Large Turtle)
ya-	feminine-zoic singular agent – it
-tsist-	noun root – fire
-a-	joiner vowel
-r-	verb root – be at a distance
-ǫ-	distributive root suffix
-ʔ	habitual aspect

Yatsistarǫka[632]	She or it often listens to a fire. (male)
[ya-tsee-stah-ron-kah]	
ya-	feminine-zoic singular agent – she or it
-tsist-	noun root – fire
-arǫ-	verb root – listen
-ka	habitual aspect

Yaweyatęsti[633]	She is making, has made the water, liquid thick. (female)
[ya-weh-ah-ten-stee]	
ya-	feminine-zoic singular agent – she
-wey-	noun root – water, liquid
-a-	joiner vowel

629. Steckley 2014:45, 130, 146, 153, 158, 182, 196, 209 and 225, Toupin 1996:189, 213, 229 and 246.

630. Toupin 1996:874.

631. This is the Large Turtle clan name held by William Walker. Connelley presents this as his clan name "Sehs'-tah-roh," meaning "'bright' and refers to the turtle's eye shining in the water" (Connelley 1900:36 and 111). Toupin 1996:907 and 938 as sistaron.

632. Toupin 1996:203 as ,atsistaronka, 858 as ,atsistaronk and 909 as ,atsitaronka.

633. Toupin 1996:850.

	-tęs-	verb root – be thick[634]
	-t-	causative root suffix
	-i	stative aspect

Yawinǫ[635] She is a (beautiful) young woman. (female)
[ya-wee-nǫ]

    ya-   feminine-zoic singular agent – she
    -inǫ   verb root – be a young woman + stative aspect

Yawinǫke[636] At the (beautiful) young woman – female Bear
[ya-wee-non-keh]

    ya-   feminine-zoic singular agent – she
    -winǫ-   verb root – be a young woman + stative aspect
    =ke   external locative clitic

Yawinǫywę[637] She is a very beautiful young woman. (female Snake)
[ya-wee-nǫ-ywenh]

    ya-   feminine-zoic singular agent – she
    -winǫ-   verb root – be a young woman + stative aspect
    =ywę   augmentative clitic

Yawi'tsinǫha'[638] She is a little girl. (female)
[yah-wee-ee-tsee-non-hah-ah]

    ya-   feminine-zoic singular agent – she
    -witsinǫha-   verb root – be a little girl
    -ʔ   stative aspect

634. The usual verb root is -tęts- but that is altered by the presence of the causative-instrumental root suffix -st-.

635. Toupin 1996:866 and 874 as ,a8innon, and 1286 as yaouinnon. In the last example, there is reference to a female having this as a name, but baptism number 1562 cannot be found in this text.

636. Toupin 1996:205, 228, 892, 896, 898, 901, 904, 925, 950–1, 954, 957, 970–2 as a8innonke, 842, 854 and 861 as ya8innonke and 241 as 8innonke. The Wendat version of the name was presented as "La8inonke", the -l- signifying a -y- sound (as in French) in Vincent 1984:165, with the meaning "la belle fille Huronne" 'the beautiful Huron girl'.

637. Steckley 2014:122, Toupin 1996:184, 1285, 205, 207, 209 and 243 as "a8innon-i8oin", and 851 as hinnono8en. What is interesting about that last entry is the in the Snake clan origin story, the first Snake clan woman marries a Thunderer, and hinnon means 'thunderer.', and this name as written would mean 'great thunderer'.

638. This was presented by Barbeau (1911:2) for a Margaret Brown as piʔitsenǒhǎ and questions whether it her "real Indian name. This makes me think that this could be a nickname

Yawistanduronh[639]
[yah-wees-tan-doo-ronh]
   ya-   feminine-zoic singular agent – she
   -wist-   noun root – metal
   -nduro-   verb root – be valuable
   -h   stative aspect

She is valuable metal, gold. (female)

Yayetęhaǫh[640]
[yah-yeh-ten-hah-onh]
She is carrying nails, claws, talons. (female)
   ya-   feminine-zoic singular agent – she
   -yet-   noun root – nails, claws, talons.
   -ęhaǫ-   verb root – carry
   -h   stative aspect

Yayǫšrase[641]
[yah-yon-shrah-seh]
It is a new partition, chair, ladder. (male)
   ya-   feminine-zoic singular agent – it
   -yǫšr-   noun root – partition, chair, ladder
   -ase   verb root – be new + stative aspect

Yažatǫhǫh[642]
[yah-zha-ton-honh]
She used to mark, write. (female Striped Turtle)
   ya-   feminine-zoic singular agent – she
   -žatǫ-   verb root – mark, write
   -hǫ-   habitual aspect
   -h   past aspect suffix

Yęhaǫh[643]
[yen-hah-on]
She is carrying it. (female Bear)
yęhaǫ   feminine-zoic singular agent – she + verb root – carry
                        + stative aspect

---

639. Toupin 1996:829.

640. This could just as well have the masculine singular agent ha-, and mean 'he carries, nails, claws, talons,' as the one example is a,etenhaon (Toupin 1996:952) and the initial -h- was sometimes missed by Jesuit linguists.

641. Toupin 1996:888 as aonchrase. It is also possible, but less likely, that the missing letter is an -h- rather than a -y-, and it refers to a new box.

642. The name is written in several different ways. Toupin 1996:208 (ahiatonhon), 824 (hiatonhonk), 829 (diatonhonk), 840 (chiatonhonk), 903 (aiatonhonk), and 925 (hahiatonhonk). Barbeau wrote what may be the same name as ayežatǫhǫ' I used to mark (Barbeau 1911:1). There is even a hohiaton which is a female's name (Toupin 1996:851).

643. Toupin 1996:214

Yętsęhaǫh	She is carrying bait for fishing. (female)
[yen-tsen-hah-onh]	
yęts-	feminine-zoic singular agent – she + noun root – bait for fishing
-ęhaǫ	verb root – carry
-h	stative aspect
Yǫnanǫhwe[644]	They (f) like, love her. (female)
[yon-anon-hweh]	
yǫa-	feminine-zoic plural agent + feminine-zoic singular patient – they – her
-nǫhwe	verb root – like, love + stative agent
Yuhšaharęht	One has a hole in its mouth. (male – mythic figure[645])
[yooh-shah-hah-renht]	
y-	partitive – such
-u-	feminine-zoic singular patient – one
-hš-	noun root – mouth
-a-	joiner vowel
-haręht	verb root – have a hole + stative aspect

---

644. She was an adopted Miami involved with baptisms from 1729 to 1741. Toupin 1996:825 as ,8annonhe, 831, 833, 841, and 847–9 as ,onannonh8e and 832 as eonannonh8e.

645. He is the young hero of the story "Two Giants and the Old Witch," in Barbeau 1960:78 #20, 79 #4 and 14, 80 #1, 30 and 39, 81 #32, 82 #30, 83 #20, 84 #10, 33 and 49, 85 #24, 31 and 39, and 86 #20 and 45.

References

Unpublished

Barbeau, Marius, 1911, "Ethnographic Study of the Wyandots: Personal Names," Geological Survey, Ottawa.

FH1697 c.1697 French-Wendat dictionary, MS., John Carter Brown Library, Brown University, Providence, Rhode Island.

Published

Bacque de la Potherie, Claude Charles Leroy, 1727, *Histoire de l'Amérique septentrionale,* 4 vols., Jean-Luc Nion et François Didot.

Barbeau, Marius, 1915, *Huron and Wyandot Mythology*, Canada Department of Mines, Geological Survey Memoir 80, No. 11, Anthropological Series, Ottawa: Government Printing Bureau.

-------, 1917, "Iroquoian Clans and Phratries", *American Anthropologist*, New Series, 19(3): 392–402.

-------, 1960. *Huron-Wyandot Traditional Narratives in Translation and Native Texts*, Bulletin 105, Ottawa National Museum of Canada.

Bardeau, Phyllis Eileen Williams, 2019, *Definitively Seneca: It's in the Word,* Lulu.com.

Béchard, Henri, 1985, "Marcoux, Joseph," *Dictionary of Canadian Biography, Volume VIII (1851–1860)* University of Toronto/Université Laval, http://www.biographi.ca/en/bio/marcoux_joseph_8E.html).

Bruyas, Jacques, 1970, *Radices Verborum Iroquaerum* (reprint of an 1862 version), New York: Cramoisy Press.

Chafe, Wallace (compiled by), 2012, *English-Seneca Dictionary*, /Users/Owner/Desktop/Wyandot%20language%20project/English-Seneca_1-18-12.pdf.

Charlevoix, Pierre-François-Xavier de, 1923, *Journal of a Voyage to North America.* 2 volumes (reprint of 1761 London edition), ed. Louise Phelps Kellogg, Chicago: The Caxton Club.

Clarke, Peter Dooyentate, 1870, *Origin and Traditional History of the Wyandotts, and Sketches of Other Indian Tribes of North America,* Toronto: Hunter-Rose.

Connelley, William Elsey, 1899a, "Notes on the Folklore of the Wyandots," *Journal of American Folklore*, 12:116–125.

-------, 1899b. *Wyandot Folklore*, Topeka: Crane and Company, Publishers.

-------, 1900. "The Wyandots," *Archeological Report of the Minister of Education Annual Reports 1899*, 92–123.

Cummins, Bryan, and John Steckley, 2013, *Full Circle: First Nations of Canada,* 3rd edition, Boston: Pearson Learning Solutions.

Curnoe, Greg, 1996, *Deeds/Nations,* London Chapter, Ontario Archaeological Society Occasional Publications #4.

Divine, Lloyd, 2019, *On the Back of a Turtle: A Narrative of the Huron-Wyandot People*, Columbus, OH: The Ohio State University Press.

Finley, James B., 1840, *History of the Wyandott Mission, at Upper Sandusky, Ohio, Under the Direction of the Methodist Episcopal Church*. Cincinnati: J.F. Wright & L. Swormstedt, for the Methodist Episcopal Church.

Froman, Fran., Alfred Keye, Lottie Keye and Carrie Dyck, 2002. *English-Cayuga/ Cayuga-English Dictionary*, Toronto: University of Toronto Press.

-------, 2012, *A Glossary of Special Gayogoho:nǫ? (Cayuga) Words and Particles, Thematically Organized*, http://cayugalanguage.ca/images/PDFs/glossary-of-special-Cayuga-words.pdf.

Gabriel, Harvey Satewas, 2014, *Kanesatake Mohawk Dictionary*, Kanesatake, QC: Self-published.

Grassmann, Thomas, 2003, "Otreouti," *Dictionary of Canadian Biography, Volume 1 (1000–1700)*, http://www.biographi.ca/en/bio/otreouti_1E.html.

Hale, Horatio, 1883, "A Huron Historical Legend," in the *Magazine of American History* 10:475–83.

-------, 1883, *The Iroquois Book of Rites*, Philadelphia: D. G. Brinton, Brinton Library of Aboriginal American Literature, Number 11.

Hancks, Larry, n.d., "Wyandot Names", Wyandot Names.PDF-Adobe Acrobat Reader DC.

Havard, Gilles, 2001, *The Great Peace of Montreal of 1701: French-Native Diplomacy in the Seventeenth Century*, Montreal and Kingston, ON: McGill-Queen's University Press.

Lajeunesse, Ernest J., 1960, *The Windsor Border Region: Canada's Southernmost Frontier*, The Champlain Society, Toronto: University of Toronto Press.

Mansky, Jackie, 2017, "The True Story of Pocahontas", *Smithsonian Magazine*, March 23.

Michelson, Gunther, 1973, *A Thousand Words of Mohawk*, Ottawa: National Series of Man, Mercury Series, Ethnology Division No. 5.

Michelson, Karin, and Mercy Doxtator, 2002, *Oneida-English/English-Oneida Dictionary*, Toronto: University of Toronto Press.

O'Callaghan, and Fernow B., eds., 1855 *Documents Relating to the Colonial History of the State of New York*, New York Colonial Documents, volumes 9: 178–9 and 10, Albany: Weed, Parsons.

O'Meara, John, 1996, *Delaware-English/English-Delaware Dictionary*, Toronto: University of Toronto Press.

Potier, Pierre, S.J. 1920, *Fifteenth Report of the Bureau of Archives for the Province of Ontario*, Toronto: C.W. James.

Powell, John Wesley, 1881, *Wyandot Government: A Short Study of Tribal Society*, First Annual Report to the Secretary of the Smithsonian Institution, 1879–80, pp. 57–69, Washington: Government Printing Office.

Sagard, Gabriel, *1866, Histoire du Canada et Voyages Que Les Frères mineurs Recollects Y Ont Faicts Pour La Conversion Des Infidèles Depuis L'An 1615*, Montreal: Edwin Tross.

-------, 1990. *Le Grand Voyage du Pays des Hurons*, Bibliotèqie Québécoise.

Scott, James C., Tehranian, John, and Mathias, 2002, "The Production of Legal Identities Proper to States: The Case of the Permanent Family Surname," in *Comparative Studies in Society*, 44(1): 4–44.

-------, 2004, "Government Surnames and Legal Identities," in Carl Watner, ed., *National Identification Systems*, Jefferson, NC, and London: McFarland & Co., Inc.

Sioui, Linda, 2007, "The Huron-Wendat Craft Industry from the 19th Century to Today," http://collections.musee-mccord.qc.ca/en/keys/webtours/CW_HuronWendat_EN.

Smith, Donald, "Tekarihogen," *Dictionary of Canadian Biography*, Vol. VI (1821–1835), www.biographi.ca/en/bio/tekarihogen_1830_6E.html.

Steckley, John L., 1988, "How the Huron Became Wyandot: Onomastic Evidence," *Onomastica Canadiana*, 70(2): 59–70.

-------, 1989, "Huron Sweat Lodges: The Linguistic Evidence," *OAS Arch Notes* 1:7–8.

-------, 1992, *Untold Tales: Four 17th-Century Huron*, 2nd edition, Toronto: Associated Heritage Publishing.

-------1998, *Wendat Names at Lorette 1762–1791*, Toronto: Petun Research Institute, Research Bulletin no. 19.

-------, 2007a, *A Huron-English/English-Huron Dictionary (Listing Both Words and Noun and Verb Roots)*, Lewiston, NY: The Edwin Mellen Press.

-------, 2007b, *Words of the Huron*, Waterloo, ON: Wilfrid Laurier University Press.

-------, 2010, *Gabriel Sagard's Dictionary of Huron*, Merchantville, NJ: Evolution Publishing.

-------, 2011, *Beyond Their Years: Five Native Women's Stories*, Toronto: Three O'Clock Press.

-------, 2016, "Hechon: The Story of a Wendat Name," *Onomastica Canadiana*, 95(1–2): 85–107.

-------, 2018, "Rescuing Colonized Names of the Wyandot", *Onomastica Canadiana*, 97(1–2): 65–187.

-------, 2020, *Forty Narratives in the Wyandot Language*, Montreal and Kingston, ON: McGill-Queen's University Press.

Sturtevant, Andrew K. 2011, *Jealous Neighbors: Rivalry and Alliance Among the Native Communities of Detroit, 1701–1766*. Dissertation, Theses and Masters Projects, Paper 1539623586, https://dx.doi.org/doi:10.21220/s2-crtm-ya36.

Terry, Frank, 1897, "Naming the Indians," *American Monthly Review of Reviews*, March.

Thwaites, Reuben, G., 1959, *The Jesuit Relations and Allied Documents* [JR], New York: Pageant Book Co.

Toupin, Robert, 1996, *Les Écrits de Pierre Potier*, Ottawa : Les Presses de l'Université d'Ottawa.

Vincent, Marguerite, Tehariolina, 1984, *La Nation Huronne: Son Histoire, Sa Culture, Son Esprit*, Quebec, QC: Éditions du Pélican

Woodbury, Hanni, 2003, *Onondaga-English/English-Onondaga Dictionary*, Toronto: University of Toronto Press.

-------, 2018, *A Reference Grammar of the Onondaga Language*, Toronto: University of Toronto Press.

Wyandotte Nation of Oklahoma Website
BIOGRAPHIES
Author: Andrews, Sallie C.

Subject: Robert Armstrong
www.wyandotte-nation.org/culture/history/biographies/robert-armstrong/.
Subject: Catherine Quoqua McKee Clark
www.wyandotte-nation.org/culture/history/biographies/catherine-quoqua-mckee-clark/
Subject: Leonard Nicholas Cotter
www.wyandotte-nation.org/culture/history/biographies/leonard-nicholas-cotter-sr/
Subject: Nicholas Cotter
www.wyandotte-nation.org/culture/history/biographies/nicholas-cotter/
Subject: Walk-in-the-Water
www.wyandotte-nation.org/culture/history/biographies/walk-in-the-water/

Author: Buser, Charles A.

Subject: Adam Brown
www.wyandotte-nation.org/culture/history/biographies/adam-brown/
Subject: Leatherlips
www.wyandottenation.org/culture/history/biographies/leatherlips/
Subject: Tarhe
www.wyandotte-nation.org/culture/history/biographies/tarhe-grand-sachem/

Author: Walker, B.N. O. (autobiography)
www.wyandotte-nation.org/culture/history/biographies/bno-walker/

BIOGRAPHICAL PANELS
Author: Andrews, Sallie Cotter

Subject: Mary McKee
www.wyandotte-nation.org/traditions/biographical-panels/mary-mckee/

Author: Turner, Jeremy

Subject: Catherine Coon Johnson
www.wyandotte-nation.org/traditions/biographical-panels/catherine-johnson/
Subject: Smith Nichols
www.wyandotte-nation.org/traditions/biographical-panels/smith-nichols/
Subject: Hiram Star Young
www.wyandotte-nation.org/traditions/biographical-panels/hiram-star-young/

Authors: Simmons, Ashley and Sallie Cotter Andrews

Subject: Mary Greyeyes
www.wyandotte-nation.org/traditions/biographical-panels/mary-greyeyes/.

General History

Buser, Charles A., "101 Names," www.wyandotte-nation.org/culture/history/general-history/names-given/.

-------, "Our Great Chiefs" (1989), www.wyandotte-nation.org/culture/history/general-history/our-great-chiefs/

Historic Rolls

1843 Ohio
www.wyandotte-nation.org/culture/history/historic-rolls/ohio-muster-roll/
1870 Muster Roll
www.wyandotte-nation.org/culture/history/historic-rolls/roll-1870/
1874 Voters List by Clan
www.wyandotte-nation.org/culture/history/historic-rolls/wyandot-voter-list-by-clan/

History: Journals

Walker, William, Walker Journal Book 2, www.wyandotte-nation.org/culture/history/published/provisional-government/journal2/

Cemeteries

Bland Cemetery, Oklahoma
www.wyandotte-nation.org/culture/history/cemetery-lists/bland-cemetery/
Huron Cemetery, Kansas
www.wyandotte-nation.org/culture/history/cemetery-lists/huron-cemetery/

Treaties

1785
www.wyandotte-nation.org/culture/treaties/treaty-of-1785/
1789
www.wyandotte-nation.org/culture/treaties/treaty-of-1789/
1795
www.wyandotte-nation.org/culture/treaties/treaty-of-1795/
1805
www.wyandotte-nation.org/culture/treaties/treaty-of-1805/
1807
www.wyandotte-nation.org/culture/treaties/treaty-of-1807/
1808
www.wyandotte-nation.org/culture/treaties/treaty-of-1808/
1814
www.wyandotte-nation.org/culture/treaties/treaty-of-1814/
1815
www.wyandotte-nation.org/culture/treaties/treaty-of-1815/
1817
www.wyandotte-nation.org/culture/treaties/treaty-of-1817/

1818
www.wyandotte-nation.org/culture/treaties/treaty-of-1818-sept-17/
1818
www.wyandotte-nation.org/culture/treaties/treaty-of-1818-sept-20/
1832
www.wyandotte-nation.org/culture/treaties/treaty-of-1832/
1842
www.wyandotte-nation.org/culture/treaties/treaty-of-1842/
1843
www.wyandotte-nation.org/culture/treaties/treaty-of-1843/
1855
www.wyandotte-nation.org/culture/treaties/treaty-of-1855/
1867
www.wyandotte-nation.org/culture/treaties/treaty-of-1867/

Wyandot of Kansas Website
www.wyandot.org

Marsh, Thelma, c. 1970, "Tarhe," www.wyandot.org/tarhe.htm
Civil War, www.wyandot.org/civilwar.htm.
Missionary Society, 1828, "Wyandot Members of Missionary Society Upper Sandusky Ohio" in the Wyandot Nation of Kansas Website, www.wyandot.org/1828us.htm.
--------, 1832, www.wyandot.org/1832.htm.

General Online References

1857 Payments
https://sites.rootsweb.com/~kswyanhp/history/1857aprwyantribeincompetents.html

Abelard Guthrie
https://www.kckpl.org/wyandot-daguerreotype/documents/AbelardGuthrie.pdf

Chief Leatherlips Monument
https://www.roadsideamerica.com/story/9791

History of Wyandotte Country Kansas and its People, 1911, edited and compiled by Perl W Morgan, Chicago: The Lewis Publishing Company, chapter VII, "Come to their Promised Land." http://genealogytrails.com/kan/wyandotte/history7.html#:~:text=Splitlog%20was%20a%20mechanical%20genius,he%20was%20his%20own%20engineer

"List of Cayuga Names of the family of Mr. and Mrs Jas. Jamieson"
https://sova.si.edu/record/NAA.MS1690), collected by J.N.B Hewitt, in 1879

Louis Callihoo
www.biographi.ca/en/bio/callihoo_louis_7E.html.

Matthew Splitlog: The Indian Millionaire
http://grandlakenewsonline.com/matthias-splitlog-the-indian-millionaire-p336-126.htm

Myeerah
www.myeerah.com/story.htm

"Oneida Chief Skenandoah" in the Native Heritage Project
https://nativeheritageproject.com/2012/05/29/oneida-chief-skenandoah/).

Haudenosaunee Confederacy Site
www.haudenosauneeconfederacy.com/government/current-clan-mothers-and-chiefs/.

About the Author

John Steckley is the author of two dozen books on a wide variety of topics, including numerous works on Indigenous topics. He taught at Humber College in Toronto for thirty years prior to his retirement in 2015. He holds two degrees in anthropology and a doctorate in education. His primary area of academic interest is the Wendat/Wyandot language, which he has been studying for the past 48 years. After retiring from Humber, Steckley worked as the Tribal Linguist for the Wyandotte Nation of Oklahoma for six years.

Books on Indigenous Topics by John Steckley

Untold Tales: Three 17th Century Huron (R. Kerton Ltd., 1981; 2nd ed., Associated Heritage Publishing, 1992).

Beyond Their Years: Five Native Women's Lives (Canadian Scholars' Press, 1999).

Full Circle: Canada's First Nations (with Bryan Cummins) (Pearson Education Canada, 2000; 2nd edition, 2007; 3rd edition, 2013).

Aboriginal Policing: A Canadian Perspective (with Bryan Cummins) (Pearson Education Canada, 2002).

Aboriginal Voices and the Politics of Representation in Canadian Sociology Textbooks (Canadian Scholars' Press, 2003).

De Religione: Telling the Seventeenth Century Jesuit Story in Huron to the Iroquois (University of Oklahoma Press, 2004; paperback reprint, 2020).

Words of the Huron (Wilfrid Laurier University Press, 2007).

Huron Dictionary: Verb Roots and Noun Roots (Edwin Mellen Press, 2007).

White Lies about the Inuit (Broadview Press [later University of Toronto Press], 2008).

Gabriel Sagard's Dictionary of Huron (Evolution Publishing, 2010).

The First Jesuit Huron Dictionary (Edwin Mellen Press, 2010).

Learning from the Past: Five Cases of Aboriginal Justice (De Sitter Publications, 2011).

The 18th Century Wyandot: A Clan-Based Study (Wilfrid Laurier University Press, 2012).

Instructions to a Dying Infidel (Humber College Press, 2013).

Indian Agents: Rulers of the Reserves (Peter Lang Publishing, 2016).

The Problem of Translating Catholic Doctrine into the Language of an Indigenous Horticultural Tribe: A Study of Jesuit Father Jean de Brébeuf's 1630 Catechism of the Wendat (Huron) People (Edwin Mellen Press, 2017).

*Forty Narratives in the Wyandot Language (*McGill-Queen's University Press, 2020).

The Wyandot Language: Structure and Dictionary (Edwin Mellen Press, 2021).

The Names of the Wyandot (Rock's Mills Press, 2023).